I0810104

IMAGES
of America

INDIAN VALLEY

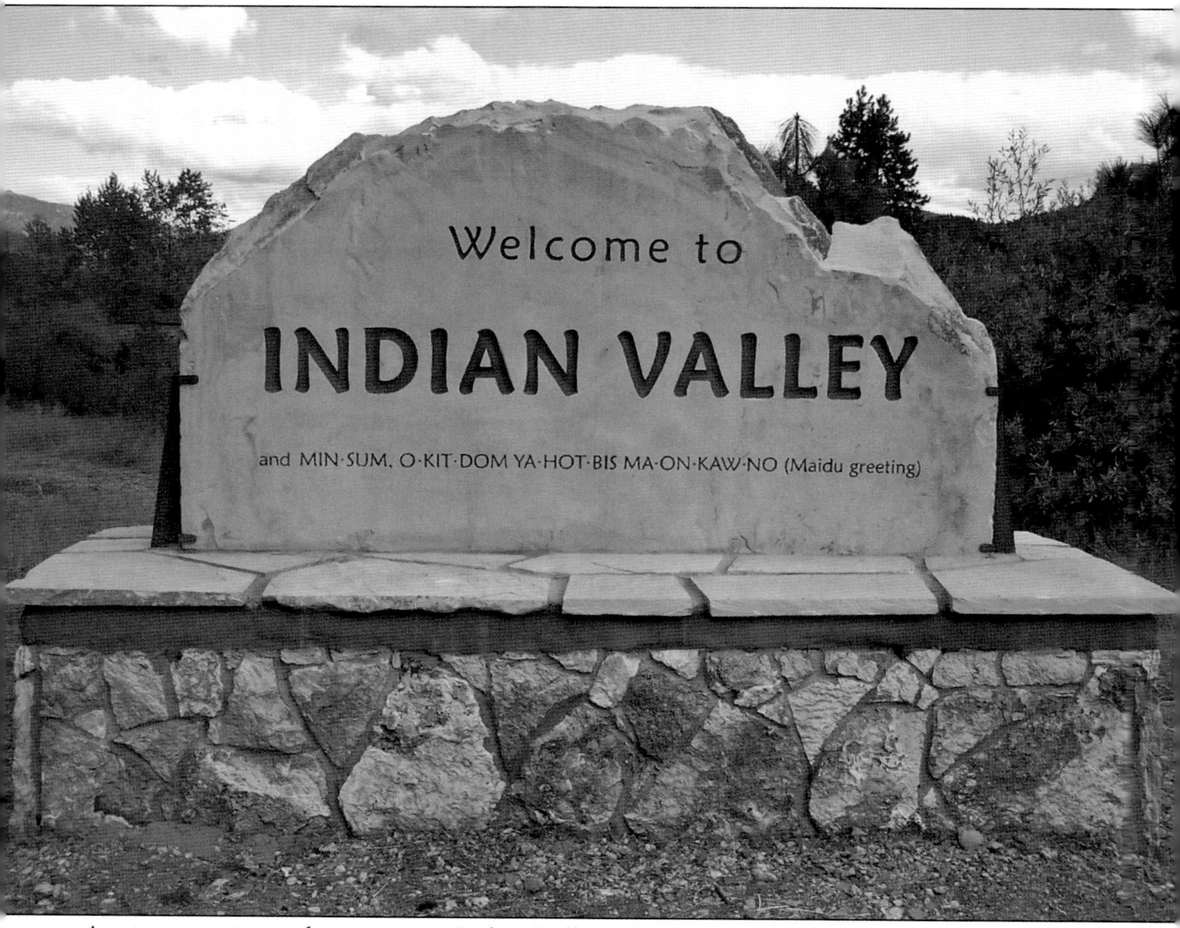

As visitors arrive at the gateway to Indian Valley, whether from the north or the south, they see this welcoming sign. It states, "MIN-SUM, O-KIT-DOM YA-HOT-BIS MA-ON-KAW-NO," a Maidu welcome meaning, "All who are coming here have a good stay. From the Maidu People."

On the Cover: Ivan and Mildred Smith are on the left, and on the right is the author's uncle Willard McCutcheon with a horse and buggy in front of the old Union School House in the North Arm of Indian Valley. Willard's dad also attended this school back in the 1800s. Willard went to high school in Greenville and was in the first graduating class out of Greenville High School in 1925. (Courtesy of Richard McCutcheon.)

IMAGES
of America

INDIAN VALLEY

Richard McCutcheon

ARCADIA
PUBLISHING

ISBN 978-0-7385-5836-3

Published by Arcadia Publishing
Charleston, South Carolina

Printed in the United States of America

Library of Congress Catalog Card Number: 2007943438

For all general information contact Arcadia Publishing at:
Telephone 843-853-2070
Fax 843-853-0044
E-mail sales@arcadiapublishing.com
For customer service and orders:
Toll-Free 1-888-313-2665

Visit us on the Internet at www.arcadiapublishing.com

This book is dedicated to Bob and Margaret Cooke. Without their efforts to start and promote the museum in Taylorsville, the history of Indian Valley could have been lost by now. Bob has passed on, but Margaret is still alive. Because of them, we now have a very nice large museum, the Indian Valley Museum, which is second to none. It has so much history of the valley that I got much of my information for this book at our local museum. (Courtesy of Margaret Cooke.)

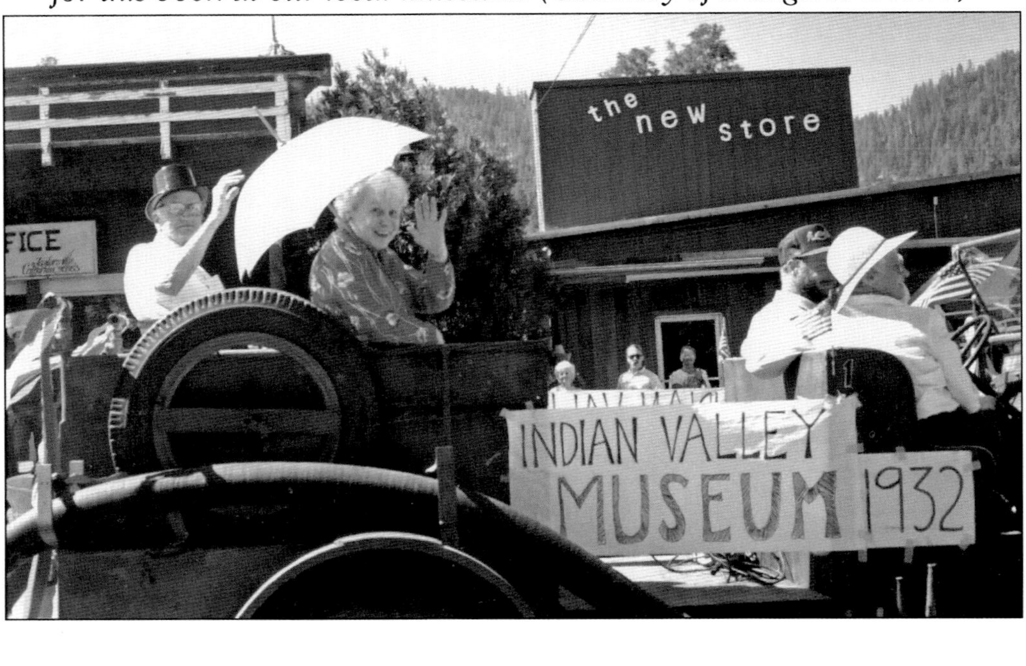

Contents

ACKNOWLEDGMENTS

A very important source for information and photographs came from the local museums in our county. The large Plumas County Museum in Quincy has lots of information, and the people there are very nice to work with. I would like to give special thanks to Scott Lawson and staff for being so helpful in my research for this book. Also, I would like to thank the local museum in my little town of Taylorsville, the Indian Valley Museum. We have a nice museum in our little town with lots of information. I would like to give special thanks to all the new staff at the Indian Valley Museum—Kathy, Francis, Ann, and Sam, and all the others who helped there.

Also thanks to the many locals who had old family albums with some very fine pictures. I will not try to name all of them because I am sure I would forget someone and I do not want to do that. They know who they are.

I would also like to give a special thank you to Patrick O'Halloran for letting me use his book, which included all the buildings in Greenville and maps of the town. It saved me lots of research and time by having access to his book. Pat spent many hours on this book and did a fine job putting it together. Also thanks to Norm Lamb of California Engels Mining for all his contributions and facts about the mines in our area. Unless otherwise stated all pictures in this book are from the Plumas County Museum or the Indian Valley Museum.

Last but not least, thanks to my editor, Kelly Reed, at Arcadia Publishing, who urged me on to do this book, and of course to my wife and granddaughter for putting up with me during this time and proofreading for me.

INTRODUCTION

They say there are three things that once gone never come back: The first is time, the second is words, and the third is opportunity. So I am going to take this opportunity to try and write this book on Indian Valley for all to enjoy.

Before the first white man came into the valley, it was occupied only by the mountain Maidu. As history tells it, they were here for over 1,000 years. The Maidus were a very peaceful people who mainly were hunters and gatherers of food. Sometimes they were nicknamed "Diggers" because they also dug for food. The valley was full of game and many wild berries. It also had the black oaks that produce a lot of acorns, which were the main staple for the Native Americans. The acorns were ground and easily stored so they had food all winter, even in the harshest winters, which were not uncommon.

When Peter Lassen came upon this valley, he must have thought, "Wow, what beauty." For miles, this valley is surrounded by the most magnificent mountains and the most fertile soil. Peter Lassen was one of the first known white men to come into the valley, according to Historical Marker No. 184. He came to stay for a short while in 1851, but it is believed that he also came through the valley at an earlier time. He was not alone. He brought with him two friends by the names of Isadore Meyerwitz and George Edward St. Felix. Lassen gave the valley its first name, Cache Valley. He built a trading post, raised vegetables, and sold them to all the people coming into the valley. The Gold Rush had started, and miners were filtering through this pretty valley. Many stayed.

The second most popular settler in the valley was a man by the name of Job (Jobe) Taylor. In early history, his name was spelled "Job," but later an *E* was added, and some papers have even been signed by Job with "Jobe" on them. Jobe Taylor visited the valley at an earlier date but came back on February 12, 1852, to stay and establish a little town named after him—Taylorsville. Later Jobe realized that the Maidu Indians had lived in the valley for many years and changed the name to what it is today, Indian Valley. This name stayed and was never changed. Jobe soon started building, and the town grew fast. There was farming throughout the valley. When Jobe came into the valley, he was the only white man here. (Peter Lassen had left for a short period, but soon came back.) It was not long before more and more immigrants came into the valley, with most coming through Beckwourth Pass and American Valley.

Taylor and his people did not raise anything at first. They purchased vegetables from Lassen and his people. Taylor was the first to raise grain in the valley, as Lassen was just raising vegetables to sell.

In the fall of 1852, the first white child was born in the valley. Dr. Cory gave birth to a little girl. That winter was a very harsh one for all the new settlers and food supplies were low, but all survived.

In 1853, Jobe built a barn, the first framed structure in the valley. He built a sawmill in 1855, and the following year, he built a gristmill. Taylorsville was on its way to becoming a large town with all the necessities of life: stores, hotels, blacksmith shops, schools, churches, libraries, and, of course, saloons.

Mining was soon the largest industry in the valley, with mines popping up all around. All the miners settling in the valley made sawmills popular; they needed cut timber to build structures. Soon there was the little town of Round Valley located just above the valley floor. I assume the elevation at Round Valley caused the town to be short-lived, because people started moving down to the lower elevations and built what is now the town of Greenville, named after Mr. and Mrs. Green. Researchers have found in studying the dates and years that they are not always the same; some claim the first house to be built in Greenville was in 1862, others claim 1861, but we do know it was around 1860 when the town was started. The little valley was later dammed to hold water and is still Greenville's water supply.

Around 1861, another town started because of the mining at the two largest gold quartz mines—the Crescent/Pet (which held two claims in the middle of town) and the Green Mountain Mine (located on the ridge above town). Crescent was located at the west edge of the valley, given that name from the crescent-shaped outcrop that acts as a backdrop for the town. Mining flourished, and soon gold stamp mills were built there. The name of the town was then changed to Crescent Mills. The first house was built in the winter of 1861–1862 by J. W. Pulsifer, who later became co-owner of the local quartz mill. At its peak, Crescent Mills had around 1,100 people in its workforce; they worked two shifts in the mines to dig miles of tunnels that ran under the town.

With the Gold Rush coming on strong, the town was growing by leaps and bounds, as was the rest of the valley. Soon Crescent Mills supported seven saloons, which never closed; a grocery store; a Chinese laundry; a seamstress; a barbershop; a doctor; and a hotel, which was owned by the town doctor, Doc Carter, and was one of the finest hotels in the valley. The hotel had an outside stairway leading to the second floor where the dance floor was located, and people danced until dawn many nights.

When not working, the men did lots of hunting and fishing. There were no seasons or licenses in those days, people just hunted to feed their families. The area had many deer, bear, duck, quail, pheasant, and grouse. It has been said there were so many waterfowl in the valley that they would darken the sky when they all took to the air.

By the early 1900s, the town started dwindling as the mines began to run dry and people were moving out to seek work elsewhere. Most of the businesses closed and moved on with the miners, leaving behind just a few. By 1920, all that remained were three saloons, a grocery store, a watchmaker, a laundry, a service station, and an ice cream parlor.

On September 2, 1926, a fire allegedly started by an arsonist destroyed most of the remaining businesses and 35 residences. The town was rebuilt in 1927 with only one saloon, a hotel, a meat market, a grocery store, and a gas station, which is about what you see today.

Just below the valley floor, another town was growing because of the mining. In 1884, a man by the name of Bob Martin homesteaded 148 acres. History states that Martin first called the town Shoofly, but it later became known as Indian Falls. Martin apparently mortgaged and forfeited the acreage to a man by the name of Thompson, who in turn sold it to W. J. Miller. Gilbert H. Goodhue bought it from Miller around 1906–1907. Goodhue sold to the Indian Falls Development Company, who subdivided the acreage into a town site. Many lots were sold, thus the start of a little town known as Indian Falls.

Around 1910, a sawmill was built by Fred Farrar. This mill operated under the name of Indian Falls Mill and Lumber Company. It cut most of the lumber for the new buildings in town, most of which were constructed by Jim Cooney. The mill did not run very long because of the problems it had in getting timber to it. Farrar spent much money building chutes down the steep mountain to get the logs to the mill. The first logs that were turned loose down the mountainside tore the chutes up beyond repair.

Soon Indian Valley was growing very rapidly. The valley has a very distinctive arm off the main valley called the North Arm, because it is off to the north. Just above the arm, copper was discovered by Henry A. Engel. It turned out to be one of the largest copper finds in the entire state. There were two Engel Mines, a lower one and an upper one. Soon a town formed near the mine called Engelmine. That town grew to be the second largest in the valley with all the necessities of life: schools, churches, stores, and so forth. Soon the town had a railroad that took the ore through Indian Valley and the little town of Indian Falls to the main railroad at Paxton. This was the beginning of the Indian Valley Railroad.

The Indian Valley Railroad ran through the middle of the North Arm, and the old railroad bed is still visible in many areas. At the onset of the arm was a depot, which was still there when the author was a kid. The depot was being used as a home. When they finally tore the depot down, parts of the nice wood floor were used in a new house up the road about one-half mile. To get to its destination, the railroad had to cross Indian Creek and the East Branch of the Feather River just before Paxton. Those crossings were visible for many years, and some you can still see.

Just to the east of Indian Valley is another arm that is not connected, but very close, and a little town called Genesee was formed. This valley was a main feeder for the stages that came from Nevada through the Sierra Valley and Clover Valley on down into Genesee Valley as well as to Indian Valley. Genesee had a store, a post office, and a few ranches in the valley. One of the main ranches was bought in 1862 by Edwin D. Hosselkus and stayed in the family for years. It covered around 1,000 acres, and their large two-story home, which was built with brick, still stands today, as does the old store. Hosselkus also owned a dairy ranch in Squaw Queen Valley. It was around 500 acres and was mostly grazing land. At the head of the valley was the Flournoy Ranch. It had a mill that made brick, which was a very popular building material even back then.

Just above Genesee was another copper find, known as the Walker Mine, which was run by the Anaconda Copper Mining Company. It turned out to be the second largest copper mine in the state, after the Engels Mine. It was instrumental to the valley even though its ore was taken out on a tramline over the mountain to another area. It soon grew to be a very large town in a higher elevation, around 6,500 feet, where the winters were very harsh. This town was called Walker Mine. At its peak, the town had a school with as many as three teachers, stores, a hospital, public dining areas, a movie theater, a post office, and a service station. For recreation, there was a baseball field and a ski hill. It had, at one time, over 200 homes counting the private and company homes and the company bunkhouses.

There are still a few families here that can trace their ancestry back to the early settlers of the valley. The author for one is the fourth generation. His great-grandfather Hugh McCutcheon came into this valley around 1870. He was a miner for several years, then settled down to ranching and farming. He also had acreage in what was called the McCutcheon Dairy. It was in the higher elevations, and he ran a dairy up there and used horses and sleighs to get the milk out in the winter. The Kingdon family is still in the valley, as is the Peter family; Jim Peter still lives on the old ranch. The Neers have been in this valley for years and still own the one ranch, as well as the McIntyres, Hamblins, Sobreros, and the Stampflis, just to name a few. The Defantis came around into the North Arm just above the McCutcheon Ranch around 1926 and still live there.

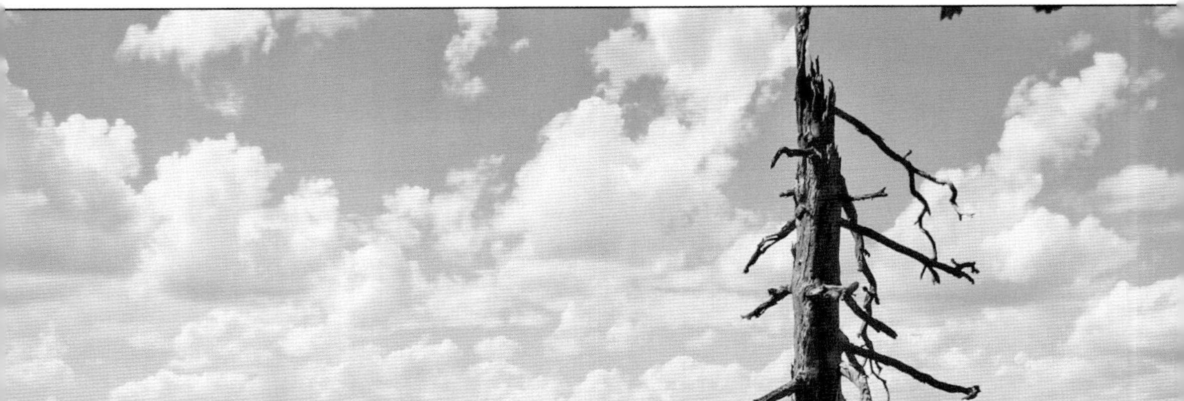

Indian Valley is a picturesque mountain meadow with an average elevation of around 3,500 feet. Surrounding the valley are many beautiful mountains with an average height of 7,700 feet. The mountains are Indian Head on Keddie Ridge; Kettle Rock; Grizzly; Jura, which is from the Jurassic Period and over 170 million years old; and Mount Hough. The mountains are so dynamic that many photographers and artists set up their tripods or easels to take pictures or paint pictures. Indian Valley is home to many events because of its beauty. One huge spring event is the Century Bicycle Ride. The ride covers the entire valley and then some, or riders can take different, shorter rides if they are not into the 100-mile ride. Indian Valley also hosts a huge rodeo on the Fourth of July and an old time Gold-digger's Day on the third weekend of July. In 2008, Indian Valley hosted what is called a "Ride and Tie" competition. The ride was on Mount Jura, so participants got a great view when they topped the mountain, which looks over the valley. (Courtesy of the author.)

One

First in the Valley

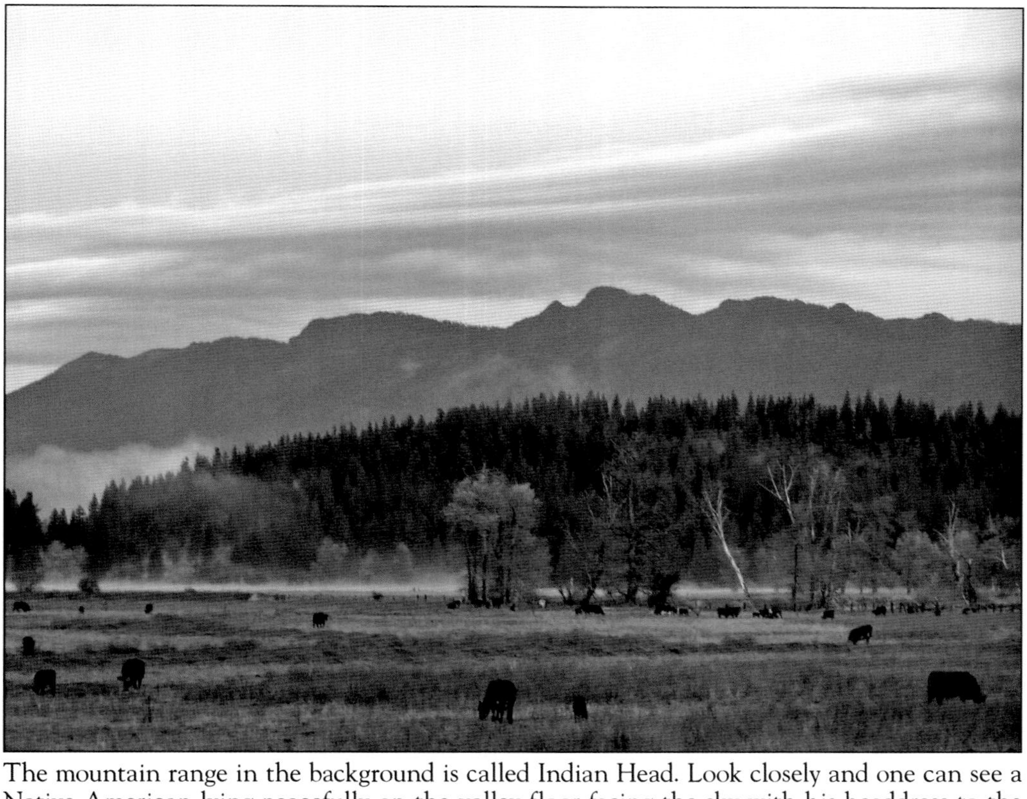

The mountain range in the background is called Indian Head. Look closely and one can see a Native American lying peacefully on the valley floor facing the sky with his headdress to the right; then his eyebrow, nose, and lips; his hands folded on stomach; and his toes up toward the sky. It is said that the Native American was out measuring the depths of the lakes. Apparently he was so tired after he measured Homer Lake, he decided to lay down to rest but fell into a deep sleep and has never awoken.

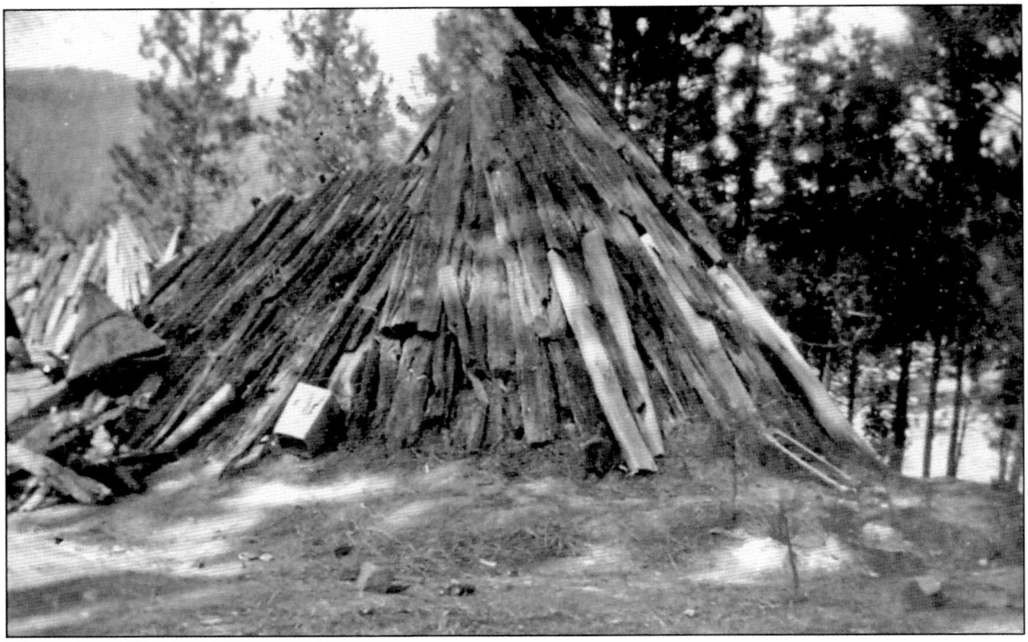

This is what the Maidus built in and around the valley for their homes. Sometimes called wigwams, they were made of bark and came to a peak at the top to shed water. This bark house was located in the lower part of Taylorsville by the millrace, a diversion ditch built by the Chinese. The water was diverted from Indian Creek.

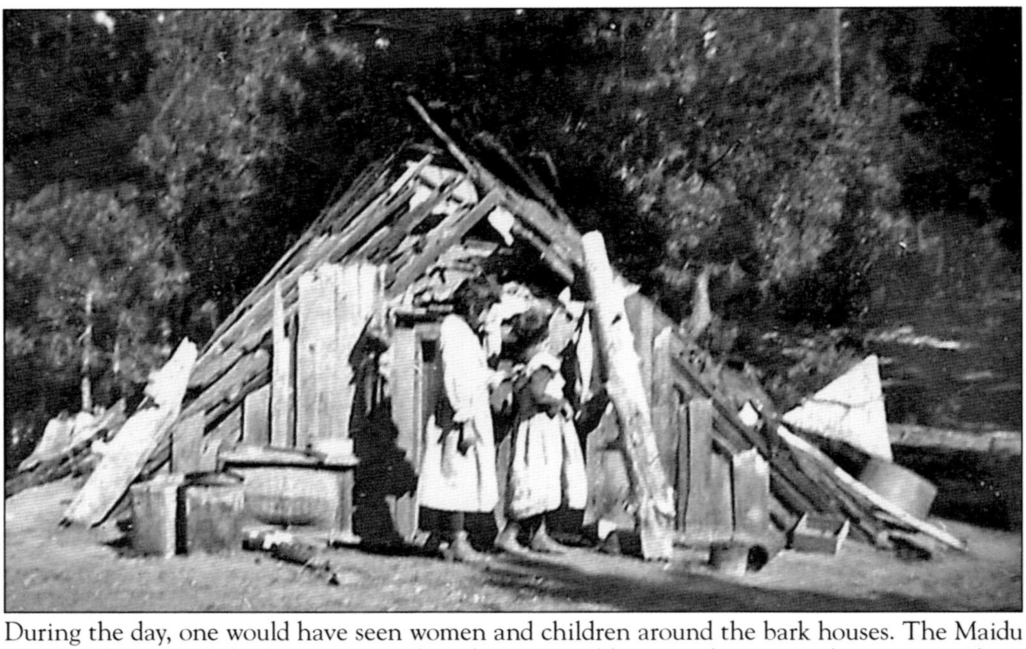

During the day, one would have seen women and children around the bark houses. The Maidu men would hunt while the women gathered acorns, wild onions, berries, and pine nuts. There were lots of wild berries, nuts, seeds, and wild vegetables. The women would usually return home first. It is certain most people today have eaten many of the items the Native Americans ate back then.

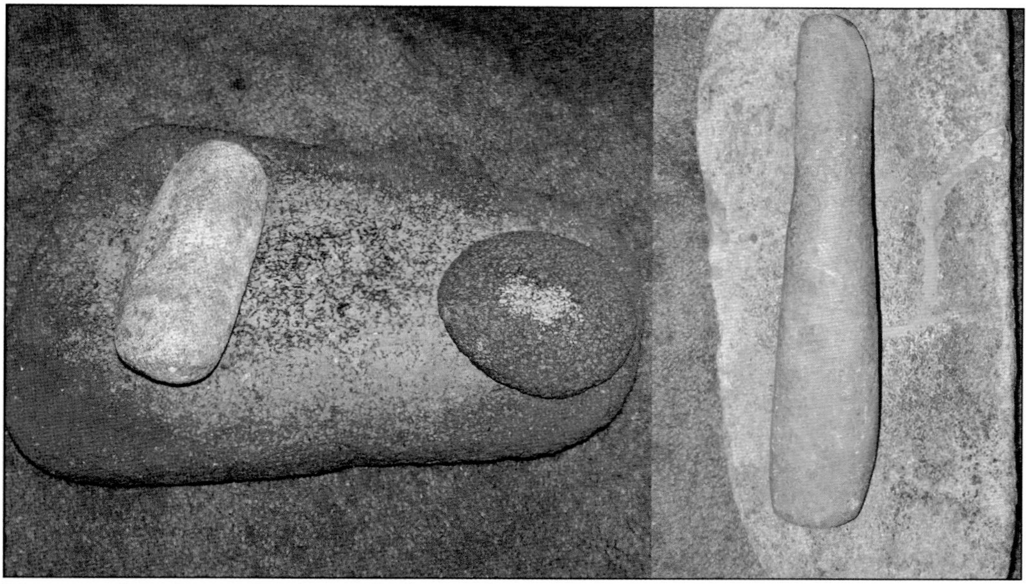

Many people today are familiar with the grinding tools the Maidus used. The author himself has found many of them while raking hay in the hayfields. They just seem to work to the top of the ground with all the plowing and moving of the earth. (Courtesy of the author.)

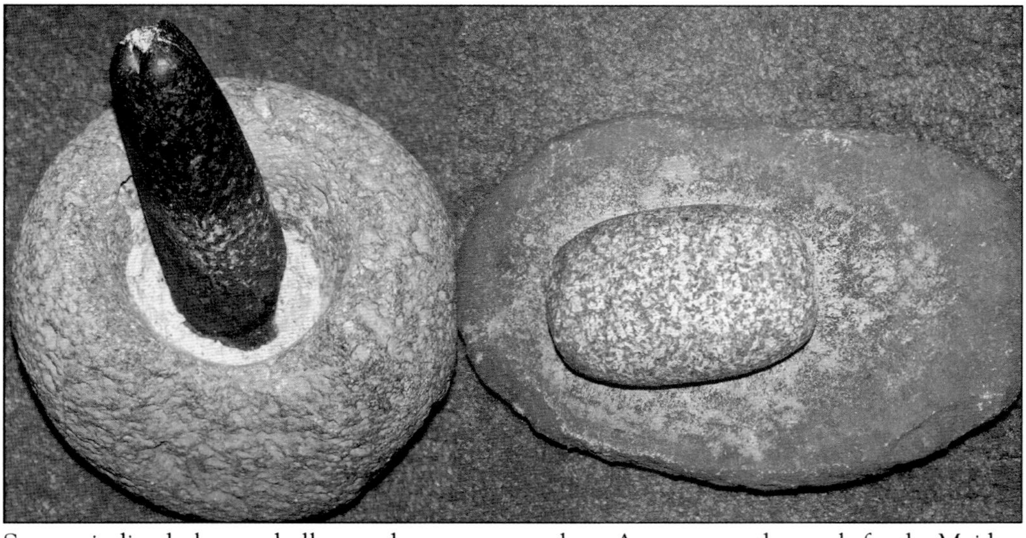

Some grinding holes are shallow, and some are very deep. Acorns were the staple for the Maidus. It took lots of grinding with these stones to crush all the acorns that had to be processed into meal then stored to last all winter, or sometimes longer, as not every year was a good one for acorns. Sometimes they had acorns that lasted for up to three years. (Courtesy of the author.)

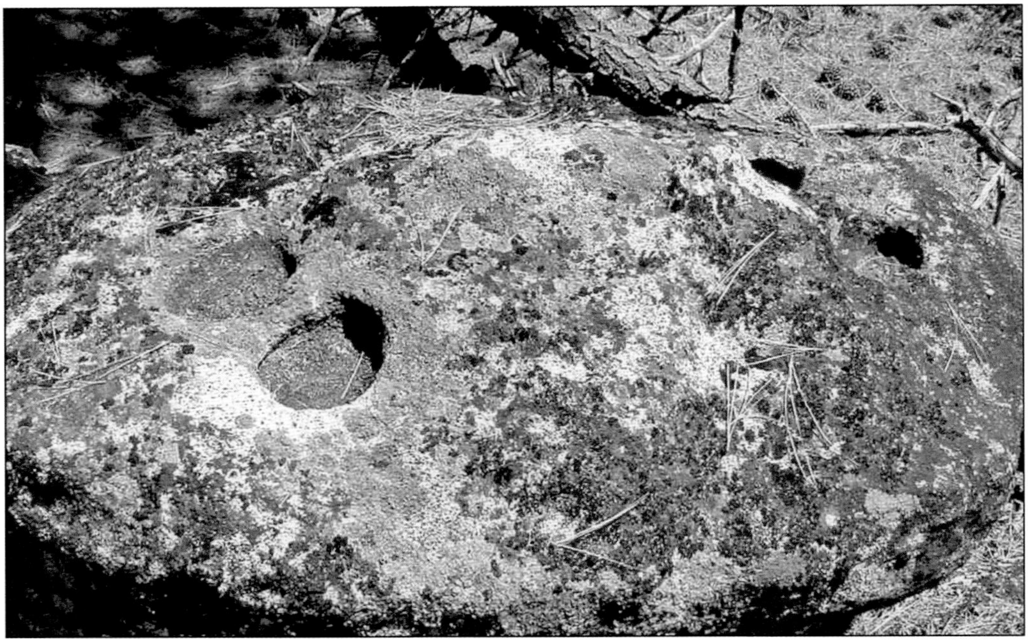

Not only did the Native Americans have the portable stones, but they also used large boulders to grind. Most of these were located near either a creek bed where there was plenty of water or a place where there were lots of oak trees and plenty of seeds and nuts that needed grinding. (Courtesy of the author.)

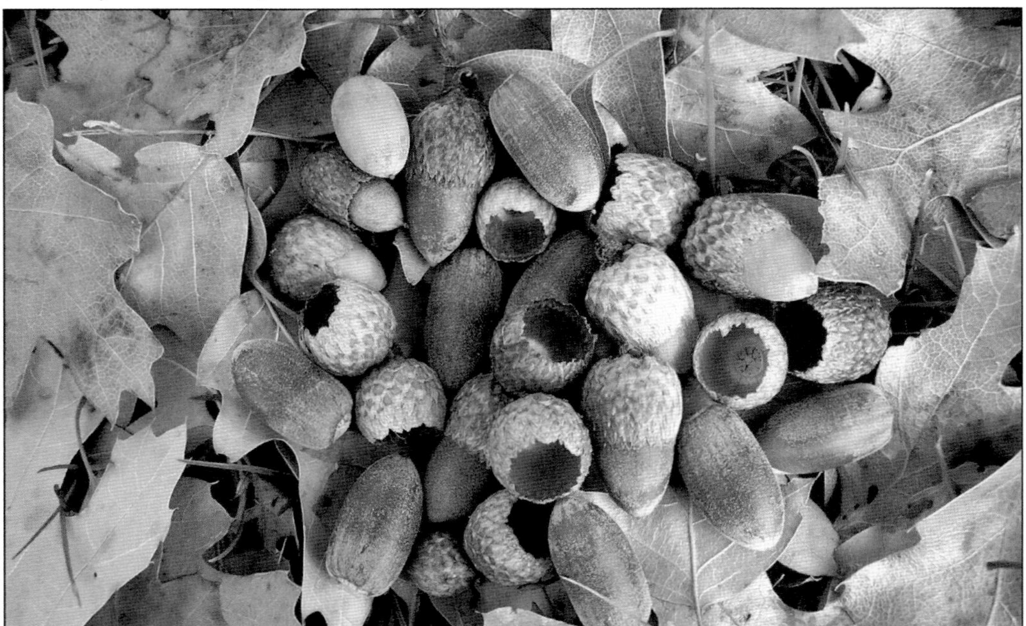

Acorns were the main food for the Maidus. Usually the acorns were stored, dried, and ground up when needed. The gathering of acorns sometimes took several days. It has been said that a Native American woman and her two or three children could gather as many as several thousand pounds in just a few days. (Courtesy of the author.)

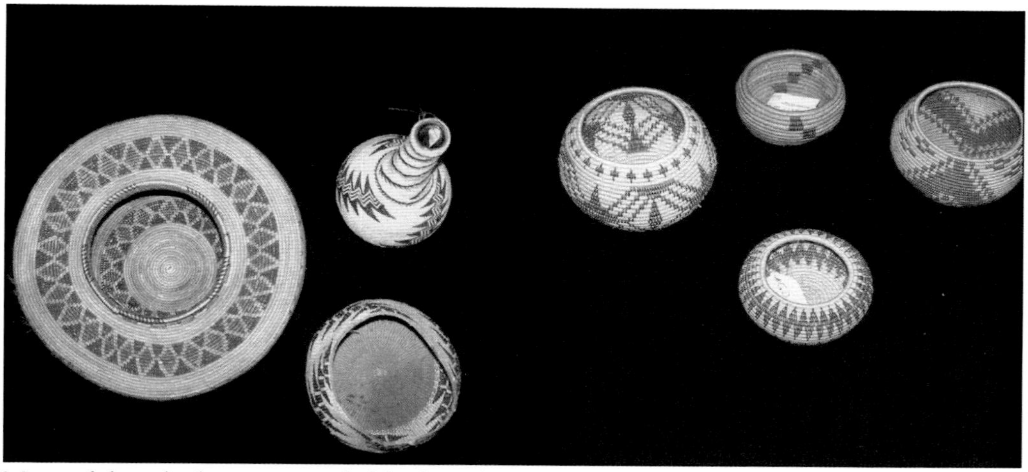

Many of these baskets were made like funnels for processing the acorn meal. The acorns had a tannic acid in them that had to be taken out. The Native Americans had a system of making a mold in clean sand and washing the meal with water that was heated by hot rocks then poured over the meal. This process leached the acid into the sand and made the acorns ready to eat. (Courtesy of the author.)

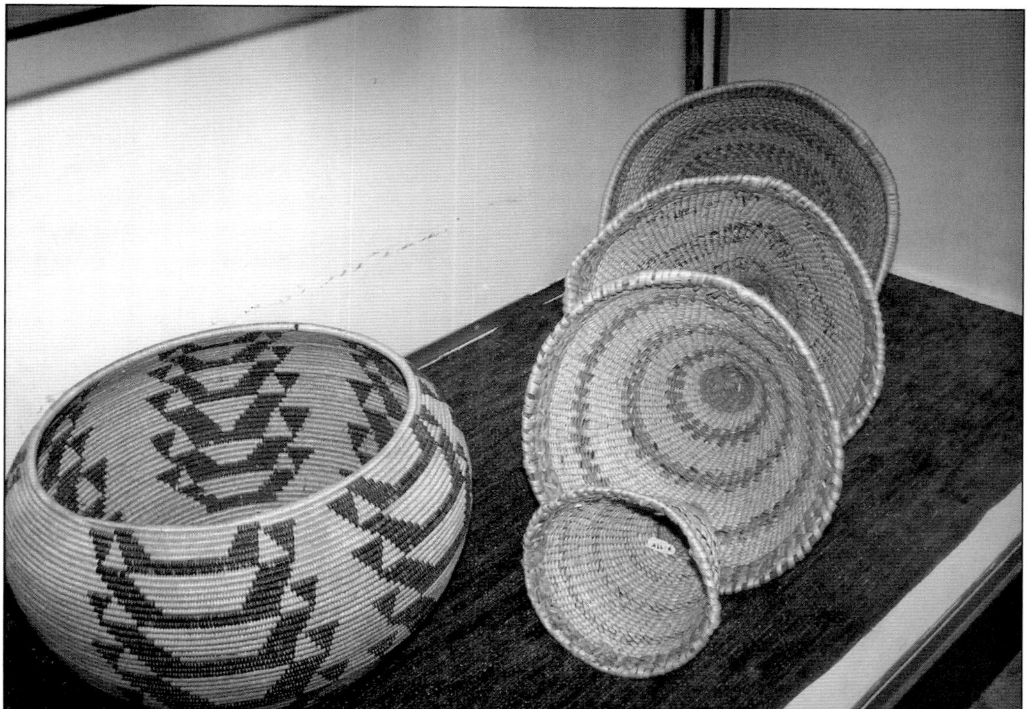

The Maidu women were always busy doing something. When not gathering acorns, seeds, and nuts, they had to weave baskets to cook with and store gatherings in. Although they could have made some of the simplest baskets, they did not. The Maidus were proud of their basketry and were known as the best basket makers in the United States. (Courtesy of the author.)

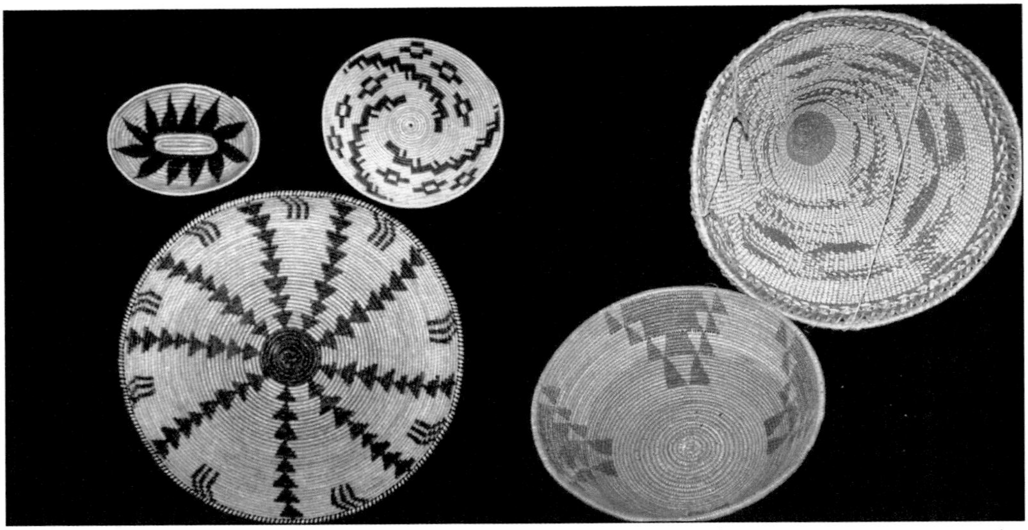

The Maidus gathered many items for their baskets. Different colors were interwoven in the baskets to create some of the finest designs imaginable. The designs were also the expressions of the person weaving the basket. The baskets were all shapes and sizes, some as large as several feet high for storing the acorns, and were also waterproof. (Courtesy the author.)

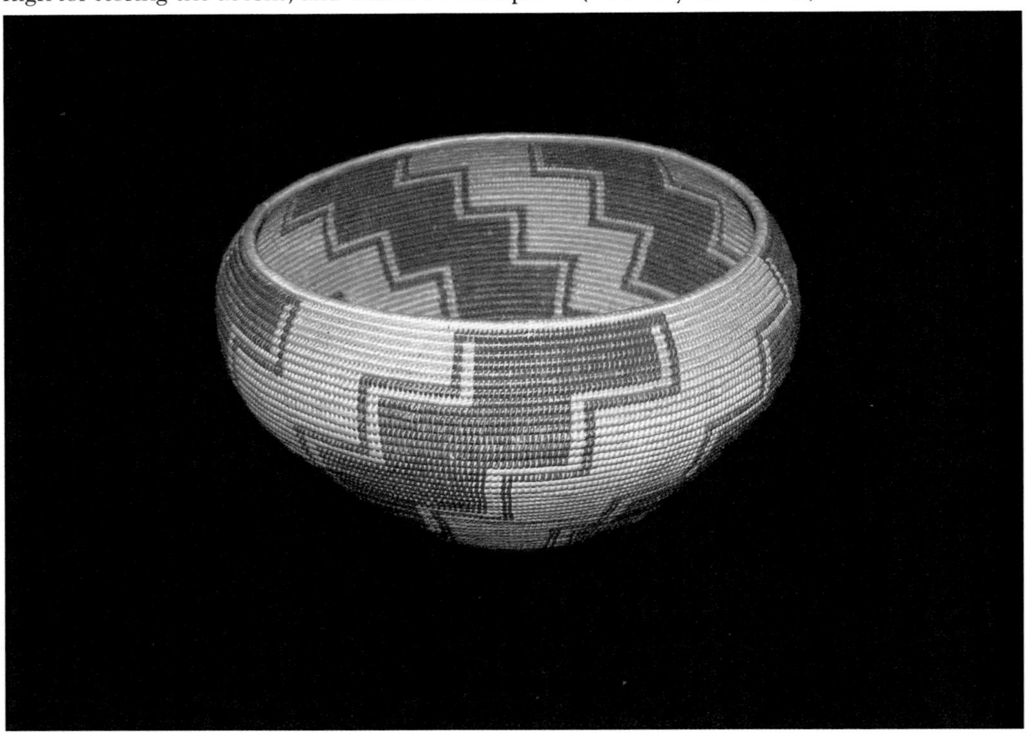

The Maidus always used willow for the foundation of their baskets. Each willow rod has to be the same size, so many hours go into scraping and sizing them. Some basket makers love the roots of the ponderosa pine because of its stickiness for starting their baskets. The pitch in the root would also help seal baskets to make them waterproof. The root has to be split in tiny, uniform strips. (Courtesy of the author.)

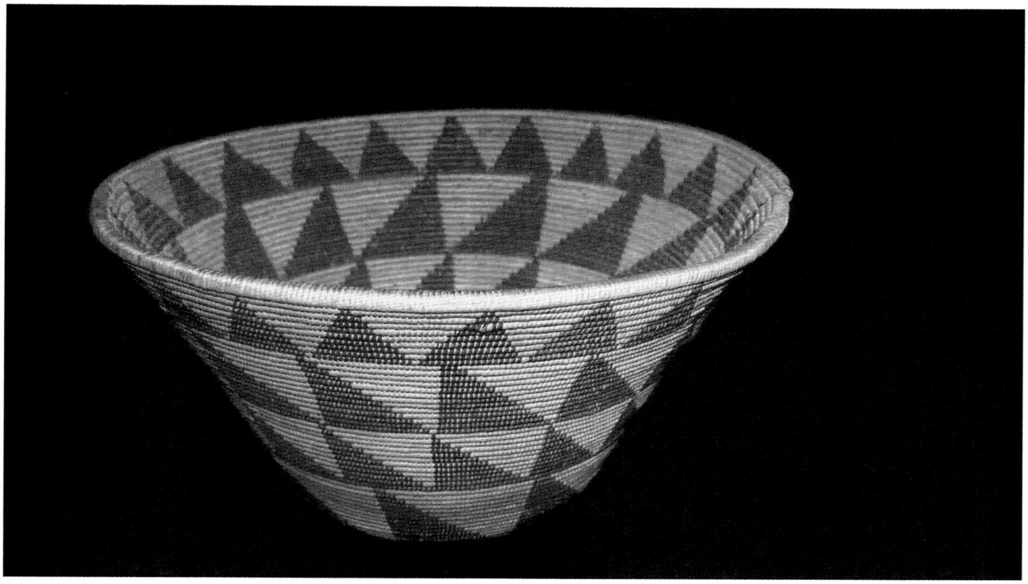

The redbud was a popular bush to get colorful strips from. The Maidus also liked bear grass and used a lot of maple, which they would burn off every year so it would grow back more uniform, which meant less time sizing it. However, much time was spent splitting material into fine strips, no matter what they were using. They usually soaked the material before weaving it. (Courtesy of the author.)

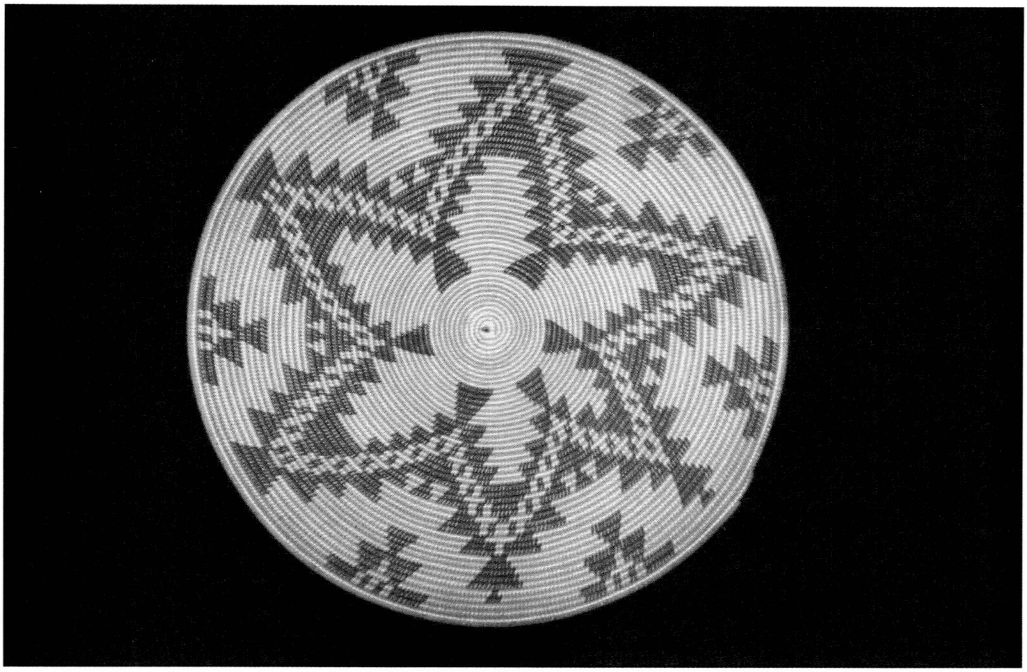

Each basket has the individual's personality in it. One could tell who had created the baskets by how there were made. In the older days, bone (or horn) was used to push the willow rods apart and lash the rows together. Those creating the baskets today use a steel awl. (Courtesy of the author.)

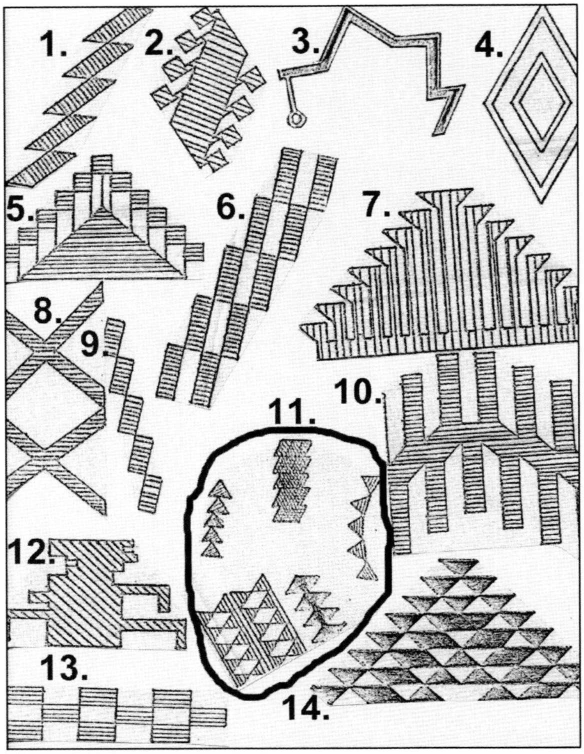

Here are just a few of the designs described by Frank Joseph, a native Maidu who donated the drawings to the Indian Valley Museum. Pictured are (1) the Earthworm; (2) the Quail Tip; (3) the Ducks Wing; (4) the Diamond Back; (5) the Bushes or Brush; (6) the Big Tongue; (7) the Pine Cones; (8) the Water Snake; (9) the Vine; (10) the Fish Teeth; (11) the Arrow Point or Flint, often combined with the Quail Tip; (12) the Sugar Pine; (13) the Caterpillar, and (14) the Flying Goose.

The men spent most of their time hunting and fishing to get protein for their diets. They had sinew-backed bows they used for larger game but relied mostly on their skills to net and trap smaller game. They also snared birds and harpooned fish or took fish with nets and some fishhooks made from sharp shell. (Courtesy of the author.)

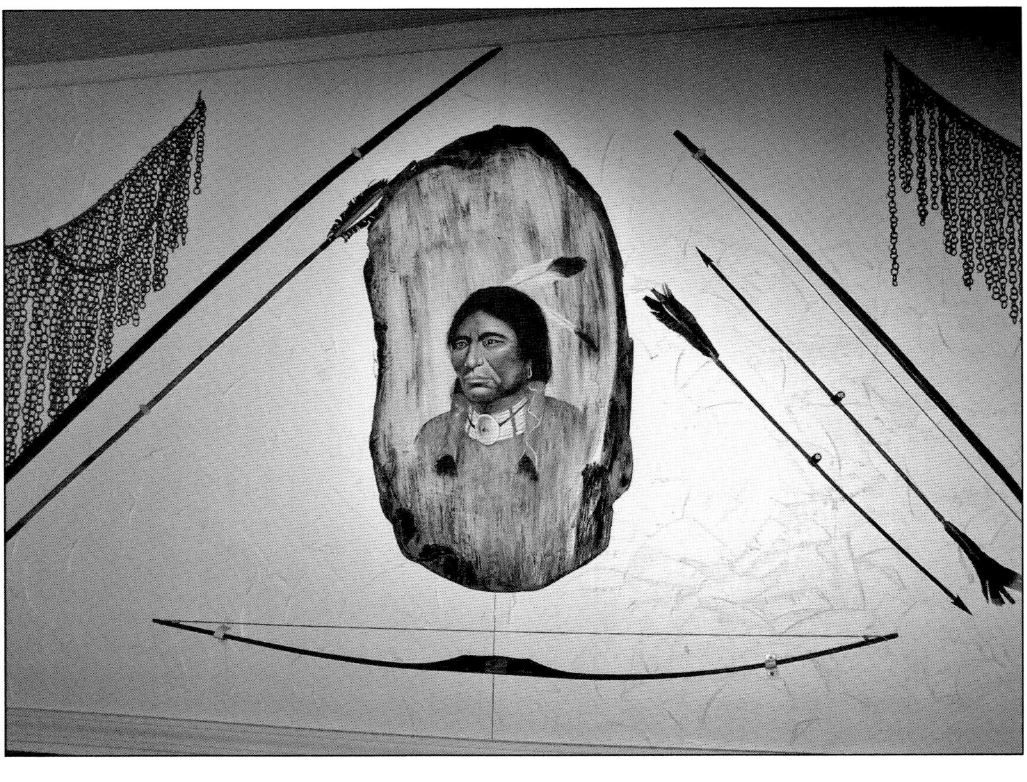

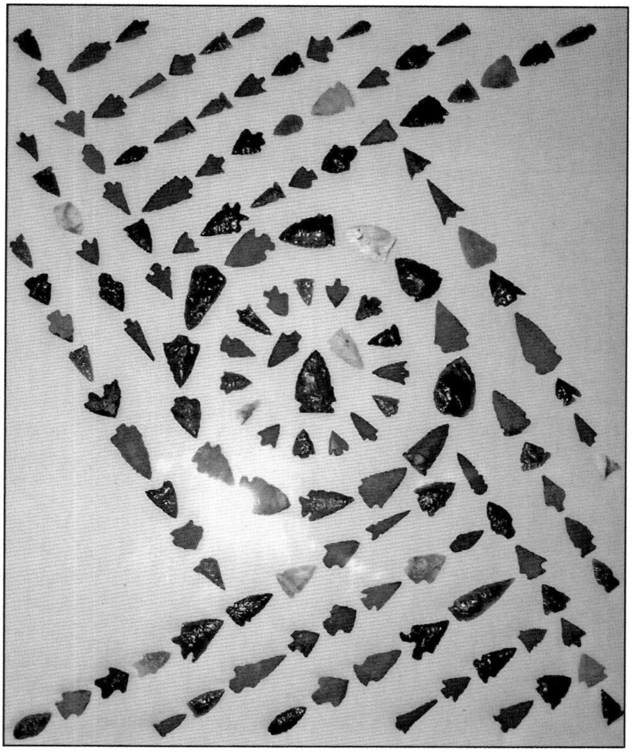

The Native Americans were very skillful in making arrowheads for their arrows. They were usually made of obsidian, flint, or other stones. They even made some arrowheads out of bone. It took much practice to achieve the exact arrowhead they wanted, slowly chipping it down to size. They even made large ones for the spearheads they used to spear fish. (Courtesy of the author.)

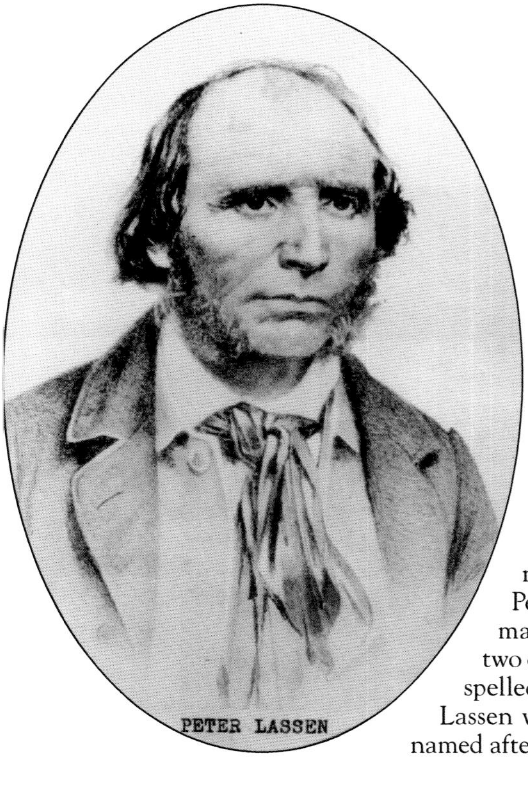

The Gold Rush was the end of the Native Americans' privacy in the valley, and it was not long before a white man by the name of Peter Lassen showed up. Lassen was the first white man into the valley but was not alone. He had two others with him, Isadore Meyerwitz (sometimes spelled Meyerowitz) and George Edward St. Felix. Lassen was the leader, so all historical markers were named after him.

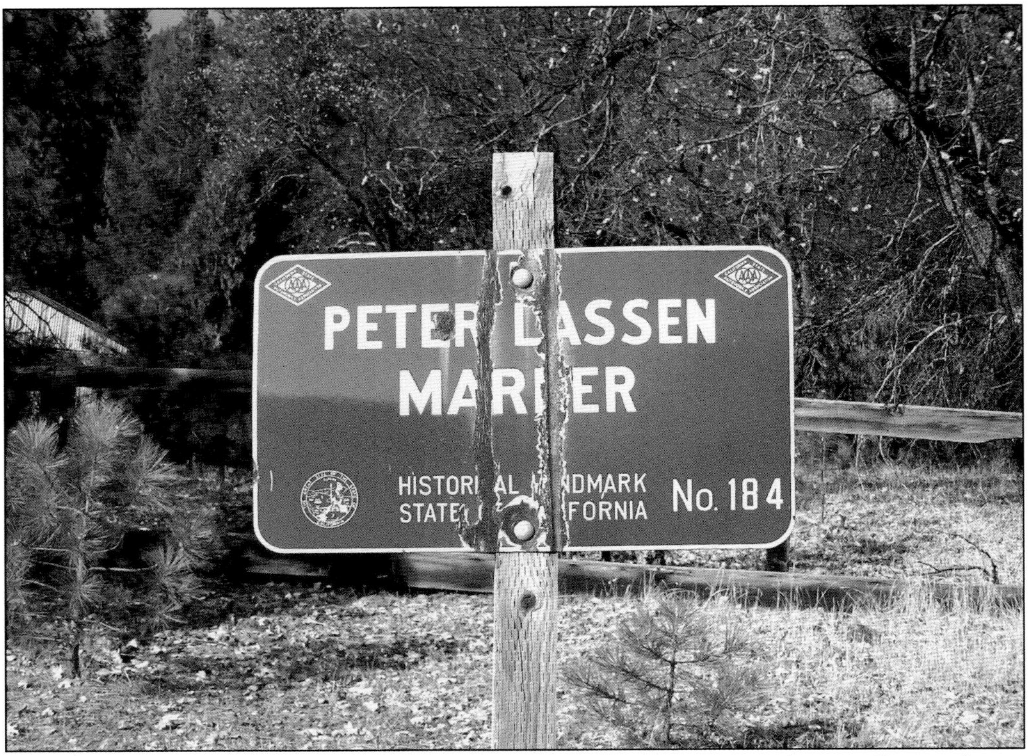

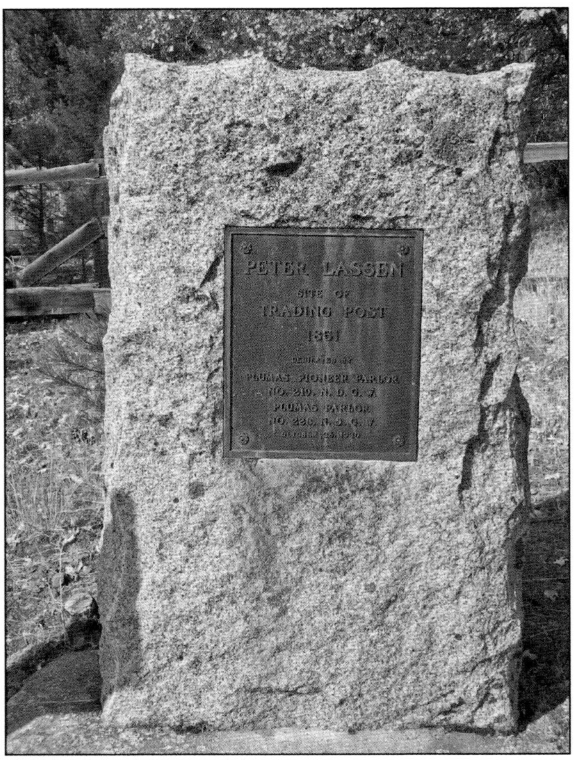

Peter Lassen was born in Denmark in 1800 but by 1840 was in California, and by 1848, he was all the way to this valley. He left but came back in 1851 to stay for a while. Lassen is the one who gave the valley its first name—Cache Valley. He built a trading post and started raising vegetables to sell to all the miners who were now filtering into the valley. (Courtesy of the author.)

Being the first white man here, Lassen had great historic impact on this valley, even though he did not stay all that long. Wanting to recognize the historical site where his trading post once stood, residents erected first a metal sign then this granite stone monument with a bronze plaque imbedded in it for all to see. (Courtesy of the author.)

Two

TAYLORSVILLE

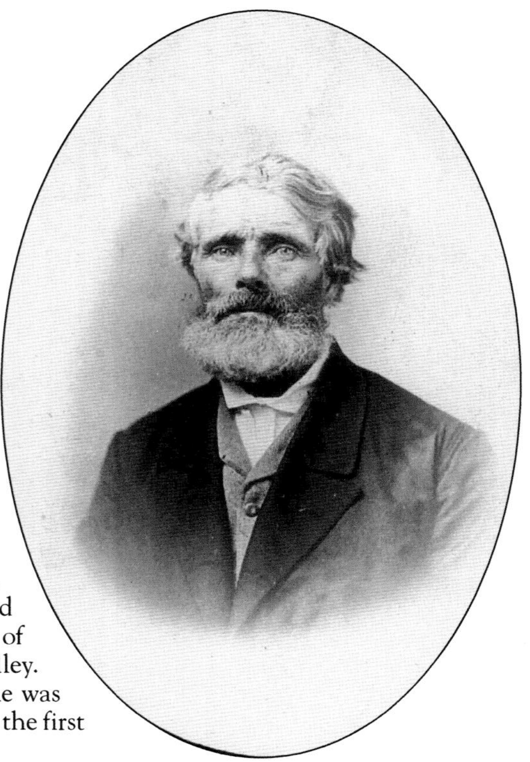

Jobe Taylor, who was originally from Pennsylvania and came to California in 1849, prospected in and around the Nelson Creek area. He then came prospecting in this valley in 1851 and camped at the site that is now Taylorsville. He came back to stay in 1852. He was the second white settler to enter the valley. Peter Lassen moved on after a short time, but Taylor stayed until his death. Taylor changed the name of the area to Indian Valley because of all the Maidu Indians in and around the valley. Taylorsville was named after Jobe Taylor, as he was the one who started building the town and was the first to construct a frame structure.

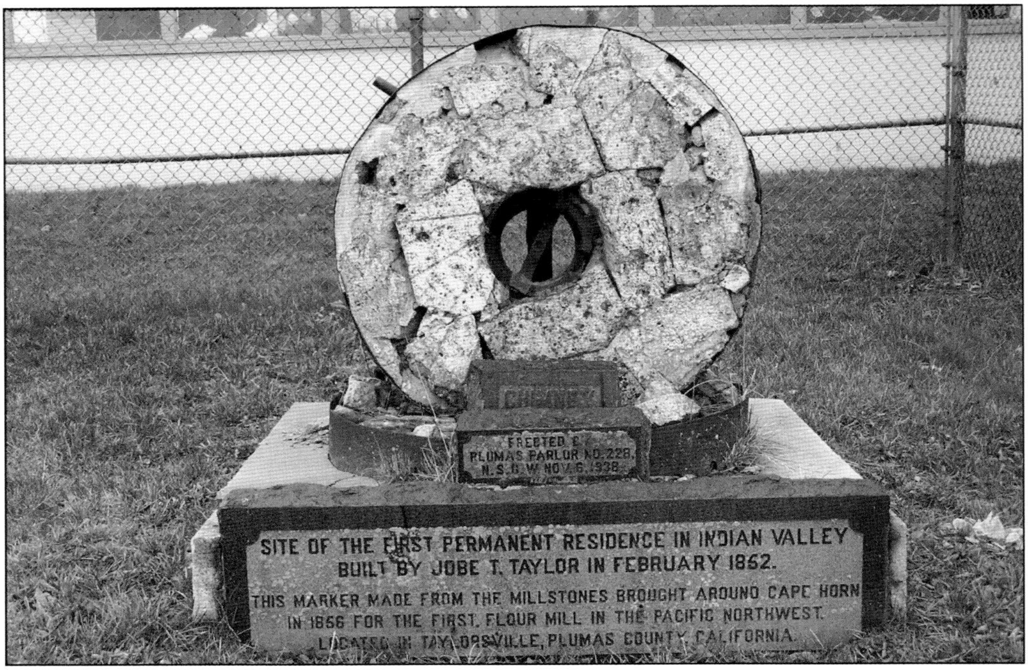

There is a millstone still marking the spot where Jobe built the first structure. This millstone came around the Horn in 1856 and was used at his gristmill. Taylor and his people bought vegetables from Lassen, as Taylor only raised grain. The white man was the first to farm the valley. The Maidus were not known for farming; they lived off the natural food that was in and around the valley. (Courtesy of the author.)

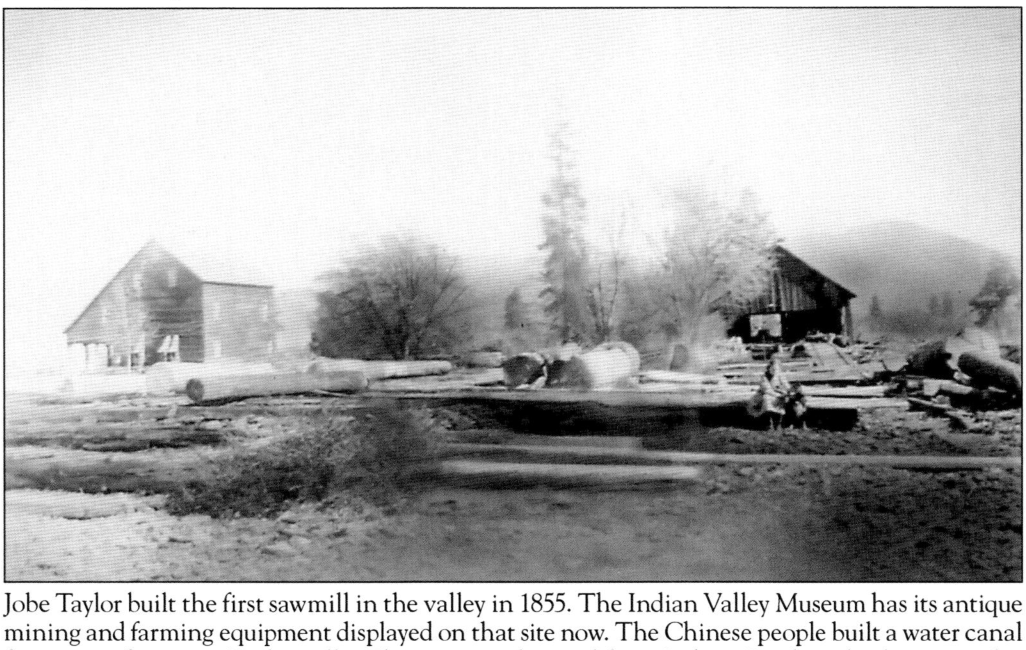

Jobe Taylor built the first sawmill in the valley in 1855. The Indian Valley Museum has its antique mining and farming equipment displayed on that site now. The Chinese people built a water canal from east of town to Taylorsville. This water is diverted from Indian Creek and is known today as the millrace because it was originally built for diverting water to Jobe's sawmill.

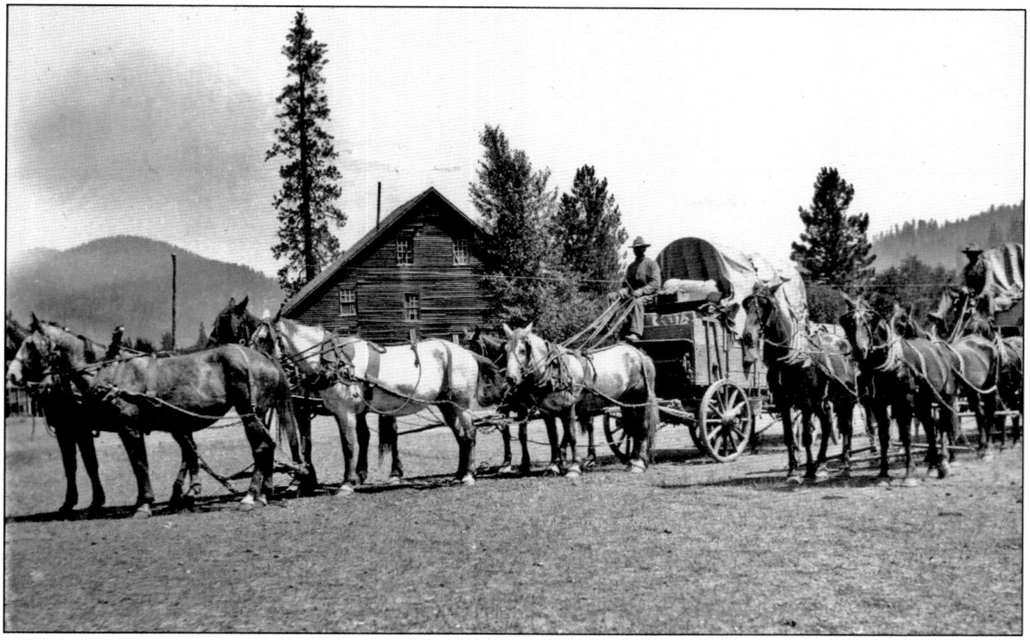

The following year, 1856, Jobe built a gristmill, located north of his sawmill. Mining and farming were becoming the most popular activities in the valley, so the gristmill was in full swing. Soon there were around 14,000 acres being used in the valley. The gristmill in the background has the Wheelock's freight line in front.

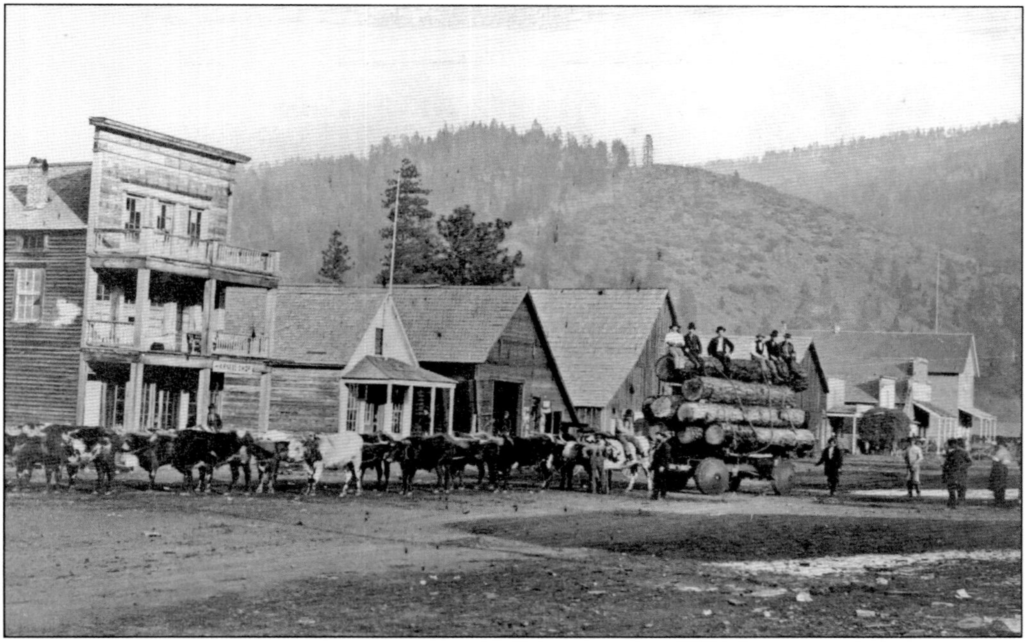

Soon buildings were going up all around town. Most were made of lumber that was cut from the sawmill in town but four or five were made of bricks; there were a couple of brick mills outside of town. Most of the logs rolling into town for milling were brought by ox and wagon or horse and wagon.

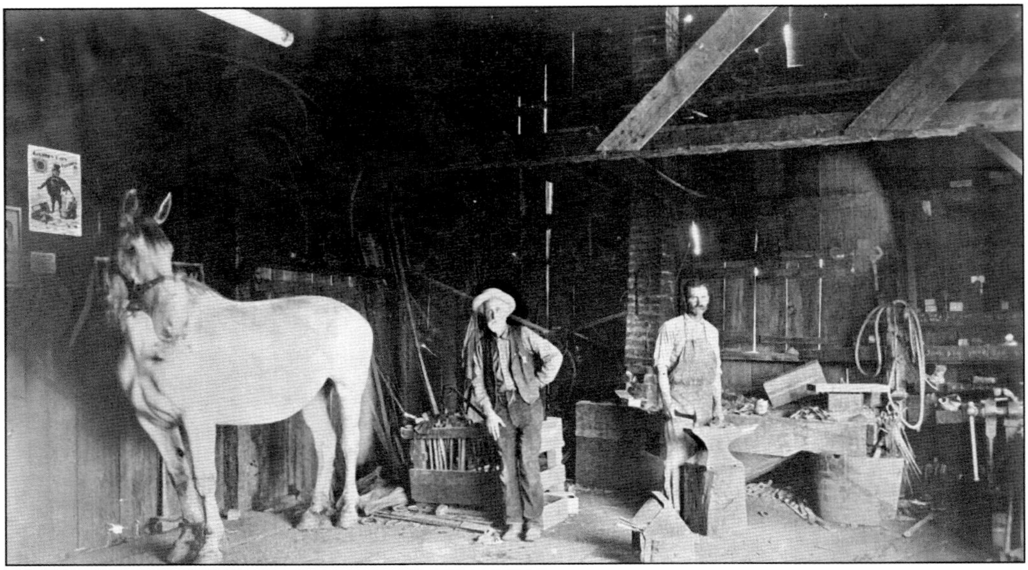

There were many businesses starting up in town. Blacksmith shops were very important with all the teams of horses coming through the area with wagons and supplies. Of course, saloons were always popular, as well as the general stores.

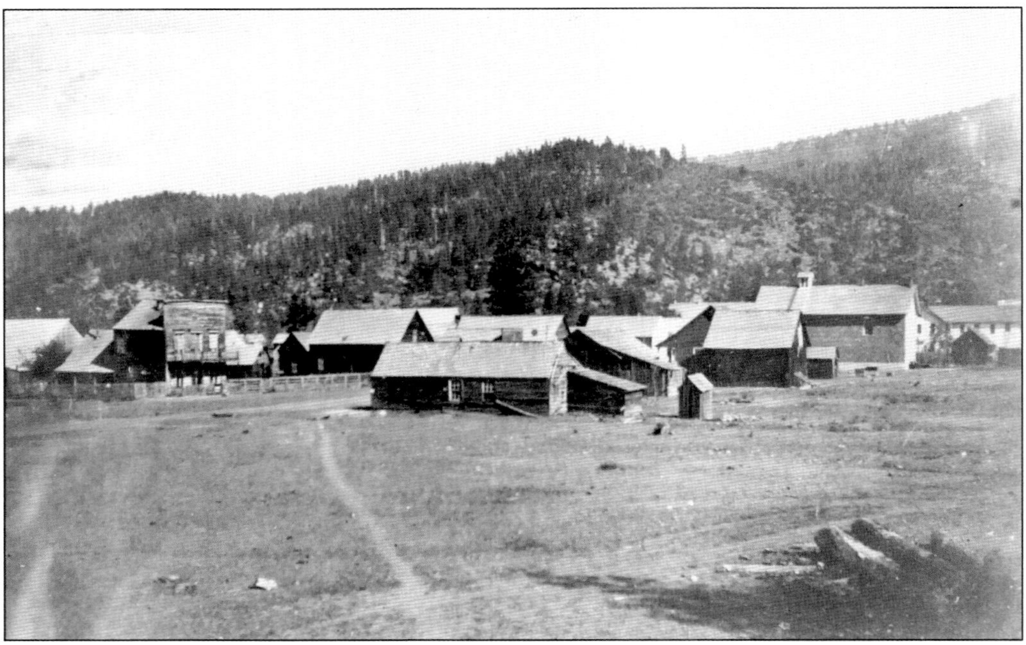

This is what the main street of Taylorsville was becoming—more structures being built and more traffic through the town; it now was a main stop for stages and freight lines and the main route from Reno to Sacramento. Taylorsville was becoming a little town nestled at the base of Mount Jura, which is one of the oldest mountains around the valley, dating back more than 140 million years.

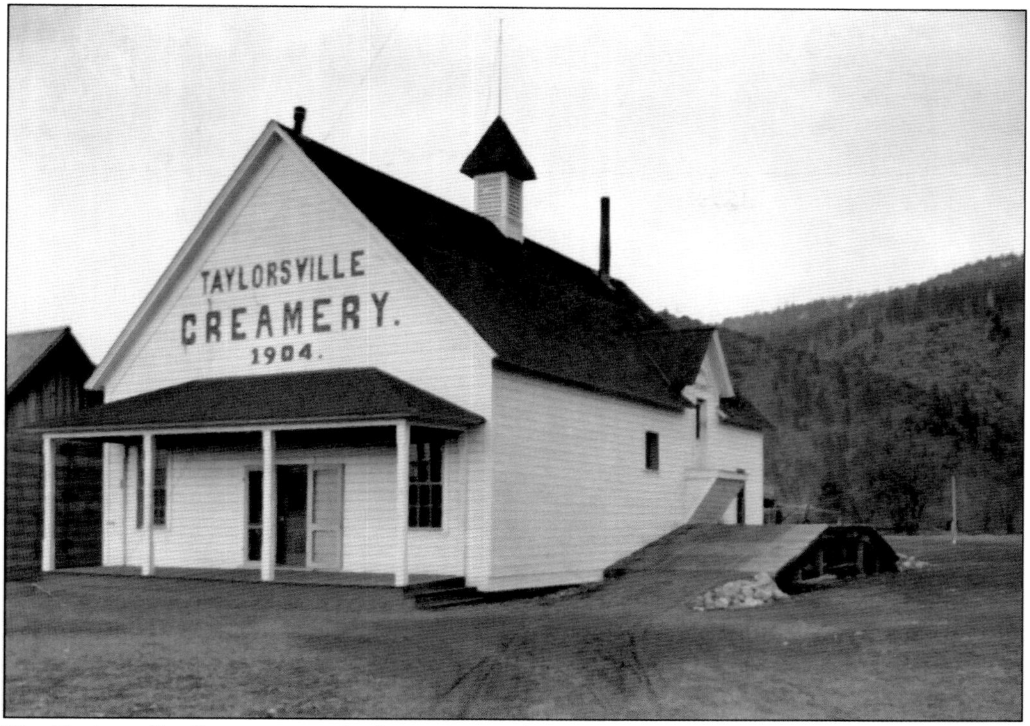

The Taylorsville Creamery was built in 1904 and was very important to the valley, with all the dairies supplying milk for it to process. Every winter they got ice from Indian Creek to use in the creamery and packed it in sawdust, which kept the ice for many months. They made butter there and shipped it all over northern California and northern Nevada. The last dairy to haul milk into the creamery was Maurice Foland's in North Arm.

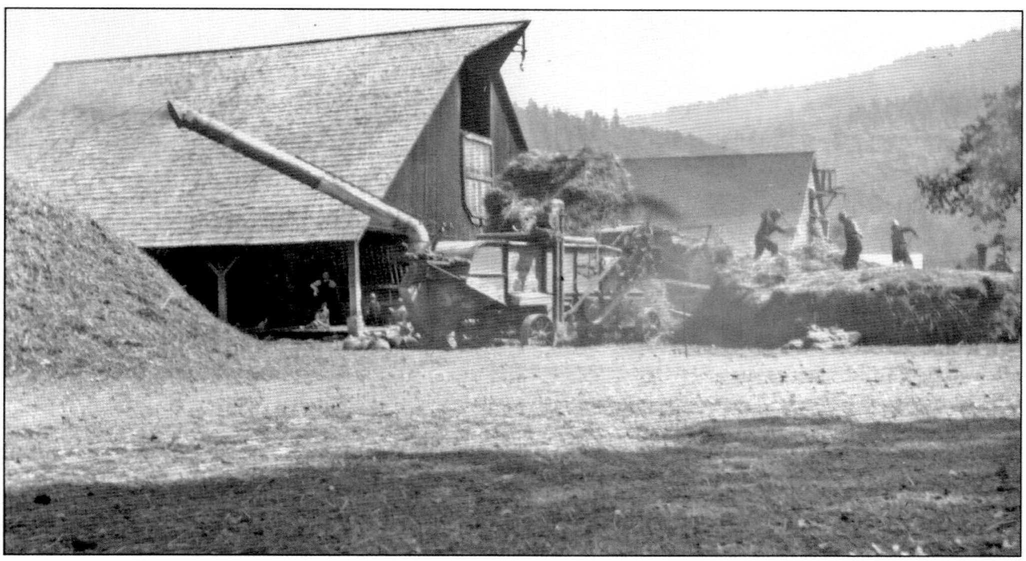
The gristmill got its grain from people in the valley getting together and thrashing. It usually took several men to do the thrashing, and they moved the thrasher from place to place. Historian Bob Cooke said he could remember this going on when he was just a small child.

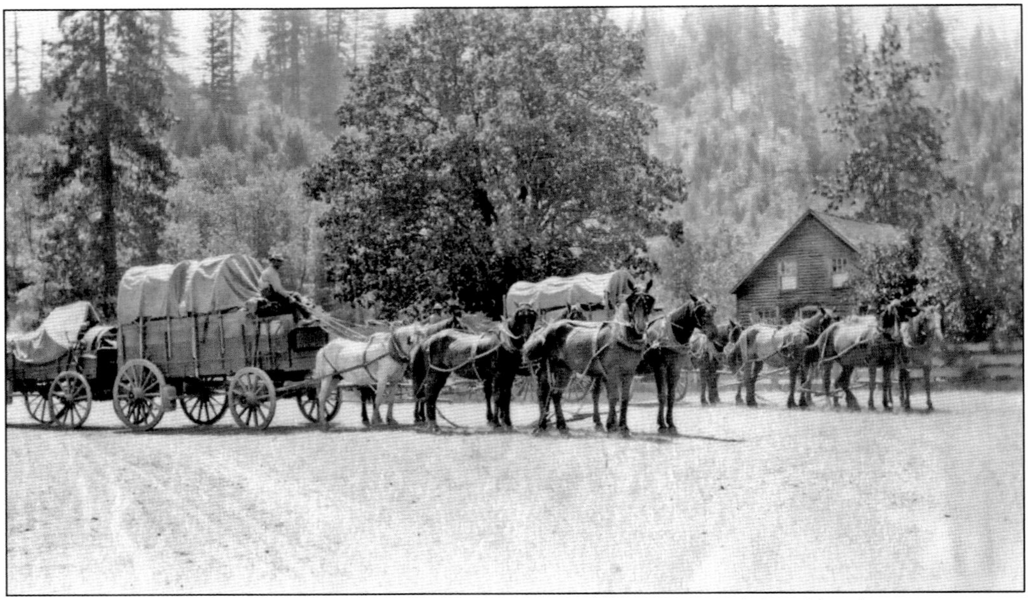

Wheelock's freight team is lined up in front of the Clary home, one of the oldest houses in town. The Clarys are relatives of the original Taylors. This street today is known as Cemetery Street because to the east of the teams in this photograph is the quaint cemetery where many early settlers rest in peace.

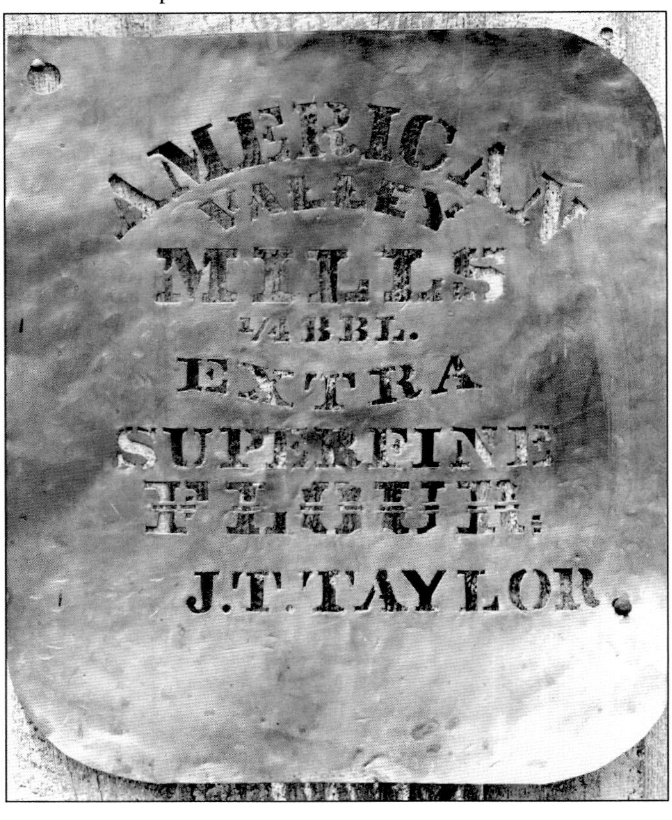

This old bronze plate was engraved with "American Valley Mills ¼ BBL. Extra Superfine Flour. J. T. Taylor." This was used to ink and stamp every flour sack that left his mill. This flour was shipped all over northern California and northern Nevada by freight teams.

Taylorsville had what they called the Peoples Popular Store, and the first IOOF lodge was above it. Built on the north side of the street, it was owned by J. C. Donnenwirth. The Peoples Popular Store has not been in existence for many years. A home now stands on that site.

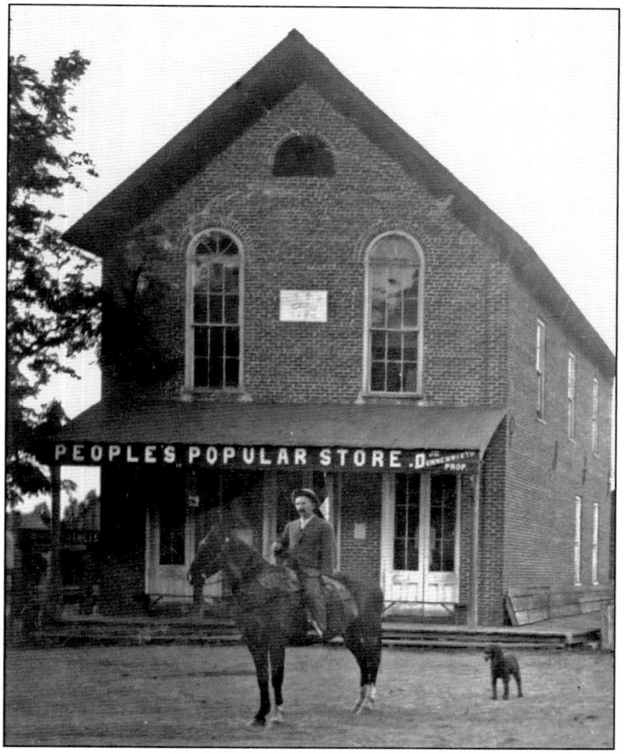

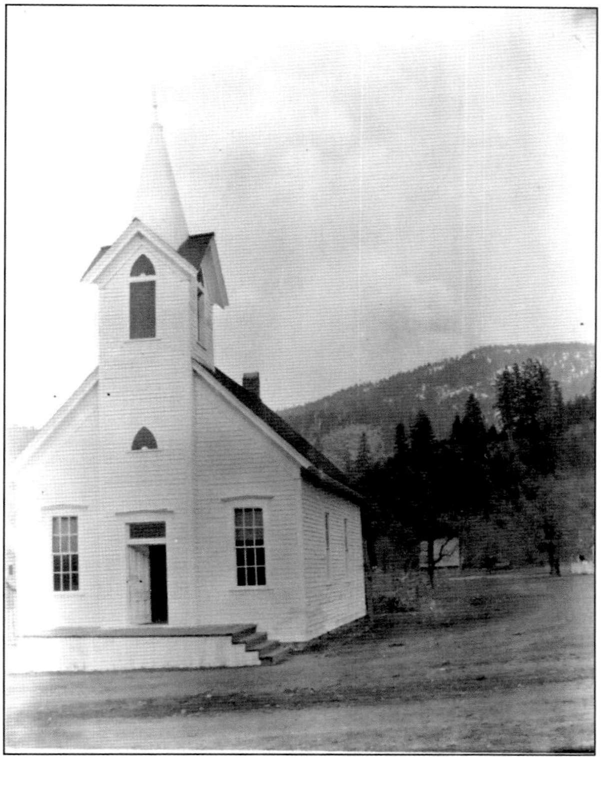

In 1875, the first church in Taylorsville opened. This church is now the Methodist Community Church and holds services every Sunday morning at 9:30. The church still has some original pieces inside, including lanterns, fixtures, and pews. The old church bell still rings every Sunday morning. The author went to Sunday school in this church and rang that bell.

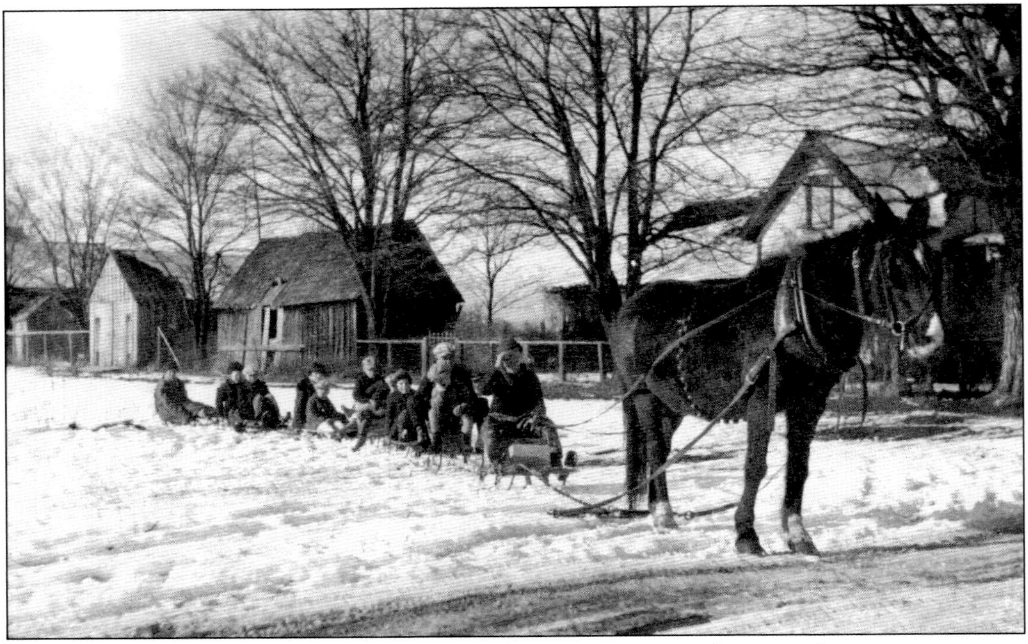

In winter, the old sleighs were a great means of transportation and, as seen here, a great means of winter play and entertainment. This horse and sleigh is approaching what is now known as Thompson Street. The author lived on this street for about nine years while he was growing up. At the end of this street is the old brick schoolhouse.

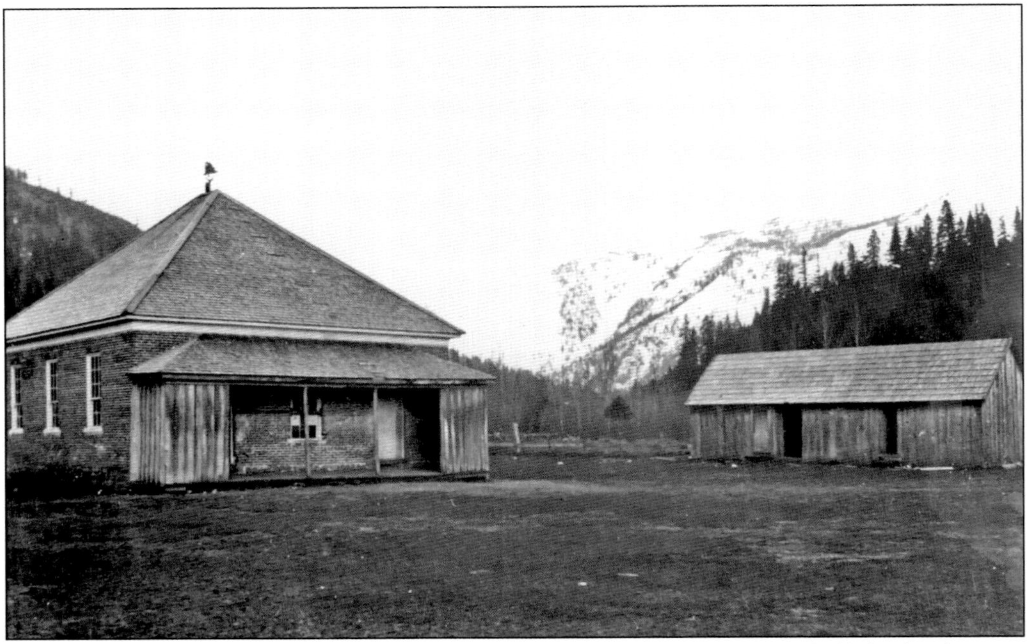

The old one-room brick schoolhouse was built in Taylorsville in 1864, and all the bricks were fired locally. It is the oldest brick schoolhouse in the state that still stands in the original place it was built. The last year the old brick schoolhouse held classes was 1949. The building was condemned that year, and the author was in the last graduating class.

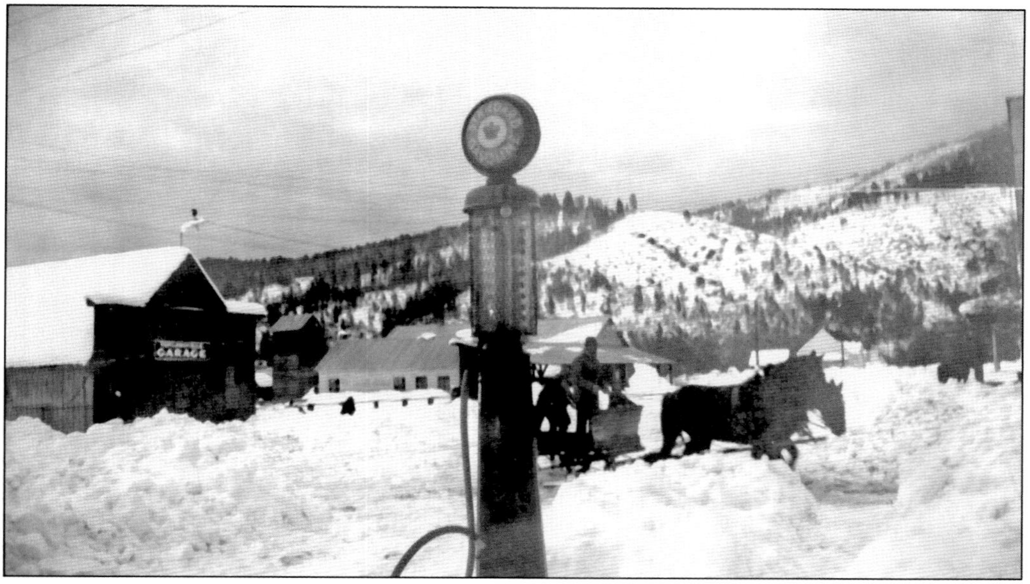

In later years, when more automobiles were coming into the valley, there was a gas pump on the corner of the Red and White store on Main Street. Looking down the street, the old creamery is visible, and to the right of the pump is the old G. R. Clark store. Both buildings are still there today, but the gas pump is gone.

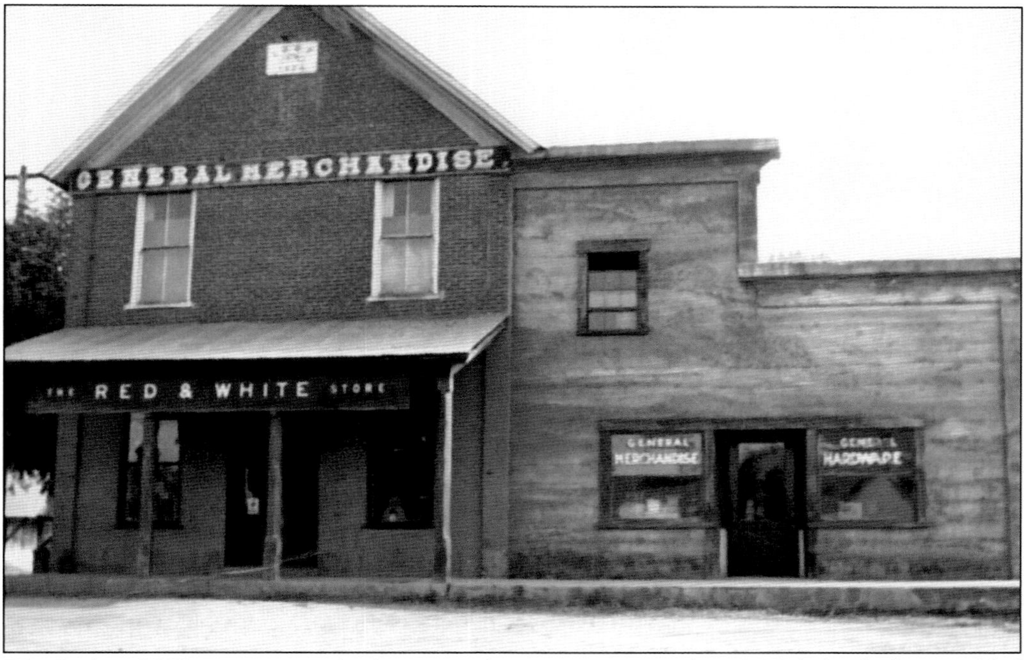

The Red and White store was built in 1862 by W. G. Young. The IOOF lodge hall was added upstairs in 1874. In 1875, Young's brother, John C. Young, came back to Taylorsville and went into business with him. In 1879, John bought his brother out. John was married October 29, 1879, to Ella Cottingham, and they had one child, Marian, born October 18, 1880. Young was also the postmaster and an agent for the Western Union Telegraph Company.

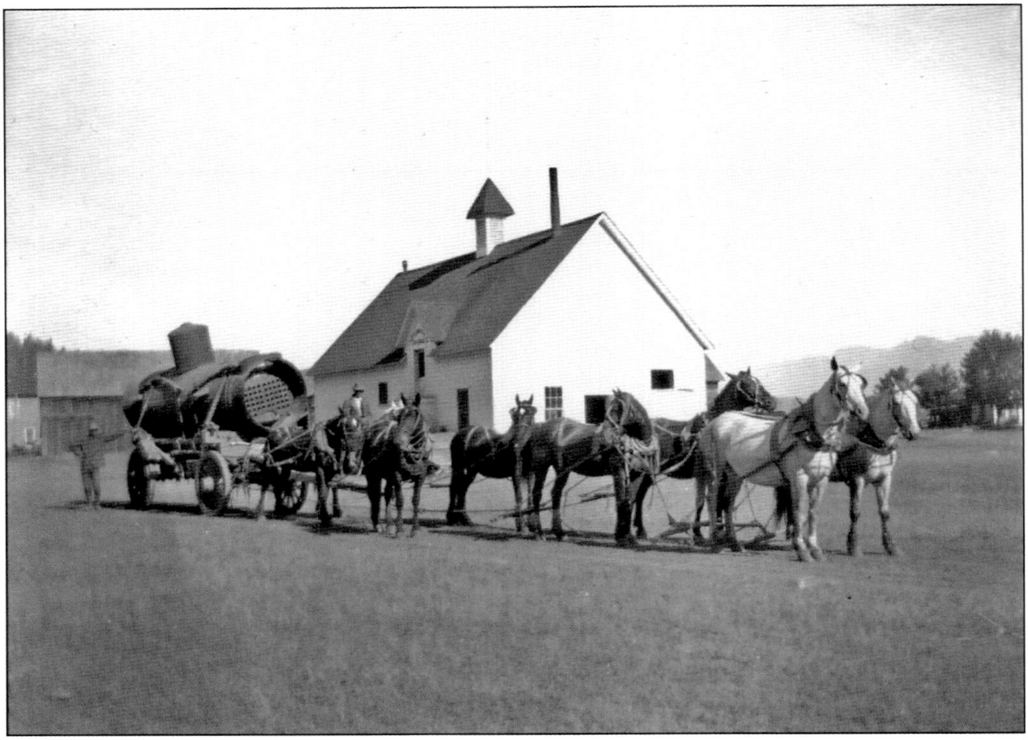

The weight of the freight ready to be transported to Engels Mine is obvious in the number of horses in the team pulling it in the photograph above. The freight lines not only hauled over the main road but also up to the mines, which were now going strong. Note the creamery in the background.

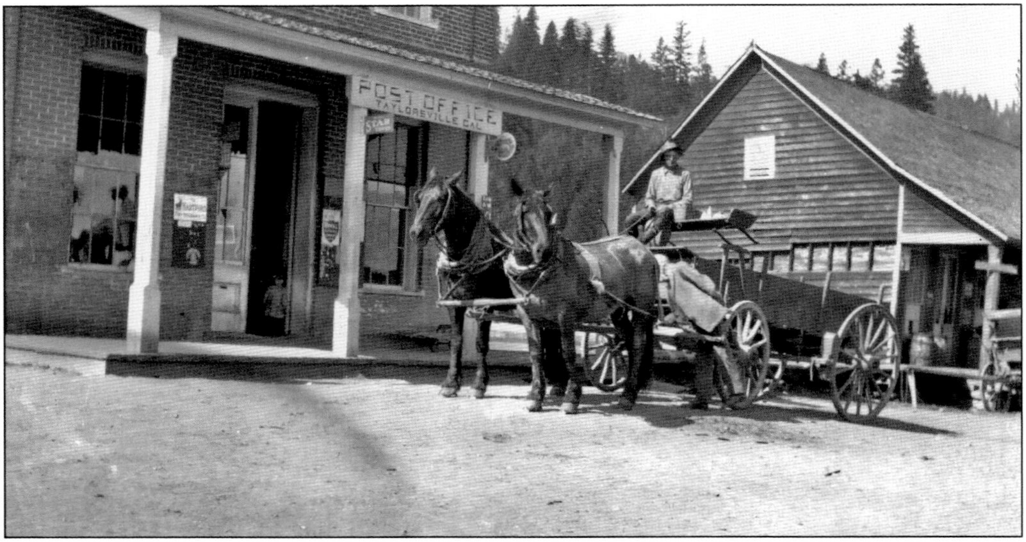

The old brick store that held the post office was a stopping place for all the wagons that were going through town, and for all the locals, too. The main street was getting more traffic all the time as the valley was growing, and the street was the main route from Nevada and the Sierra Valley to the Sacramento Valley.

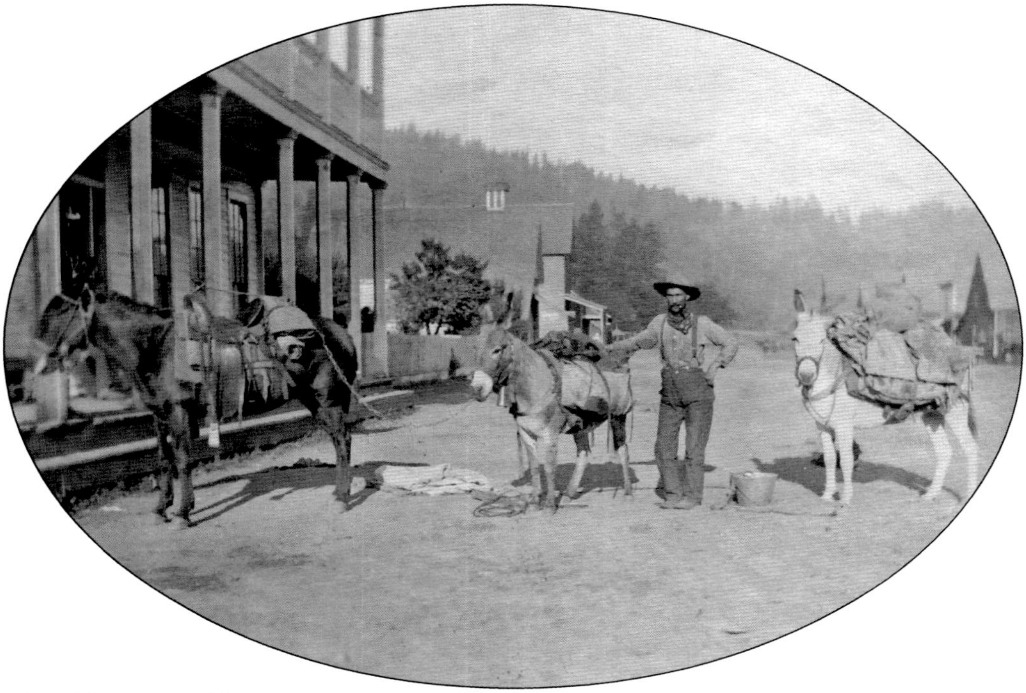

This old miner and his mule came into town for more supplies and possibly to rent a room for the night and have a shower. He is standing in front of the old Vernon House Hotel. The picture is looking to the west with the miner on the south side of the street. This was a common sight when Taylorsville was booming.

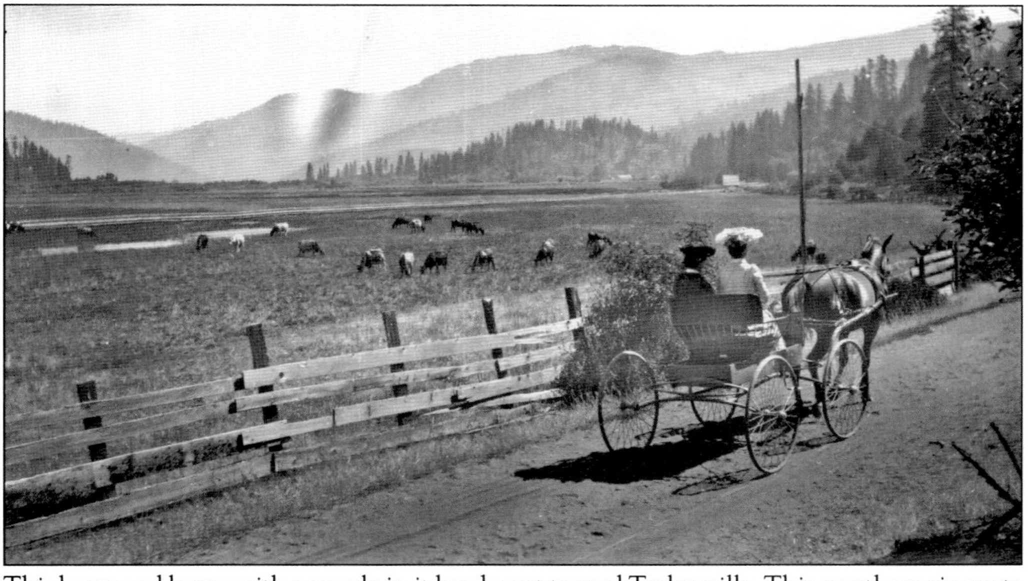

This horse and buggy with a couple in it heads east toward Taylorsville. This was the main route from Reno to the Sacramento Valley. Note all the nice pastureland and a barn in the background. They are probably out for a Sunday ride.

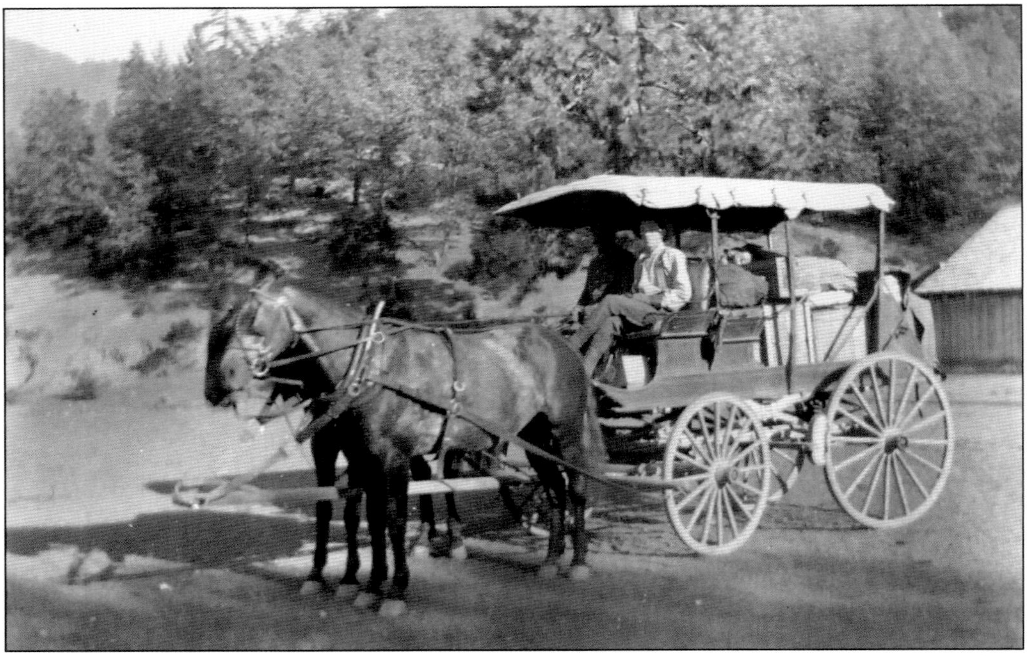

This photograph shows one of the many stagecoaches that passed through town on the way from Nevada to the Sacramento Valley. The driver of this stage is Lloyd Hardgrave; his nickname was "Doc." The Hardgraves were one of the early families in this valley. The Vernon House was owned by a Hardgrave.

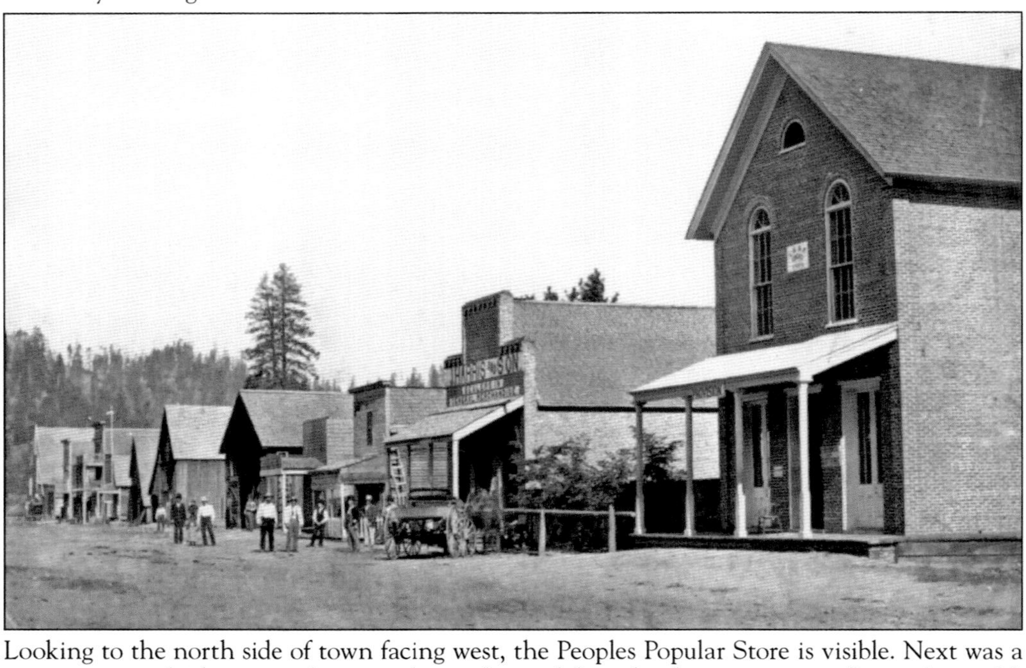

Looking to the north side of town facing west, the Peoples Popular Store is visible. Next was a grocery store, which is now a business that makes and ships dried arrangements all over the world. Next are old blacksmith shops, which are no longer there. Now there is a small private school and an abandoned service station.

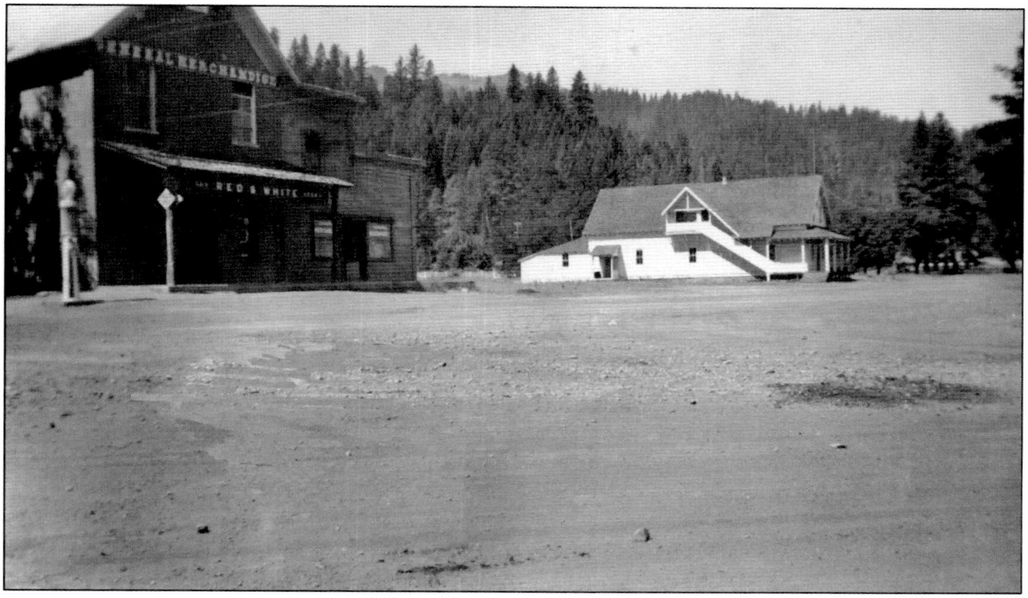

On the left is the brick market, and down the street is the old Grange Hall, which was known for its dance floor that also served as a basketball court. Many dances were held in this building. The author's father, John "Tuffy" McCutcheon, played trumpet in a dance band there many Saturday nights. They had a huge lodge hall upstairs and a kitchen.

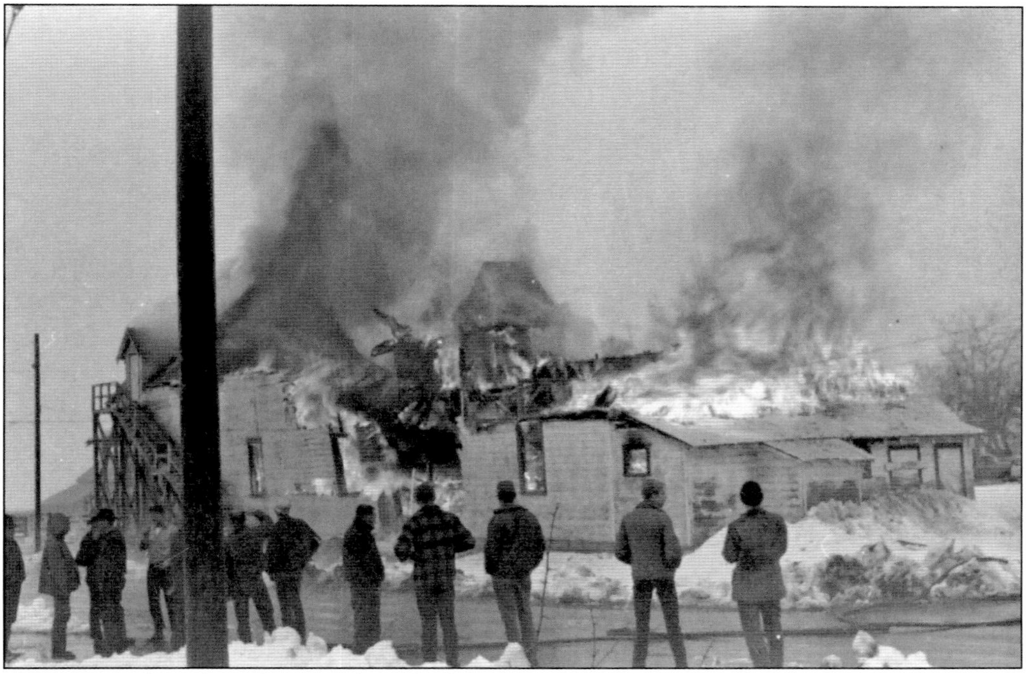

It was a sad day when the town lost the huge Grange Hall to fire on January 28, 1967. It was burning very strong before anyone was even aware it was on fire. With the hall being so old and the lumber so dry, it quickly burned all the way to the ground. The local fire department saved the buildings close by. (Courtesy of Loren Kingdon.)

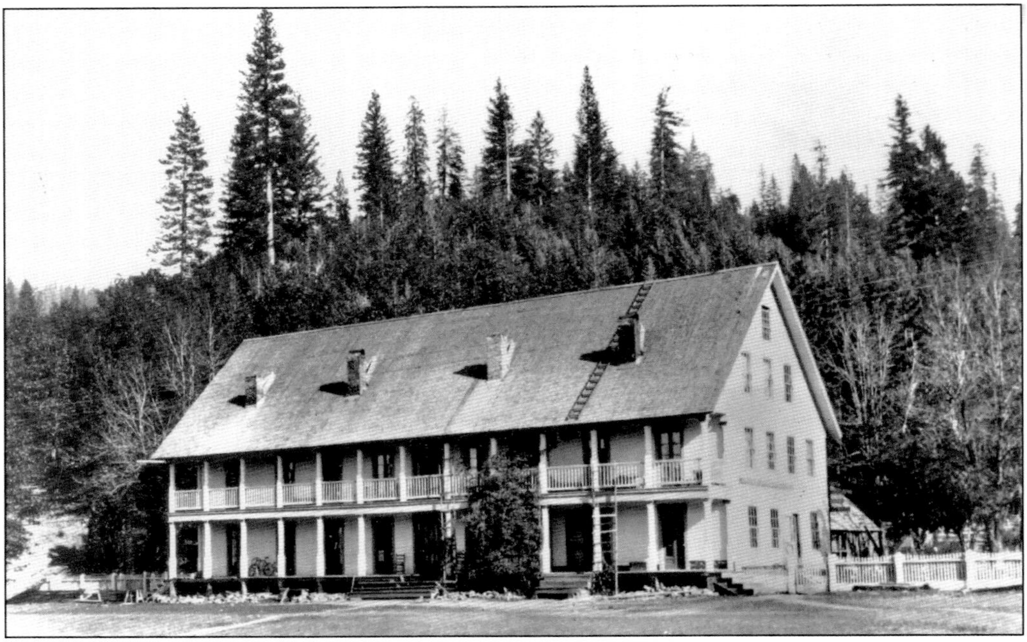

Pictured here is the Taylor Hotel, which stood on the site where the grammar school is today. It was a three-story building and, at one time, had many rooms rented in it. In later years, Marian Donninwirth owned the hotel. At one point, Marian was the only person living in the entire hotel. The author also lived in this hotel for a short time.

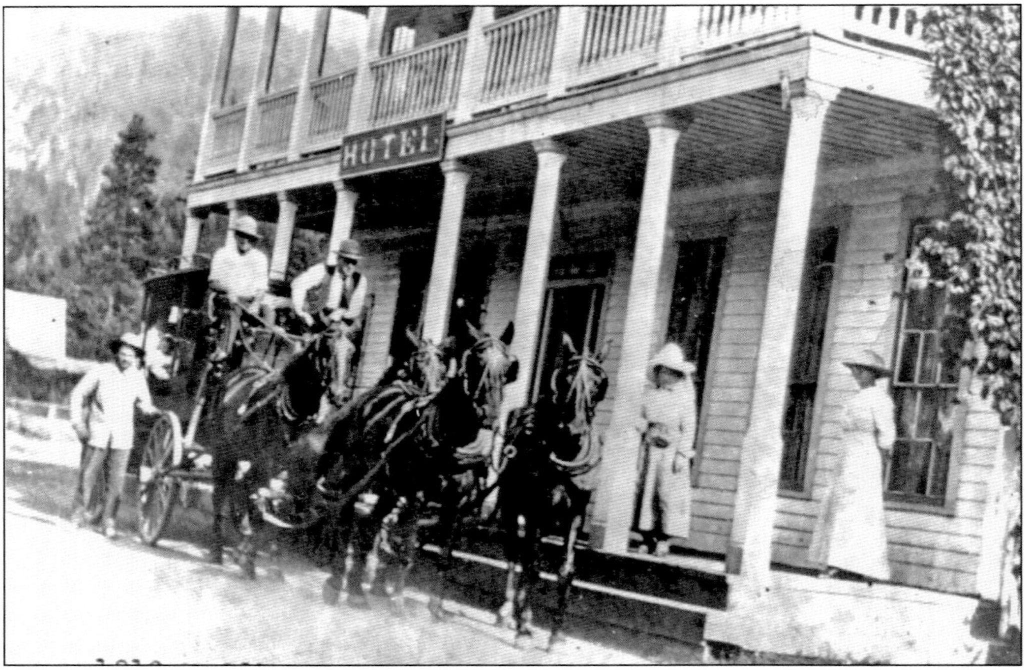

The second huge hotel in Taylorsville was built downtown and was called the Vernon House. It was owned by John Hardgrave. This hotel was torn down in the 1940s. The town had no use for it once stages were not coming through anymore and people began modernizing the area.

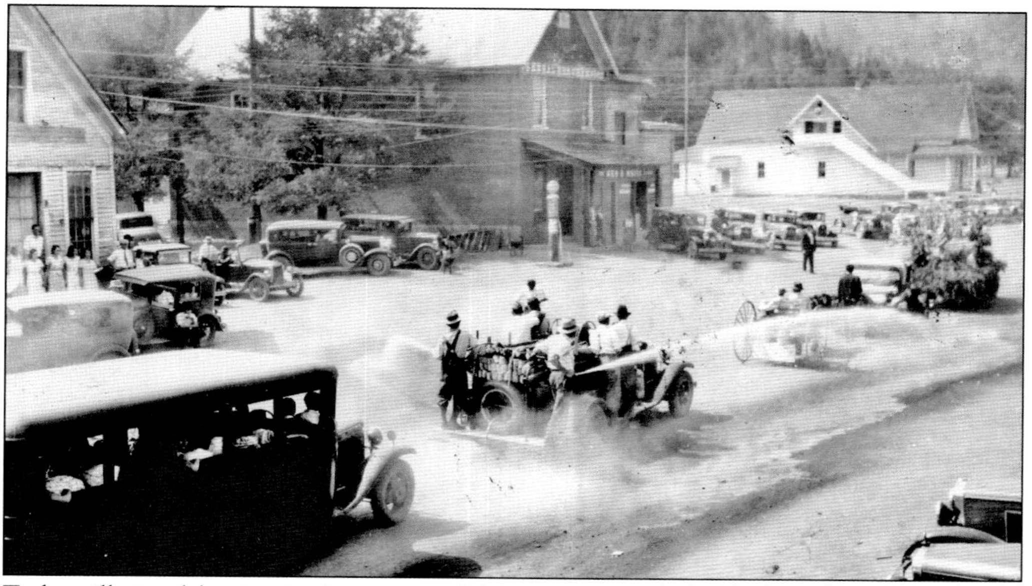

Taylorsville is celebrating in this picture of the main street. In the old days, a parade was quite common down the main street of town, and still is today. The Fourth of July is parade day in Taylorsville now. This photograph shows the old fire trucks spraying water and a good view of the market and Grange Hall.

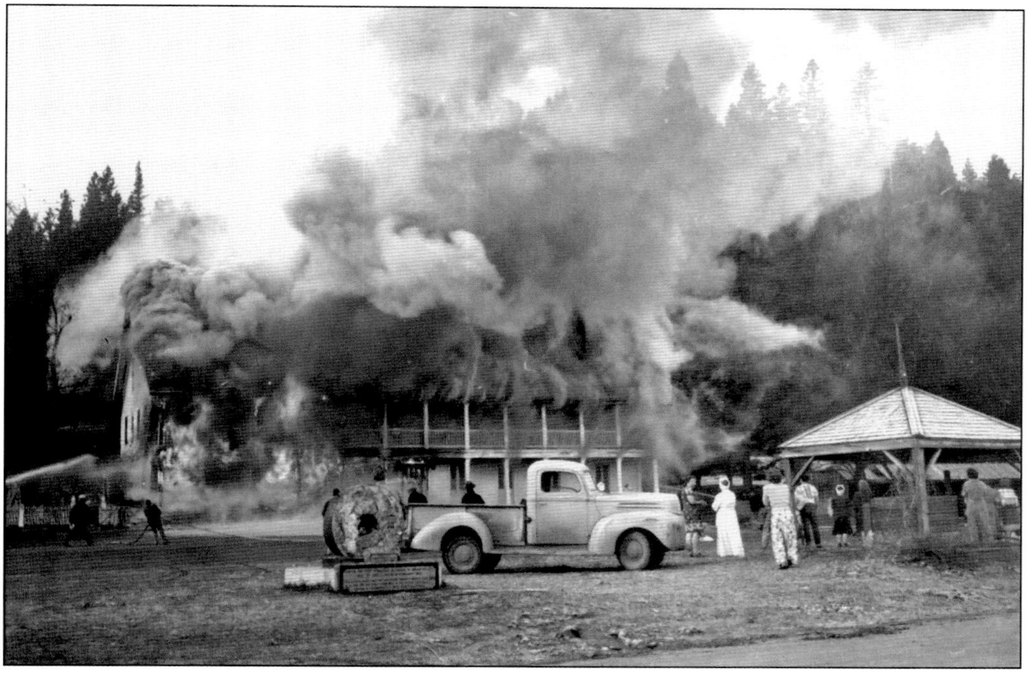

It was a sad day when the fire alarm went off on April 1, 1949. It was thought at first to have been an April Fools Day prank but soon was seen to be real, as fire trucks raced to the old Taylor Hotel. All they could do was keep the fire from destroying anything else. The author took a picture himself with a little Kodak 127 his aunt had given him for Christmas. (Courtesy of the author.)

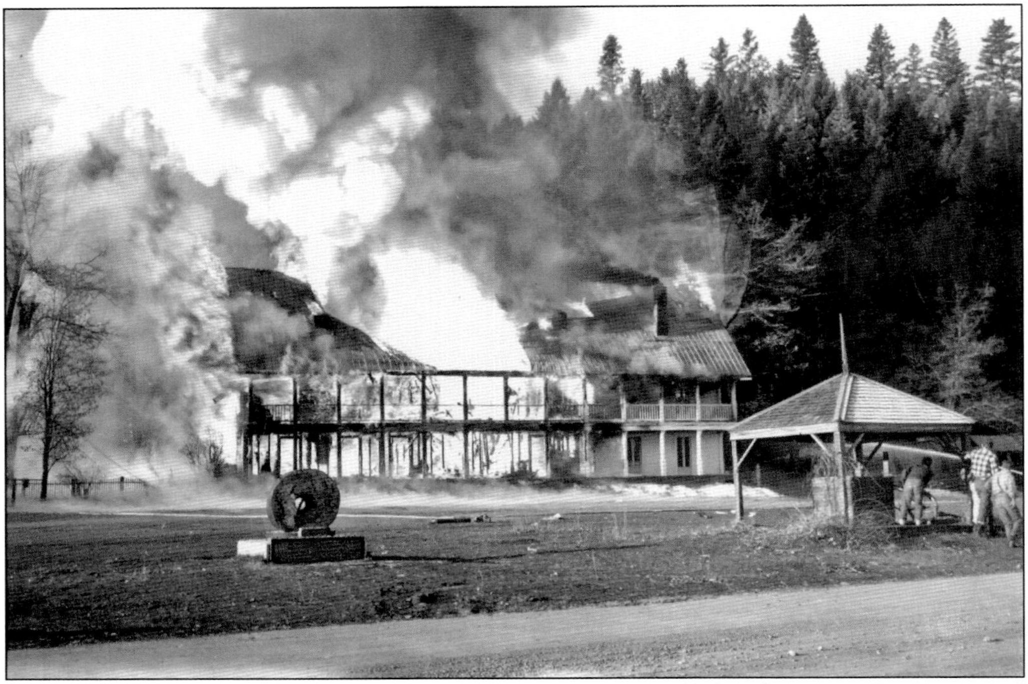

It did not take long for the huge three-story building to be engulfed in flames. In the foreground is an old well with a roof over it and the millstone that came around the Horn from Pennsylvania. The hotel was being restored at the time of the fire and had a fine dining room and a small soda fountain. (Courtesy of the author.)

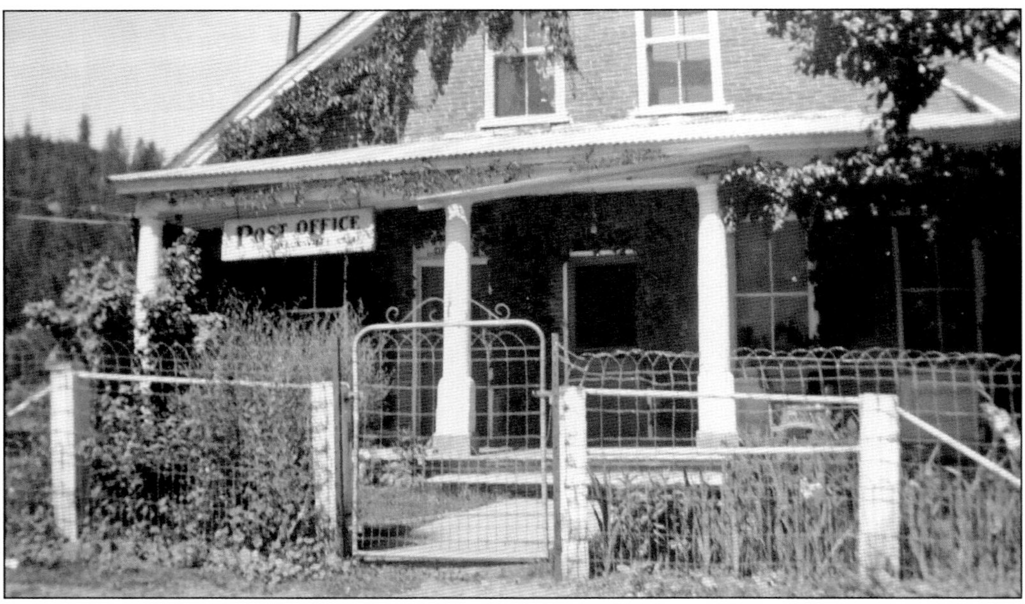

This is the old Boyden home that at one time was also the post office, which was run by the Boydens. The post office was in the front part of their house. This brick building is still there today and is one of the oldest houses in Taylorsville—probably one of the five oldest in town.

Three

GREENVILLE

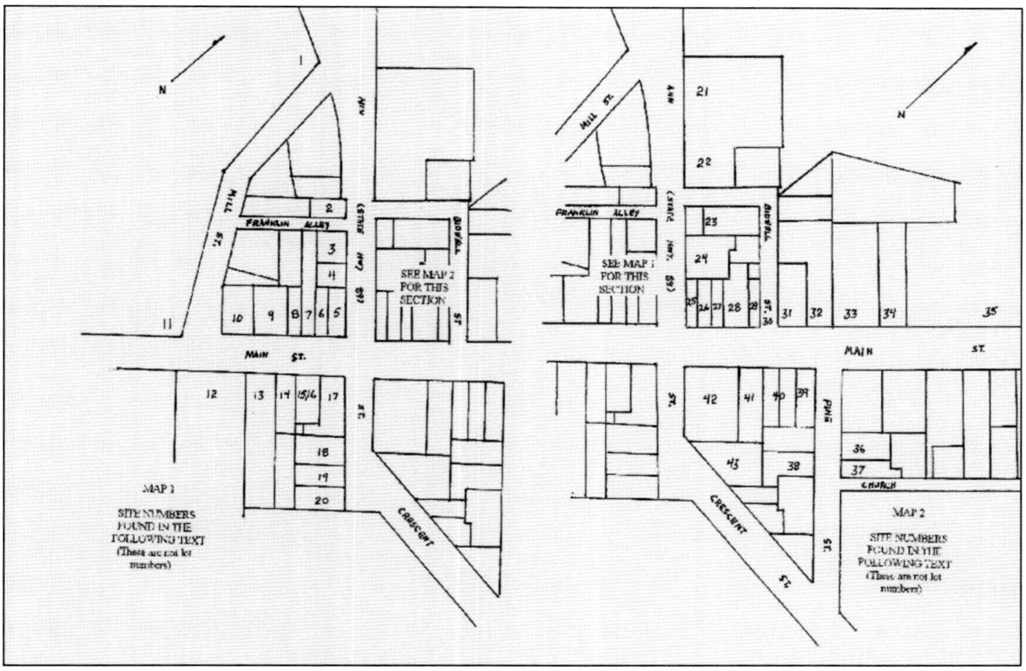

This map, created by Patrick O'Halloran of Greenville, helps show the placement of many of the old buildings in town, some of which are still there, and gives perspective for where things are today. Greenville was named after Mr. and Mrs. Green, some of the first settlers in the area. Mr. Green drowned when the first dam that was built to form Round Valley Lake collapsed. In 1862, a man by the name of Henry C. Bidwell came to Greenville and was probably one of the first to start a business there; he built a trading post. The Bidwell name was a common one in the area and is still heard quite often today. The Bidwells soon owned the water system in Greenville. Soon other businesses moved down from the town of Round Valley. (Courtesy of Patrick O'Halloran.)

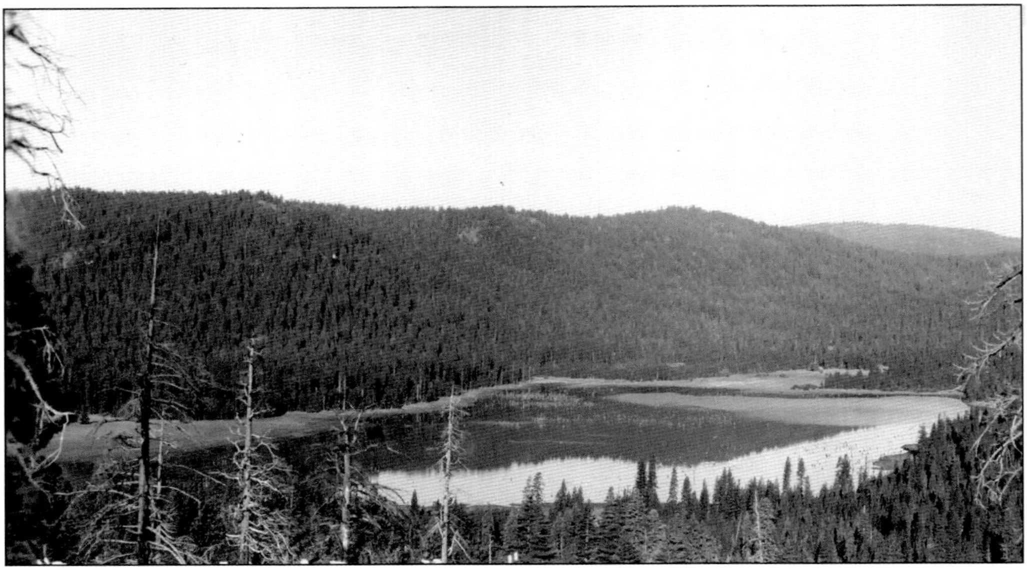

This older picture shows Round Valley Lake, which was dammed years ago and is the water supply for the town of Greenville. The town of Round Valley was once off to the northeast, but it was short-lived because of the harsh winters. Eventually the town moved to a lower elevation and became Greenville.

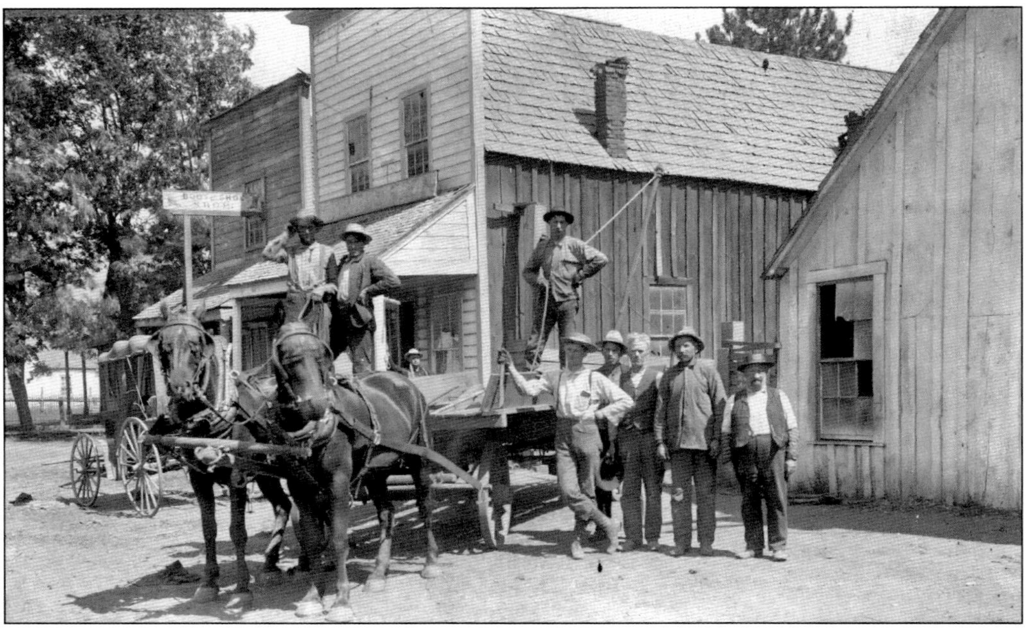

Pictured is one of the older buildings in Greenville during the horse-and-buggy days. At the far left is No. 39 on the map at the corner of Main and Pine Streets. On the left were two buildings, but today there is only one structure on that site. Greenville was growing due to all the mines. The New York, Indian Valley, McClellan, Southern Eureka, Cherokee, Arcadia, and Wolf Creek quartz mines made Greenville very popular to people entering the valley.

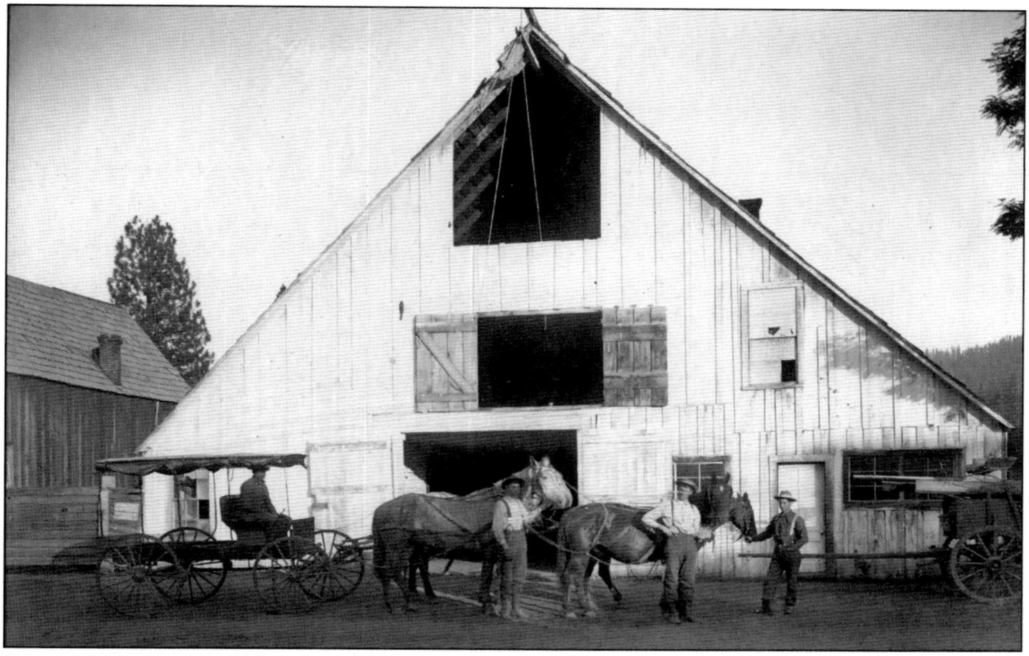

Pictured here is an old barn and livery stable in Greenville (No. 40 on the map). Horses and freight wagons were the only transportation in those days, and both needed to be taken care of, which is why there were so many barns and blacksmith shops on Main Street. The author assumes the blacksmith shops were only second to the saloons in number.

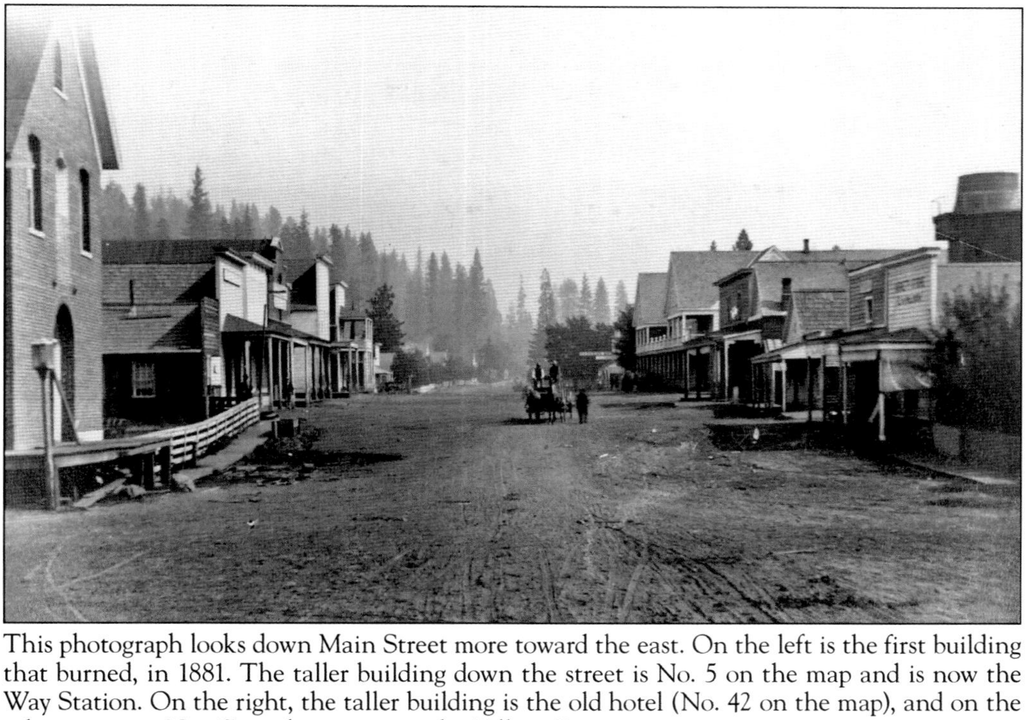

This photograph looks down Main Street more toward the east. On the left is the first building that burned, in 1881. The taller building down the street is No. 5 on the map and is now the Way Station. On the right, the taller building is the old hotel (No. 42 on the map), and on the other corner is No. 17 on the map, now the Village Drug.

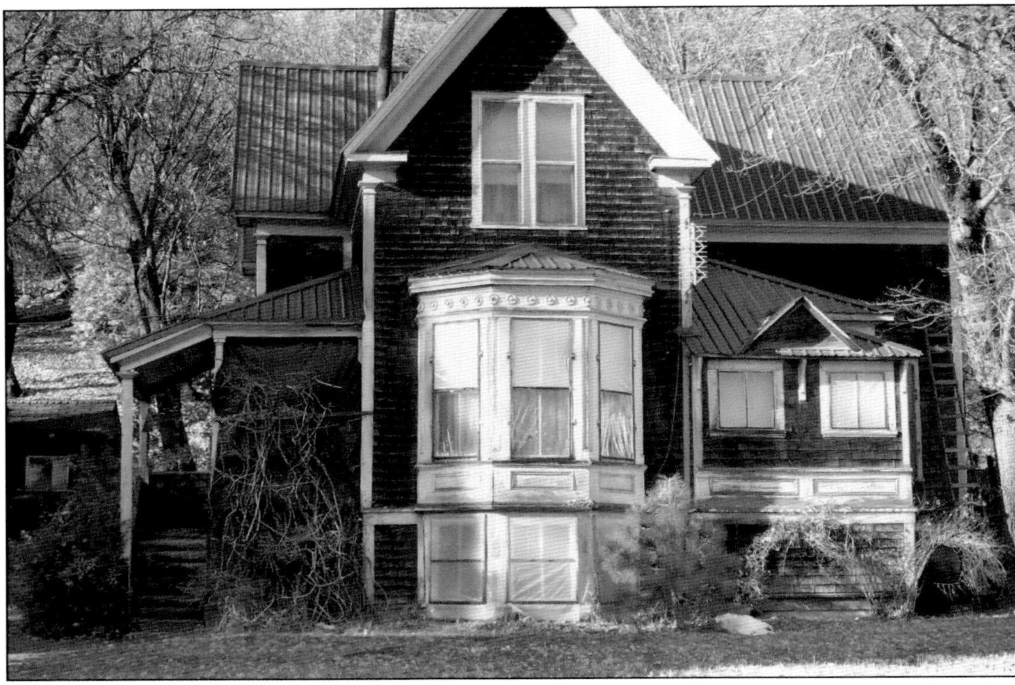

This house, owned by Elmer Hunt and his family, is one of the older homes in Greenville. It had the same floor plan for many years. Elmer's wife, Sophia (known as Dolly), and son, Raymond, continue to occupy the house. This home is on the hill side of Main Street toward North Valley Road. (Courtesy of the author.)

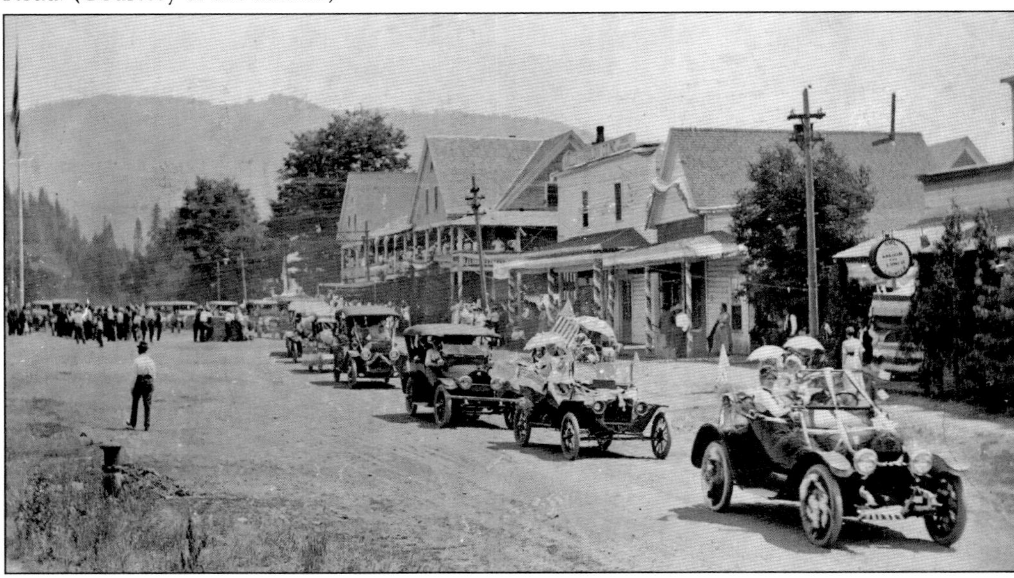

This is Main Street in Greenville in the late 1910s and early 1920s. As evidenced in the photograph, they had lots of celebrations and parades back then. Greenville was growing very rapidly with all the mines in the area. By 1883, Greenville had a population of 500 people and a sawmill, flour mill, stables, saloons, restaurants, bakeries, barbershops, and several general stores. Everything people needed was right in town.

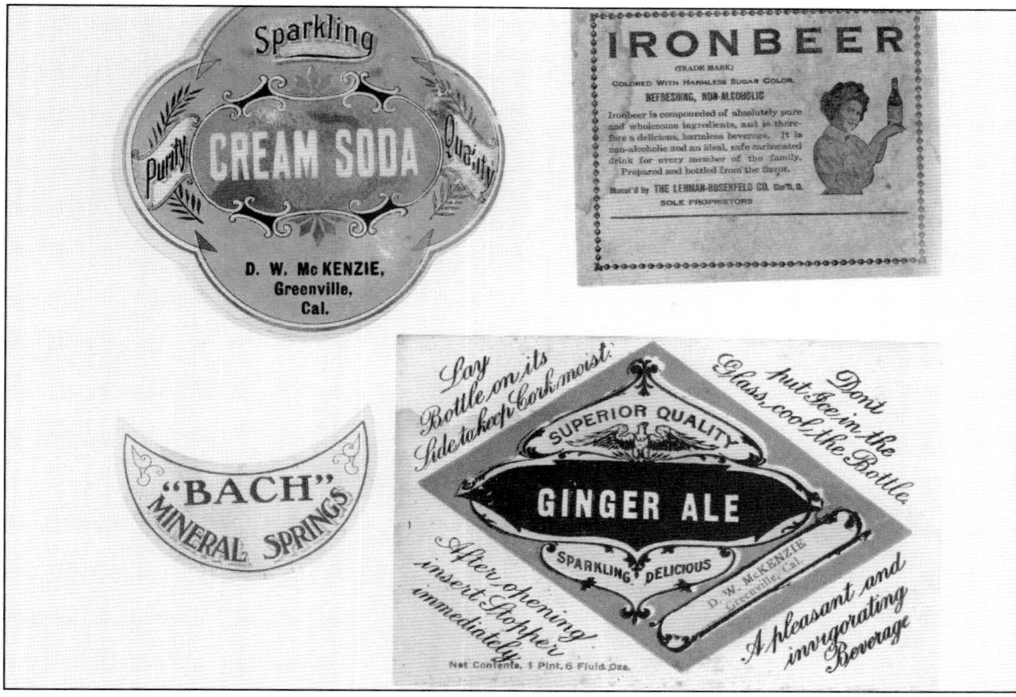

Pictured here are some of the old soft drink logos—Ironbeer, made by the Lehman-Rosenfeld Company; cream soda made by D. W. McKenzie; and ginger ale, also by D. W. McKenzie. Ironbeer was a nonalcoholic beer that could be enjoyed by everyone. The sparkling ginger ale came with instructions telling people the best way to drink it and how to keep the sparkle in it after it was opened.

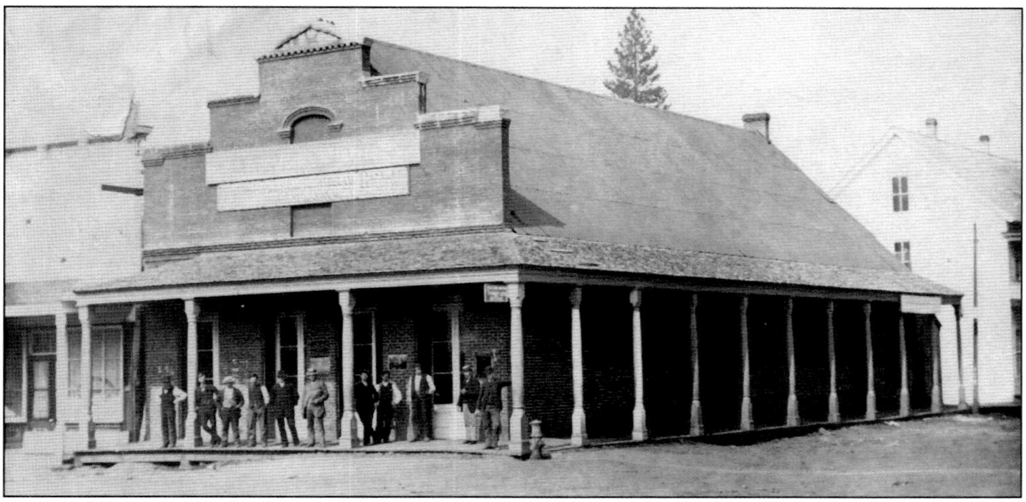

The first mention of this building (No. 5) was in 1875. Owned by J. H. Whitlock, the building had many uses through the years. It was a variety store, a general store, a saloon, and a restaurant. It was owned by J. H. Whitlock, an agent for the telegraph and Wells Fargo Express. It was thought that he ran the Wells Fargo Express on another site. In 1877–1878, this corner was bought by McIntyre and Company. McIntyre is still a well-known name in Greenville. Today this building is the Way Station.

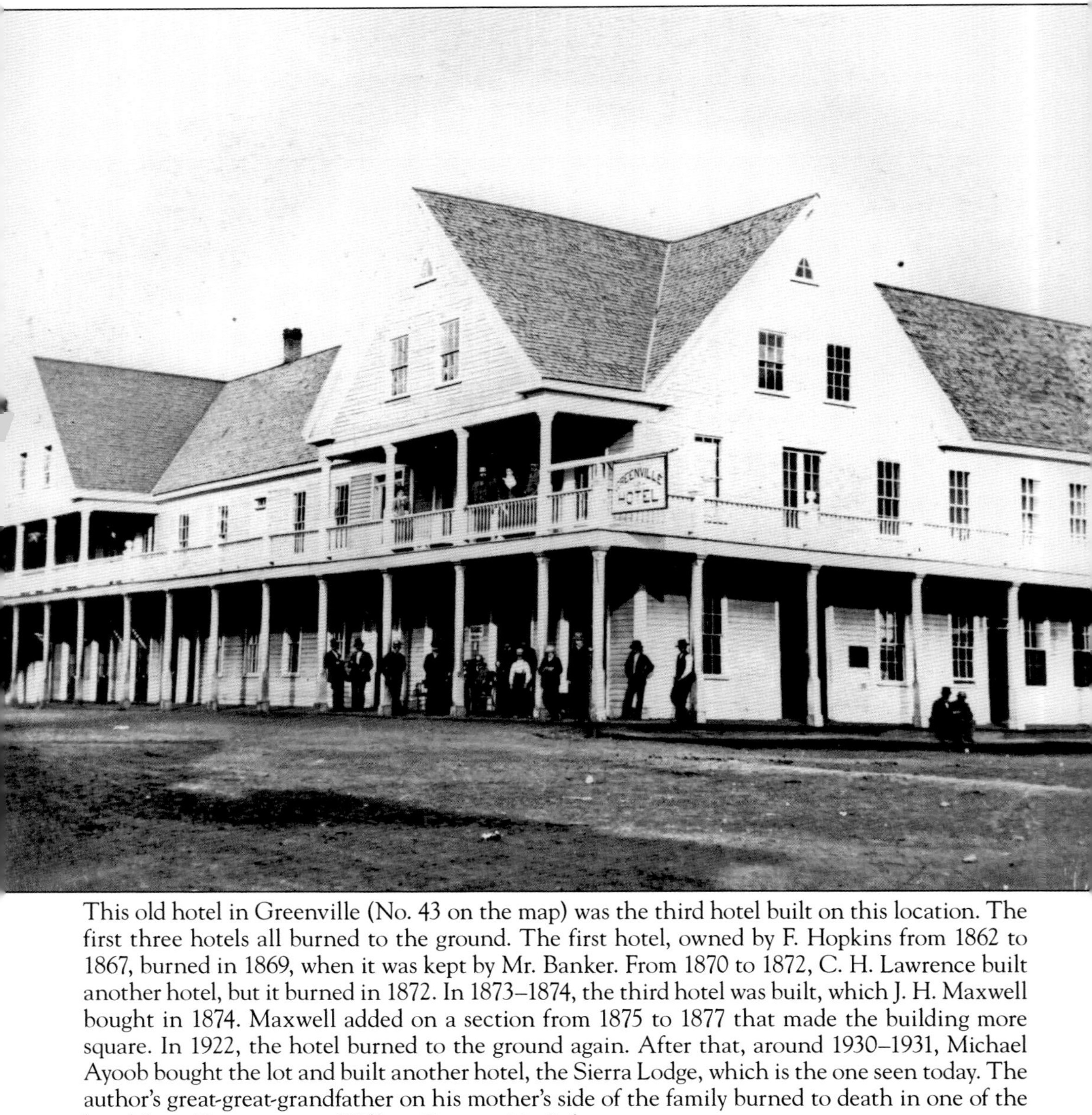

This old hotel in Greenville (No. 43 on the map) was the third hotel built on this location. The first three hotels all burned to the ground. The first hotel, owned by F. Hopkins from 1862 to 1867, burned in 1869, when it was kept by Mr. Banker. From 1870 to 1872, C. H. Lawrence built another hotel, but it burned in 1872. In 1873–1874, the third hotel was built, which J. H. Maxwell bought in 1874. Maxwell added on a section from 1875 to 1877 that made the building more square. In 1922, the hotel burned to the ground again. After that, around 1930–1931, Michael Ayoob bought the lot and built another hotel, the Sierra Lodge, which is the one seen today. The author's great-great-grandfather on his mother's side of the family burned to death in one of the hotel fires. His name was William Bascom McColm.

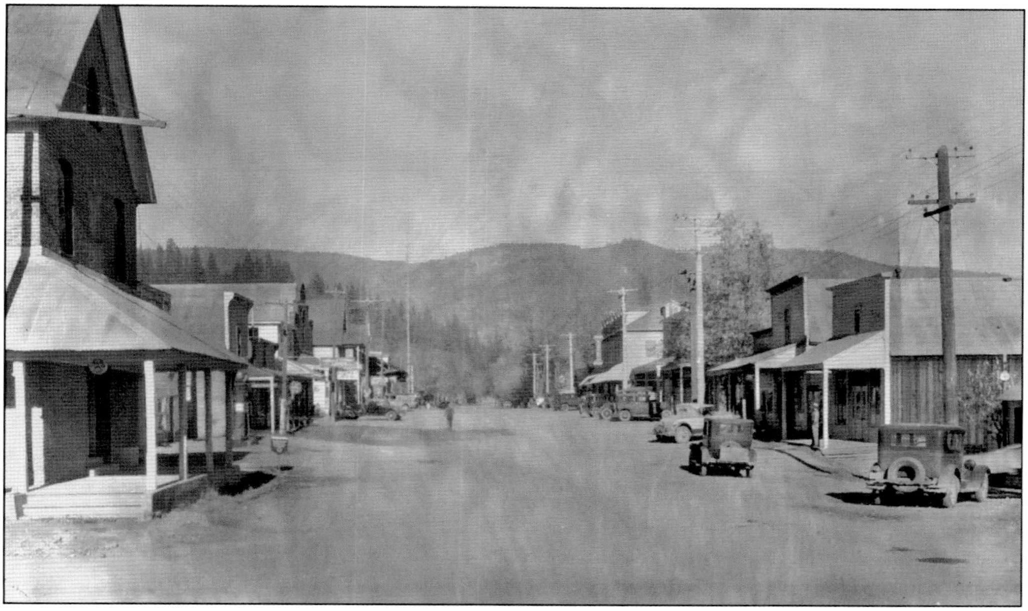

Pictured here is Main Street in Greenville. It is amazing just how many of these old buildings still stand today. Many have been remodeled and are now businesses. The biggest change on Main Street is that there used to be more than seven saloons, and today there is only one. Check the map—on the left are No. 9, No. 5, No. 6, and No. 25, and on the right are No. 14, No. 17, and No. 42, the old hotel.

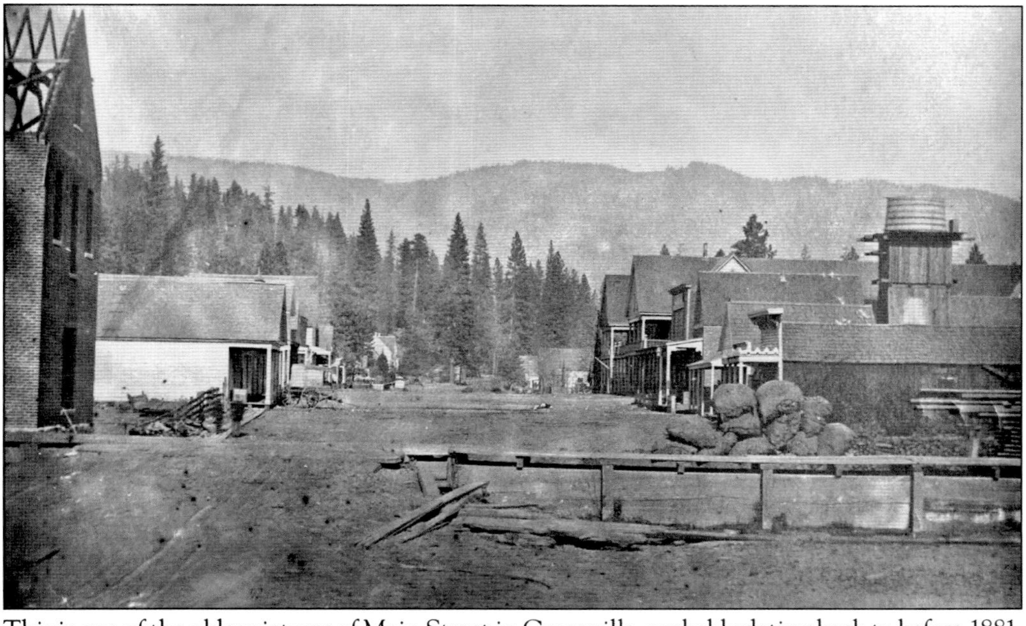

This is one of the older pictures of Main Street in Greenville, probably dating back to before 1881. The first white building on the left burned in 1881. On the right are some of the same buildings in the previous photograph from before the beginning of the 20th century.

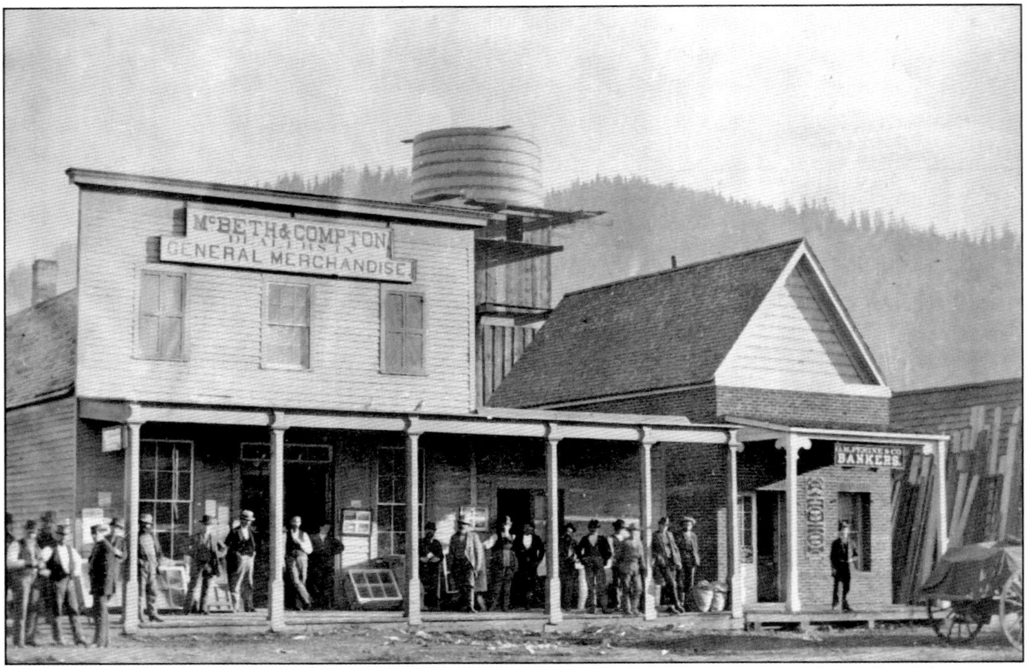

Taken around 1876, this photograph shows No. 17 on the left and No. 16 on the right. This is the corner of Main Street and Highway 89 and is now Village Drug. The right part of this building used to be a bank, and in later years, it was made into one building.

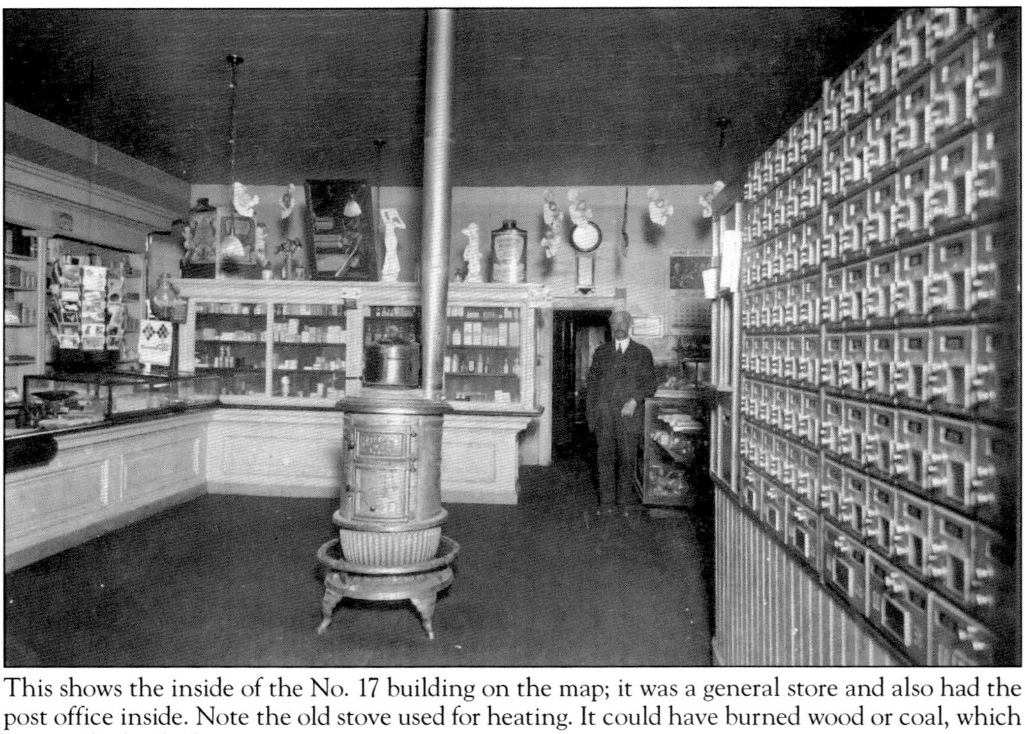

This shows the inside of the No. 17 building on the map; it was a general store and also had the post office inside. Note the old stove used for heating. It could have burned wood or coal, which was used a lot for heating.

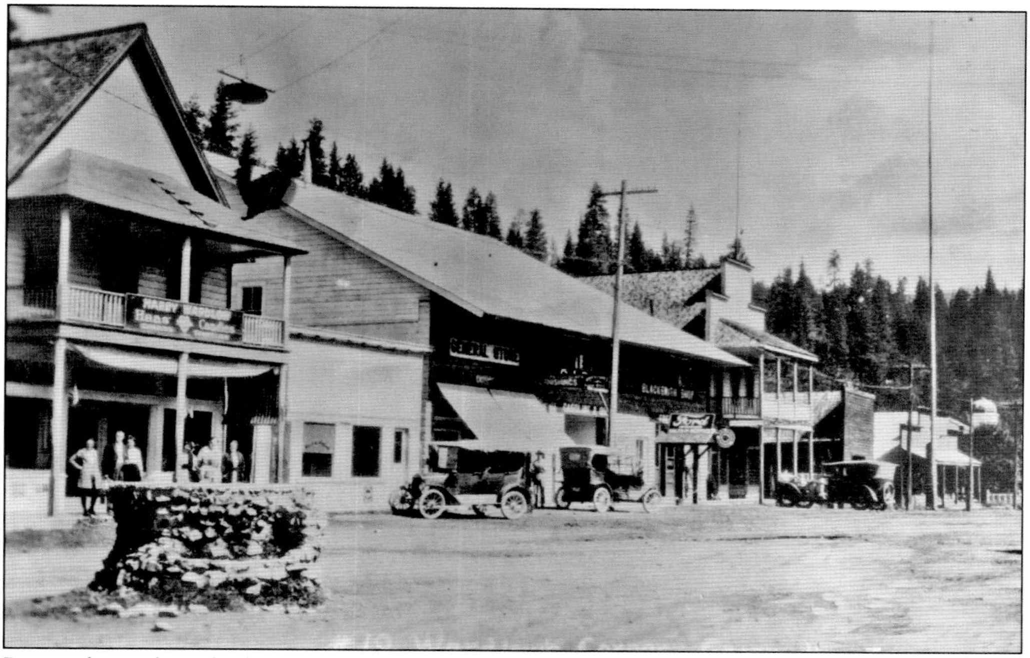

Pictured is a closer look at Main Street before 1931. Main Street was paved in 1931 and the old rock fountain was removed. From left to right, No. 25 was a saloon for years, No. 26 is a vacant lot now, No. 27 and No. 28 had two businesses under the one roof, No. 29 was also a saloon, then after the alley are buildings 31 and 32. Building No. 31 used to house fire equipment and later became a hotel.

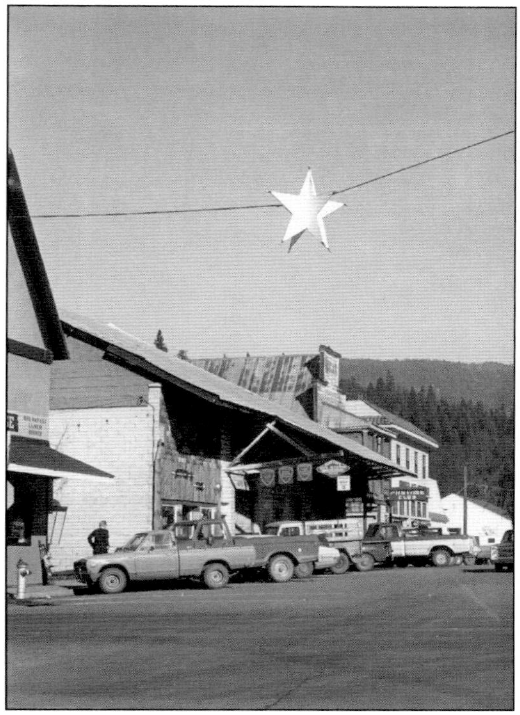

This is a better look at the buildings on Main Street. The long roof over the three businesses collapsed in the winter of 1993. The right portion went down, which was W. Hamblin's Garage, previously a pool hall. The building on the left is still there and was a saloon for many years; it is now Angie's Frame Shop. The buildings were constructed separately but under the same roof, which is why the one part stayed up.

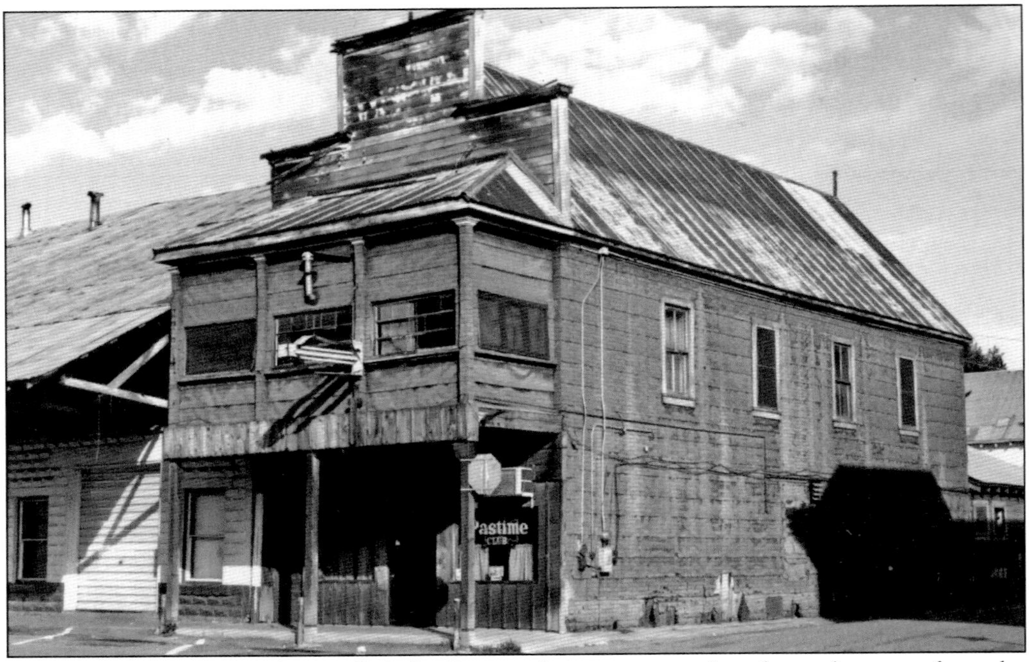

Building No. 29 was a saloon called the Pastime for many years. Just down the street from the Pastime was the old Batson Hospital. One night, a patient came up missing and a search was on. The hospital finally realized that this patient had a drinking problem, so the hospital staff went to Pastime. Sure enough, he was standing at the bar with his open hospital gown on.

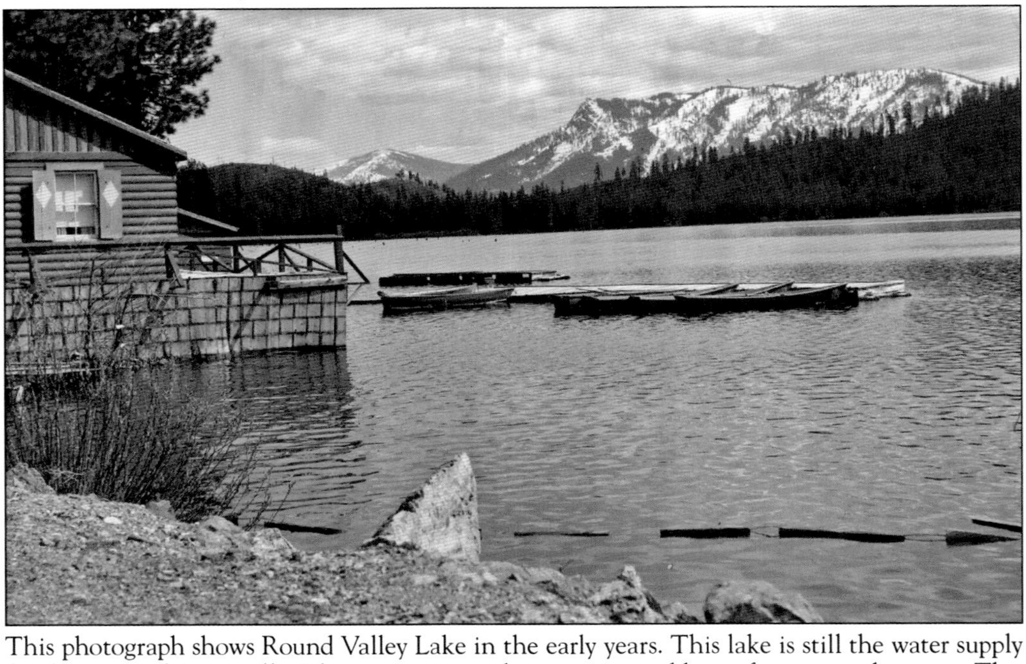

This photograph shows Round Valley Lake in the early years. This lake is still the water supply for the town of Greenville. There was a store, boat ramps, and boats for rent in the town. This lake is still very popular for its bass, catfish, and bluegill, and some organizations still have an annual bluegill derby for the children. Note the boat ramp in the lake.

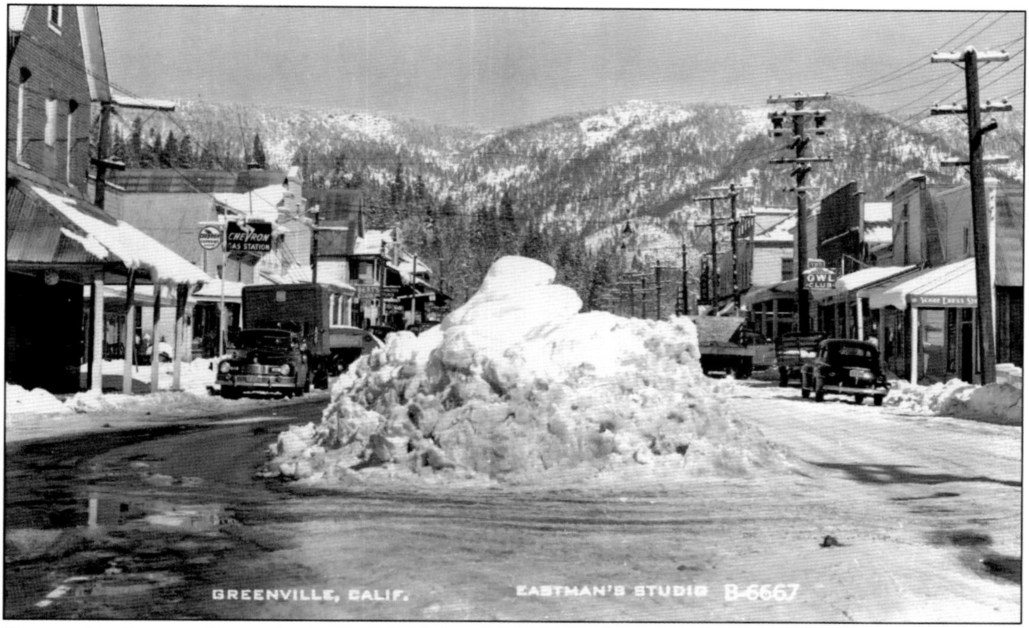

Pictured is Greenville in the later years. Most of these buildings are there today but have changed some and have different businesses in them. This picture was taken looking toward Keddie Ridge with the old lodge hall on the left, which is still there. In the winter, many vehicles got their hoods smashed when the snow fell off the roofs of Hamblin's Garage and the hotel.

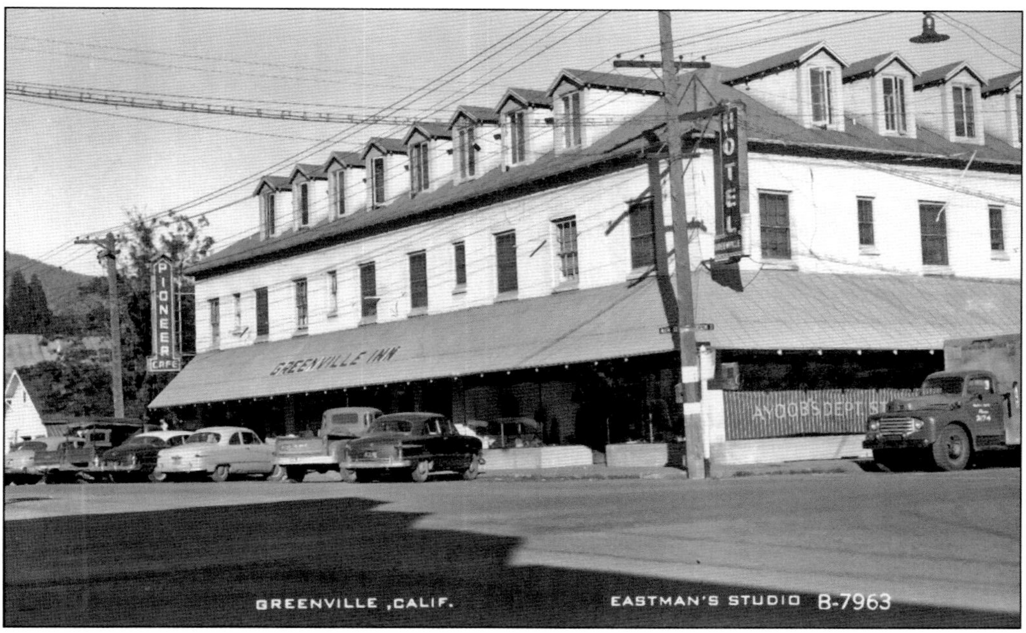

This picture shows the final hotel, built by M. D. Ayoob in 1931, which still stands today. It has been remodeled and has many rooms for people to stay in when they come to visit. This building once hosted a bar, restaurant, and clothing and sporting goods store known as Ayoob's. The cars date the photograph to the 1950s.

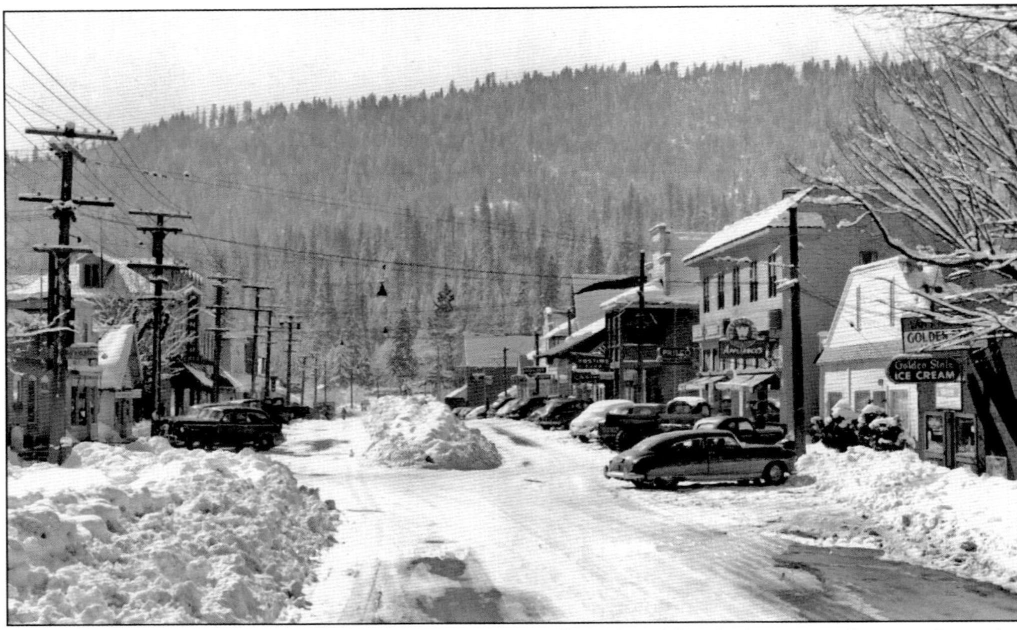

This image is looking down Main Street in Greenville. The old soda fountain, first on the right, is no longer there, but the second building, which used to be Batson's Hospital, is still there but is no longer a hospital. Next was a drugstore and soda fountain in the right side of the store. It then became a grocery store and hardware store, and now the entire building is Hunters Hardware.

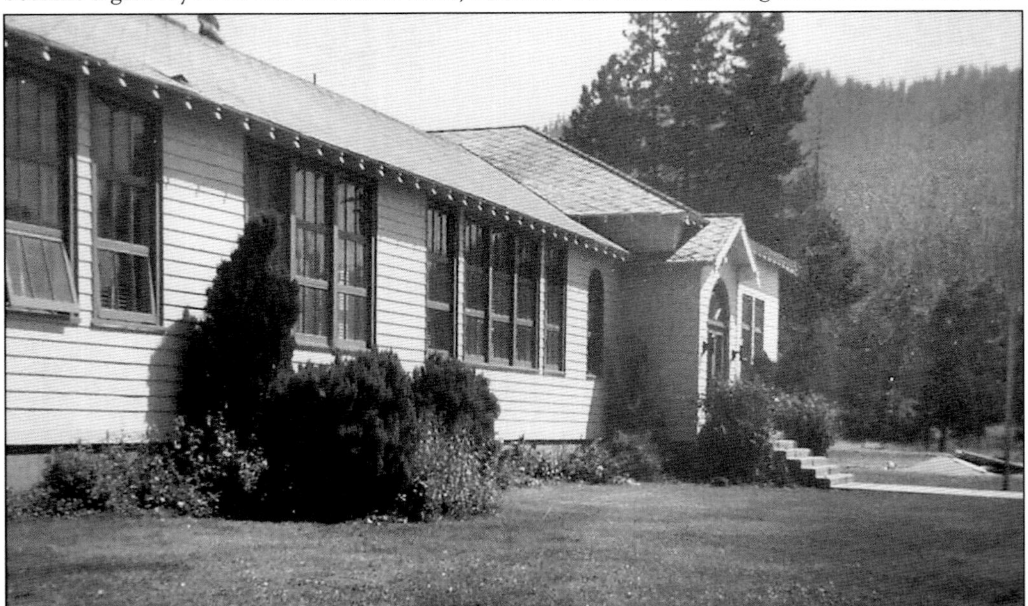

This is what Greenville High School looked like before it was torn down and a new one built in 1971. It had to be torn down because of the new laws on earthquake proofing for public buildings. Four generations of the author's family have graduated from Greenville High School—his father, John; the author and his sister, Barbara Gayel; his two sons, John and Ron; two grandsons, John and Mathew; and a granddaughter, Megan. (Courtesy of Sylvia Gloster.)

Four

Crescent Mills

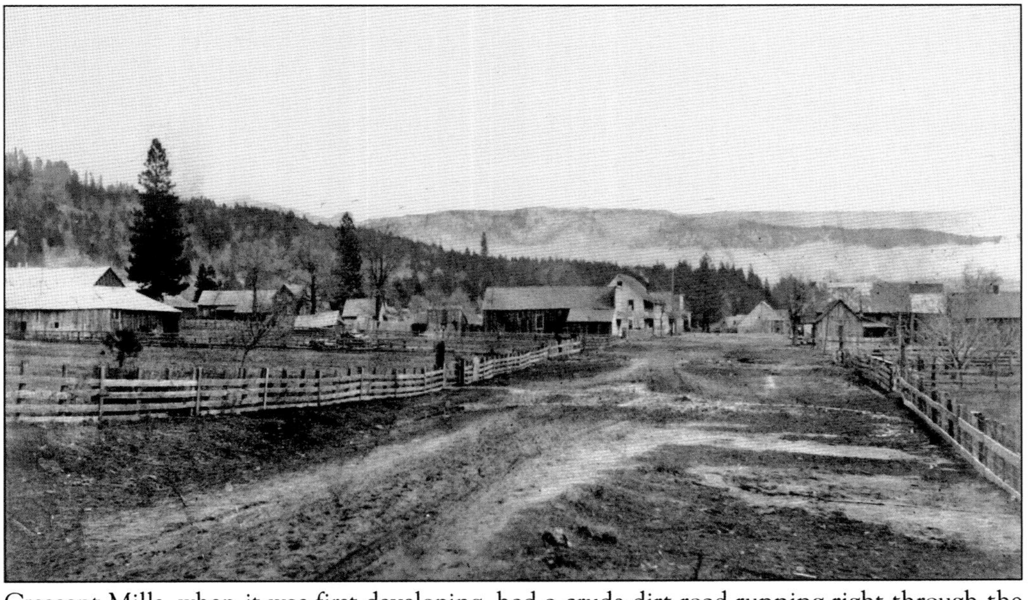

Crescent Mills, when it was first developing, had a crude dirt road running right through the town. This road connected many different places. To the north is Greenville and across the valley by the main stagecoach line is the Sierra Valley and Nevada. Travelers went through Greenville and Humbug Valley on their way to the Sacramento Valley. Now the road is a major route, Highway 89.

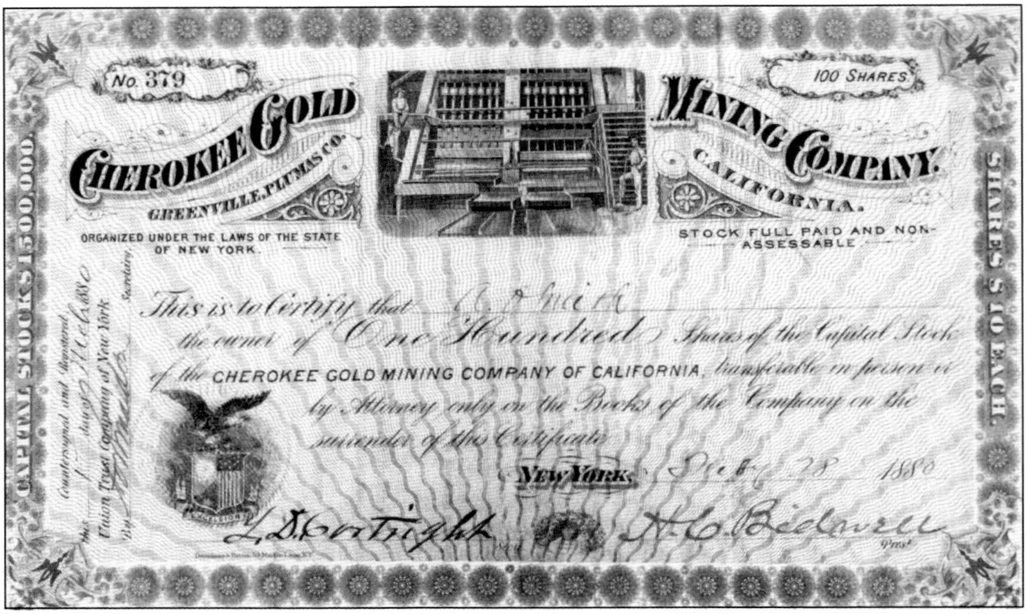

The Cherokee Gold Mining Company of California was incorporated on January 12, 1880, in New York. Henry C. Bidwell, known as the father of Greenville, was its president. Bidwell was also the president of the Green Mountain Gold Mining Company of California at Crescent Mills and the Gold Stripe Mining Company of California and the Round Valley Water Company, both of Greenville. The Cherokee Mine above Crescent Mills had been discovered around 1860 and was first called the Kettle Mine. The photograph above shows a stock certificate from the Cherokee Gold Mining Company of California dated February 28, 1880, and signed by H. C. Bidwell as president and Lewis D. Cortright of Hyde Park, Illinois, as secretary. Below is the Cherokee Mine shaft in 1938, used to work the Caledonia vein and 75-ton-per-day flotation mill. It employed 33 men. The mine closed in 1942 at the beginning of World War II. (Courtesy of Norm Lamb.)

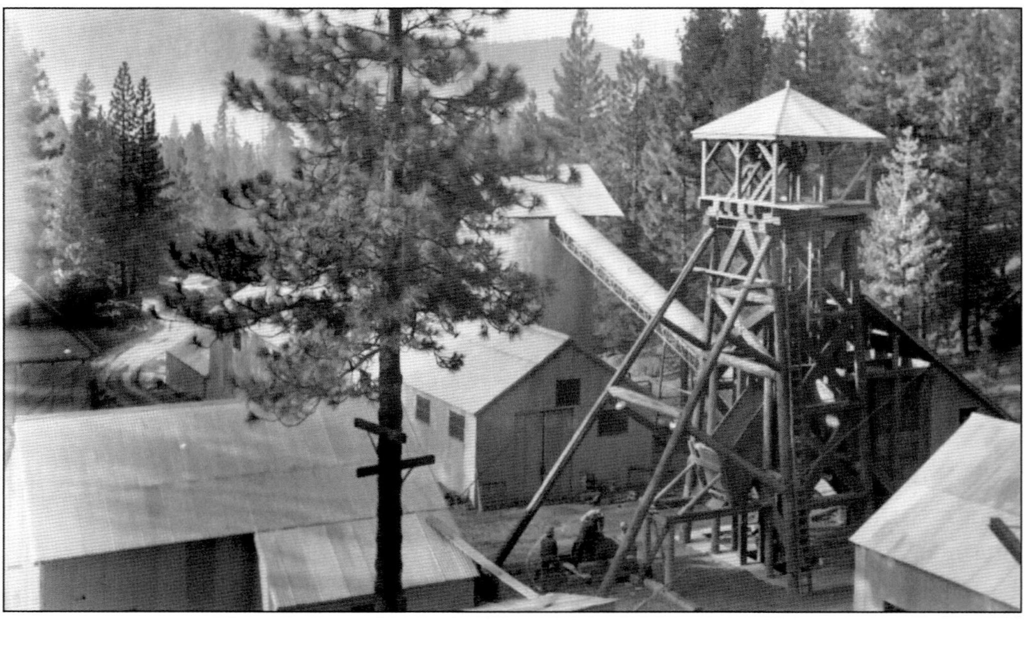

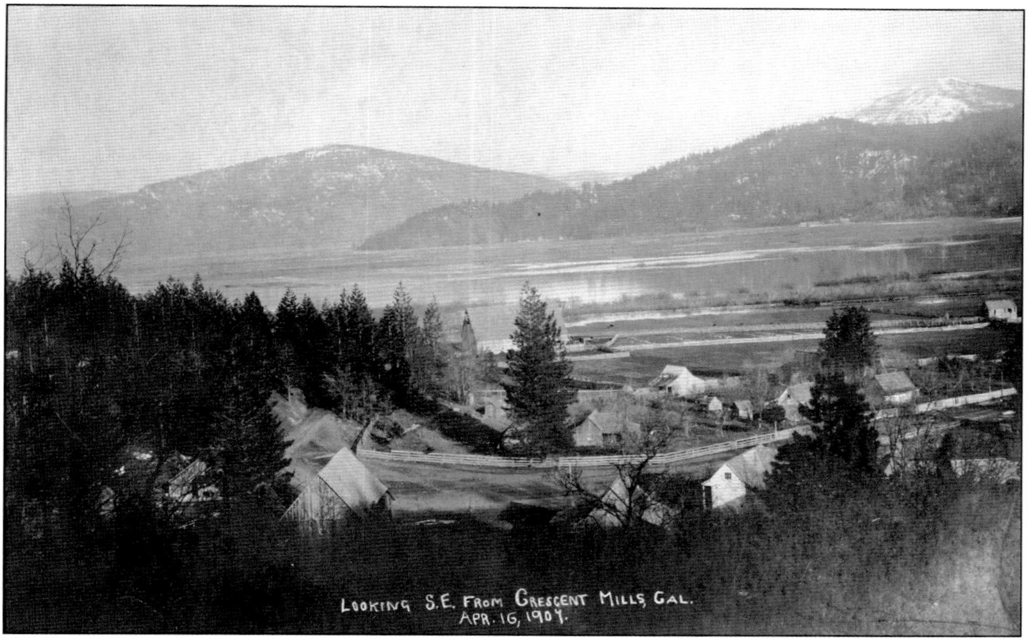

An older picture of Crescent Mills, looking down onto Crescent Mills with the valley in the background, is shown here. Notice all the water in the valley. The water table is still very high in the valley today. At the lower end of the valley is a natural rock wall not too far from the surface that holds the water in the valley. One can see why there is so much waterfowl in the valley, with all the marshland for them.

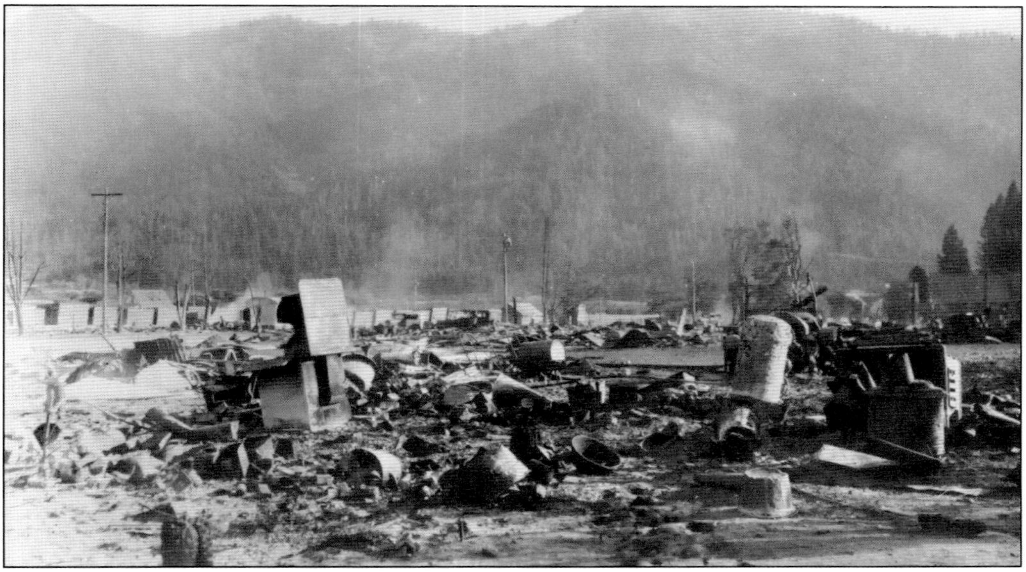

Like many older towns, Crescent Mills had a devastating fire in 1926, and it burned most of the town. When the fire started, it spread from one building to the next until almost all were demolished. It was a sad day for the town, and a great loss.

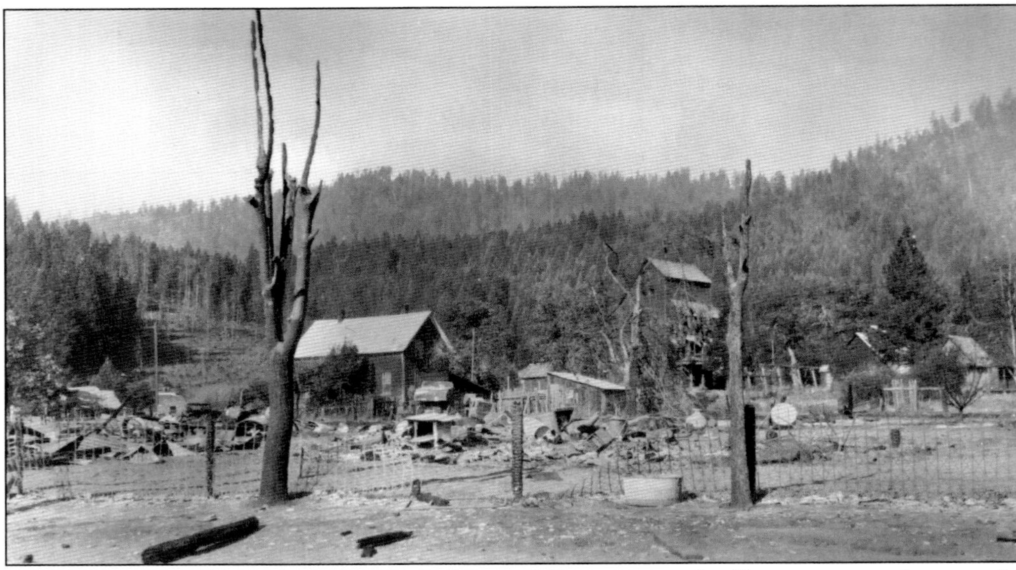

This photograph shows the upper part of town. The two-story building seen standing on the left is still there today; it has been restored by a family member who was related to the original owners. On the right is part of a mine building that did not burn.

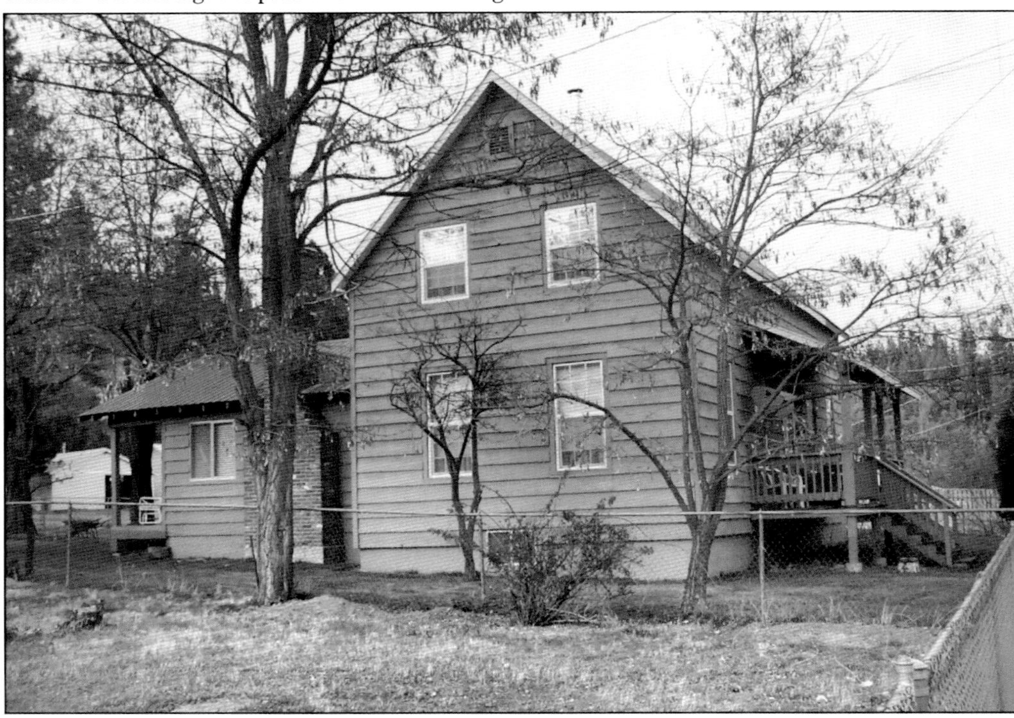

This is one of the oldest houses in Crescent Mills that was left after the fire. This house was built in 1864; a beam in the basement had "1864" carved on it. The home used to house some of the miners that worked at the mine just above it. Monday and Marie (Sobrero) Esani moved from Genesee to this house in 1920. It was restored in 1975 by some of the family members. (Courtesy of the author.)

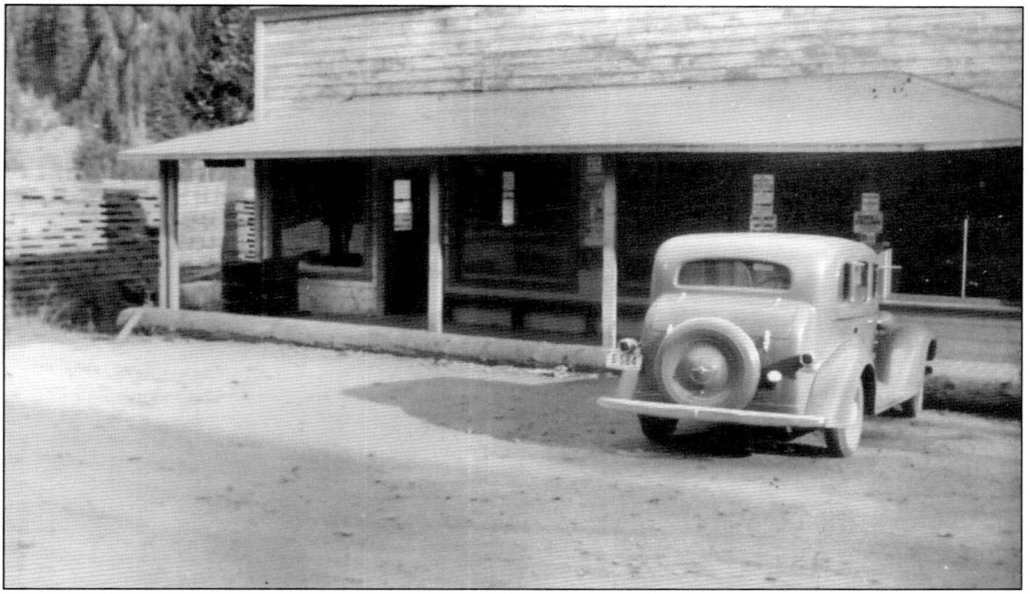

Leaving Crescent Mills, only a couple of miles to the south, was a place on the road at the base of Dixie Canyon called Frizzies. The area had a grocery store, housing, and a small mill. This is a picture of the office building that was near the mill site. It also had the cookhouse beside the office.

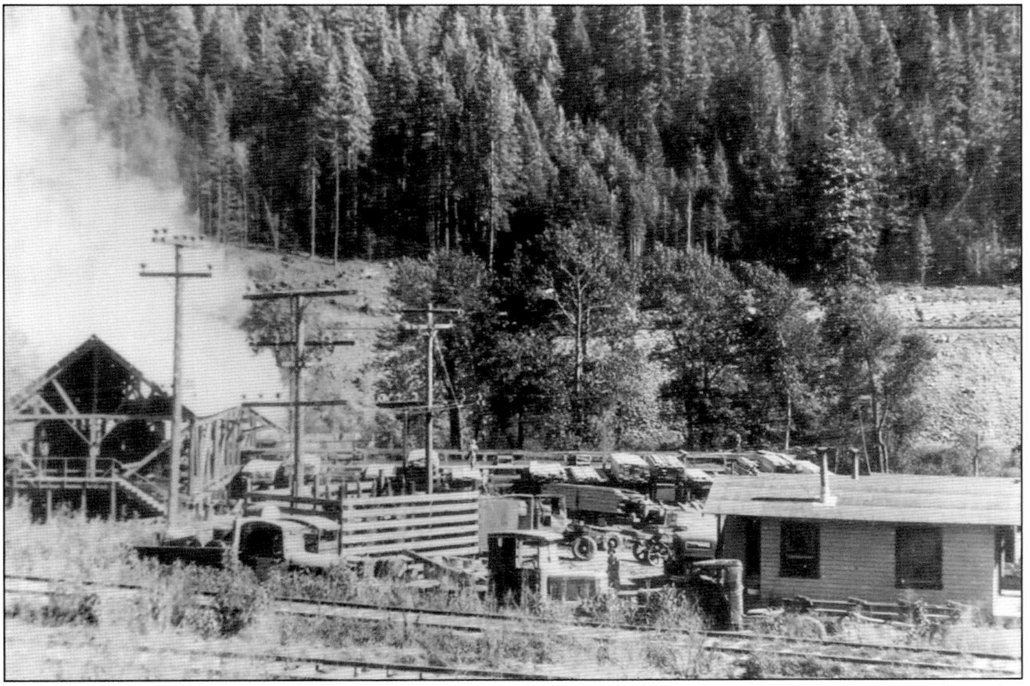

The old mill was called Frizzie Mill and, like all of the older mills, had a circular sawmill and a millpond. Pictured here are the mill and green chain and the office building. In the foreground is the railroad that ran by the mill. Western Pacific Railroad came into the valley as only a freight train.

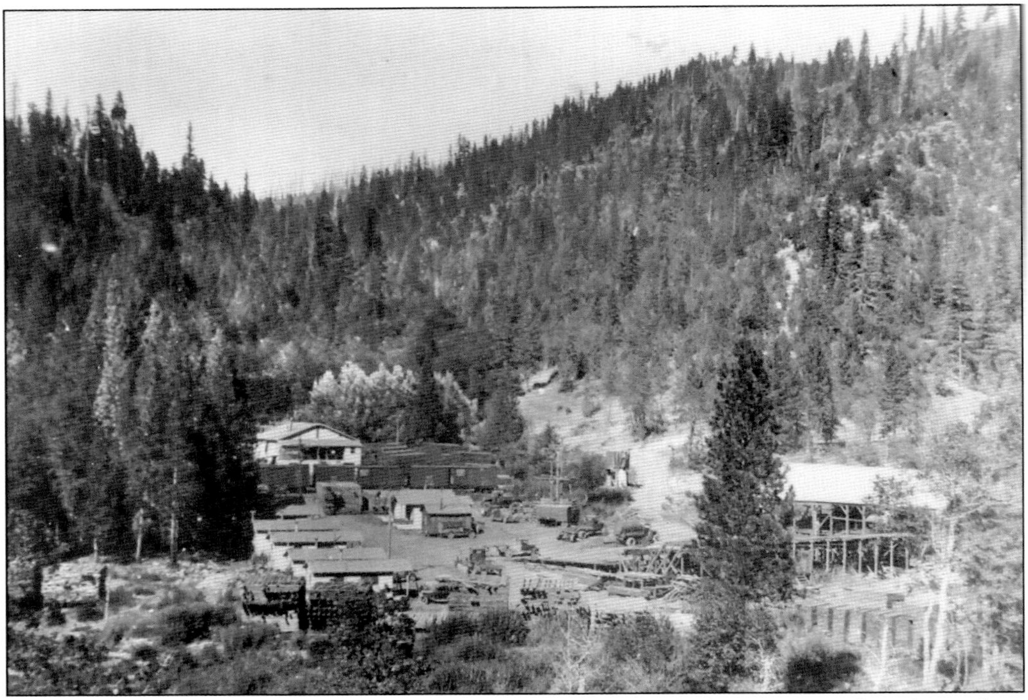

Another picture of Frizzie Mill shows more of the housing they had to accommodate the workers at the mill. Frizzie also had loggers who went up the canyon just above the mill to work every day. The cookhouse made their lunches and also fed the mill crew. The mill closed in winter, but a few people stayed around and lived there, so the cookhouse was open year-round.

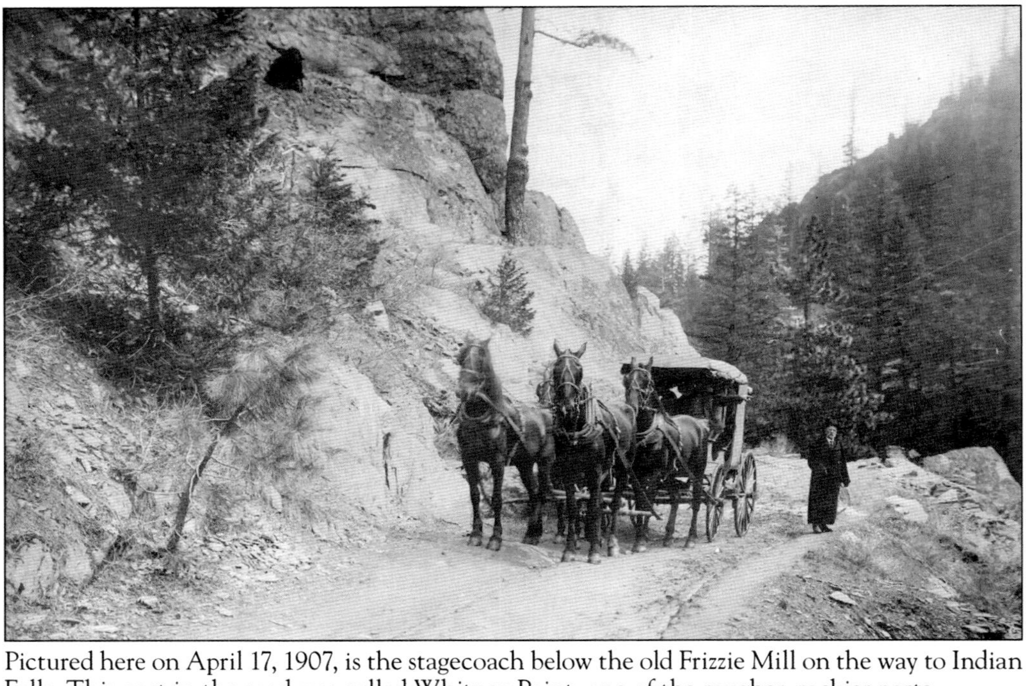

Pictured here on April 17, 1907, is the stagecoach below the old Frizzie Mill on the way to Indian Falls. This part in the road was called Whitney Point, one of the rougher, rockier parts.

Five

INDIAN FALLS

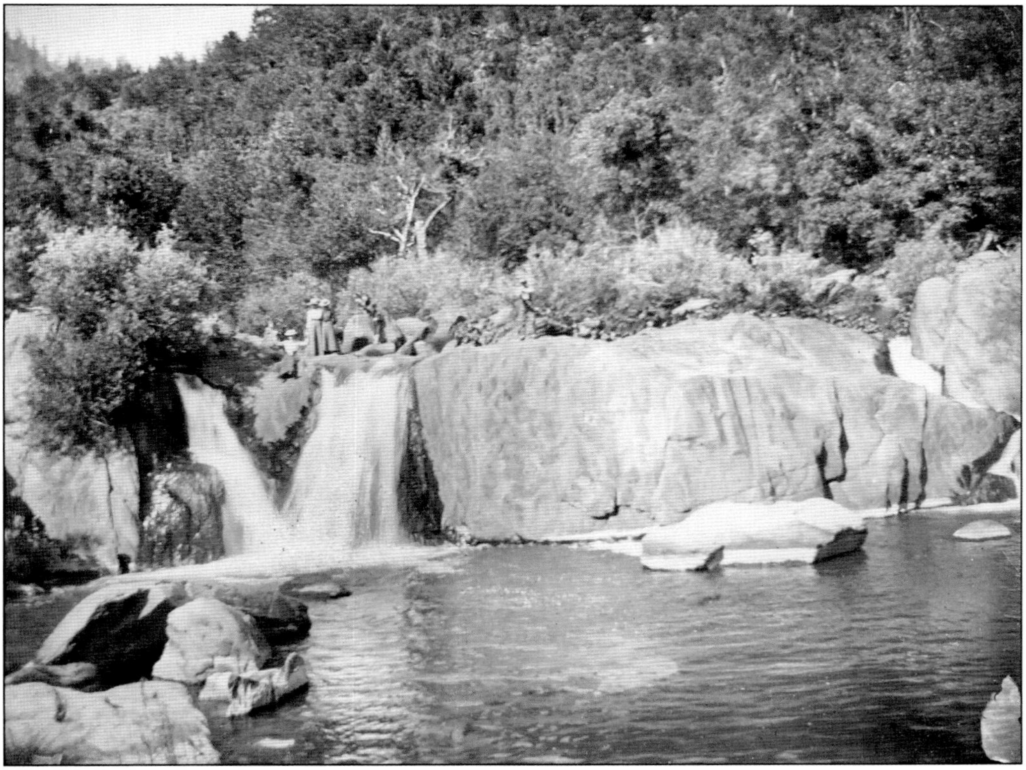

Pictured here is Thundering Falls, now known as Indian Falls. The Native Americans named it Thundering Falls and thought it had something evil about it. They said it looked like a lovely lady sitting on a rock, and the falls were her hair draping over the rock and down into the pool below. If people got too close, she would snare them and pull them into the pool to drown.

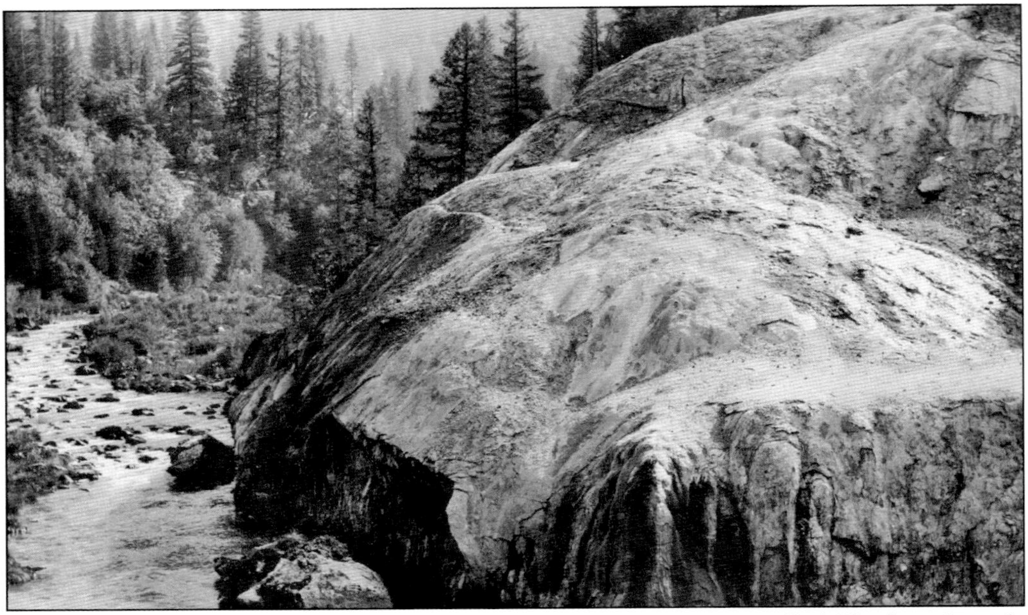

Just down around the turn from the falls is what the Native Americans called *Chuchuya* (or soda rock). The Native Americans saw it as a woman bent over toward the creek. They also saw two other women, one on each side of the larger one, with arms outstretched toward the creek. This was also an evil place, and according to Native American legend, if one got too close to these arms they would take one to the creek to drown.

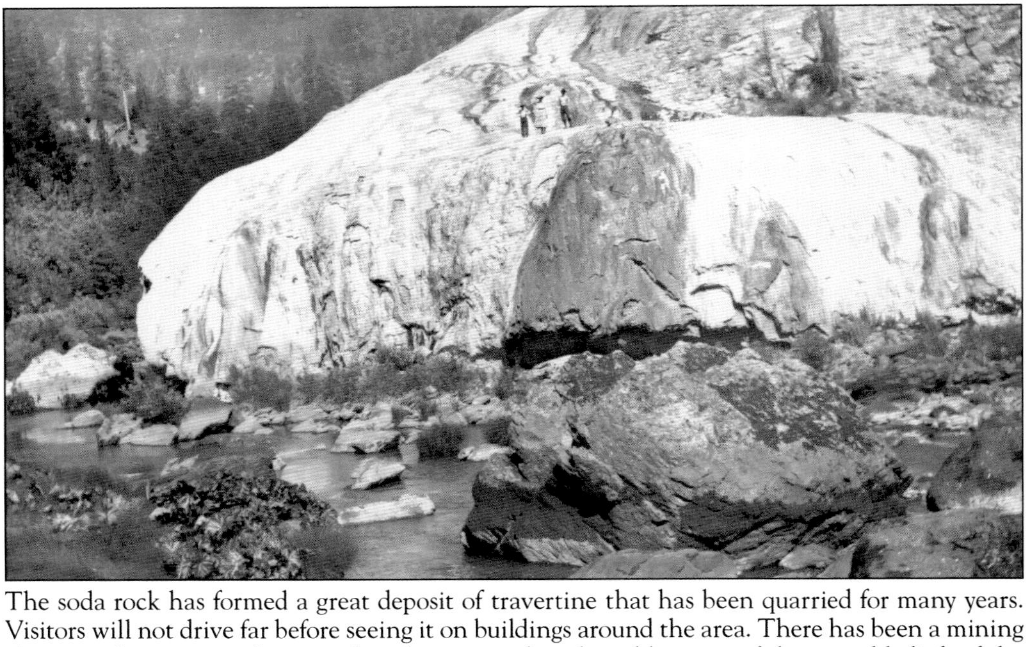

The soda rock has formed a great deposit of travertine that has been quarried for many years. Visitors will not drive far before seeing it on buildings around the area. There has been a mining claim on the property for years, but the mining has slowed because of the sacred beliefs of the Native Americans. They are afraid that if the mining continues, it will eventually take away the soda rock that has been there for years.

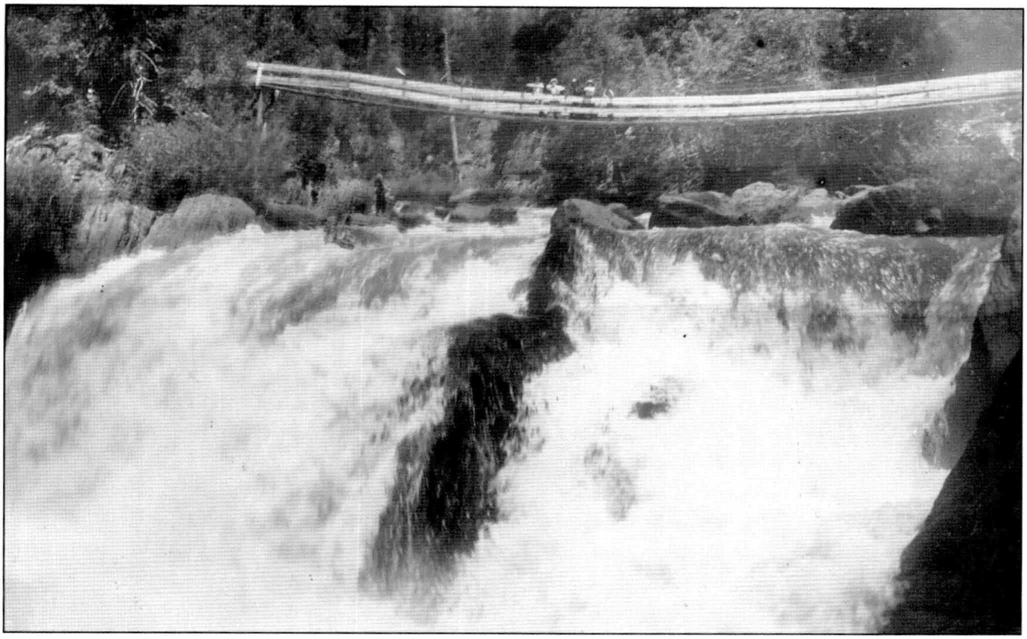

Another picture of Indian Falls shows a footbridge built to walk over Indian Creek above the falls. This bridge led to a trail that went all the way to a little crystal-clear lake called, as one would guess, Crystal Lake. This was a popular spot for the Maidu people to spear salmon that were at the end of their run because of the height of the falls.

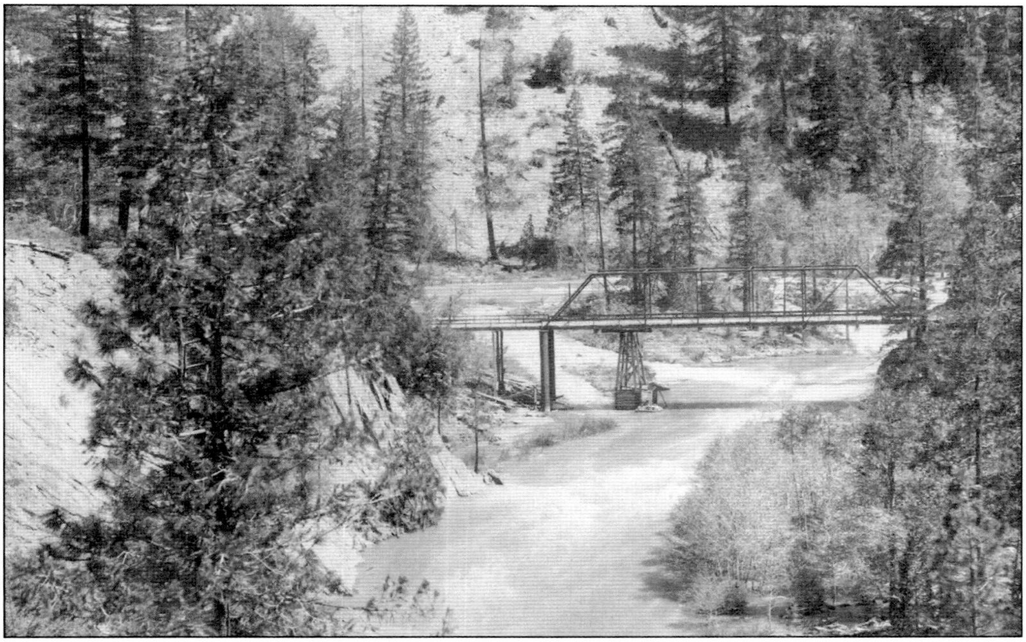

Between the falls and the soda rock is one of the oldest steel bridges still in its original location. This bridge is known as the Shoofly Bridge, and it crossed Indian Creek on the old highway to Quincy. It got its name from the shoofly the old miners built on the bend in Indian Creek. Shoofly is a term still used today meaning a diversion.

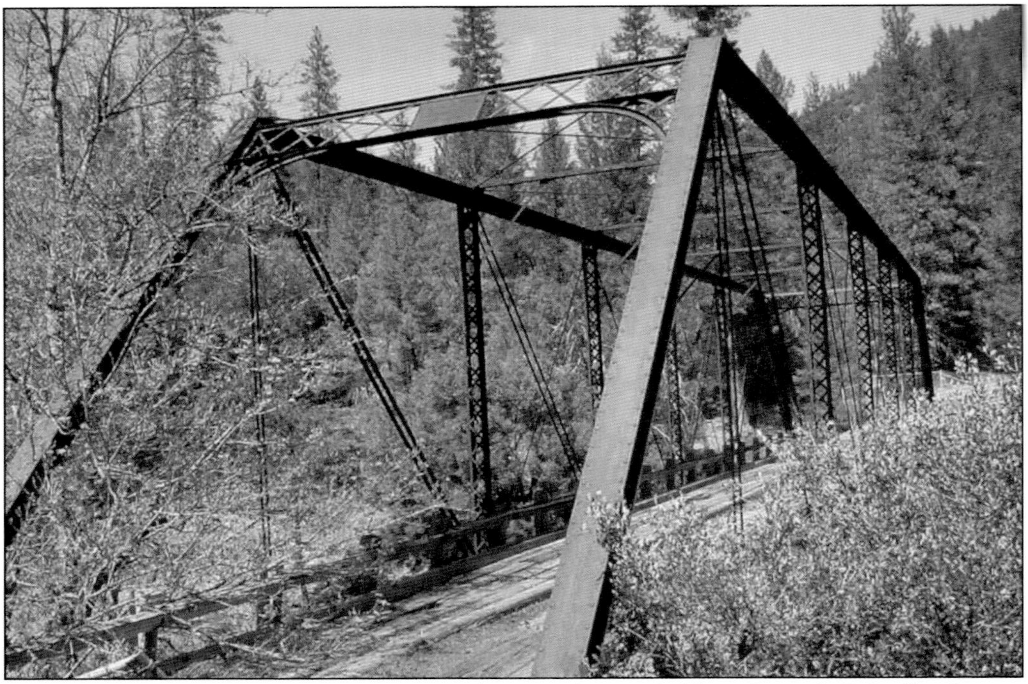

The Shoofly Bridge was built in 1889 over Indian Creek. It probably withstood all the floodwaters because of the bend in the river just above it. The bridge was used every day for years by travelers en route to Quincy until a new highway was built around 1938. Now the bridge is off limits for all vehicles, and only foot traffic is allowed. (Courtesy of the author.)

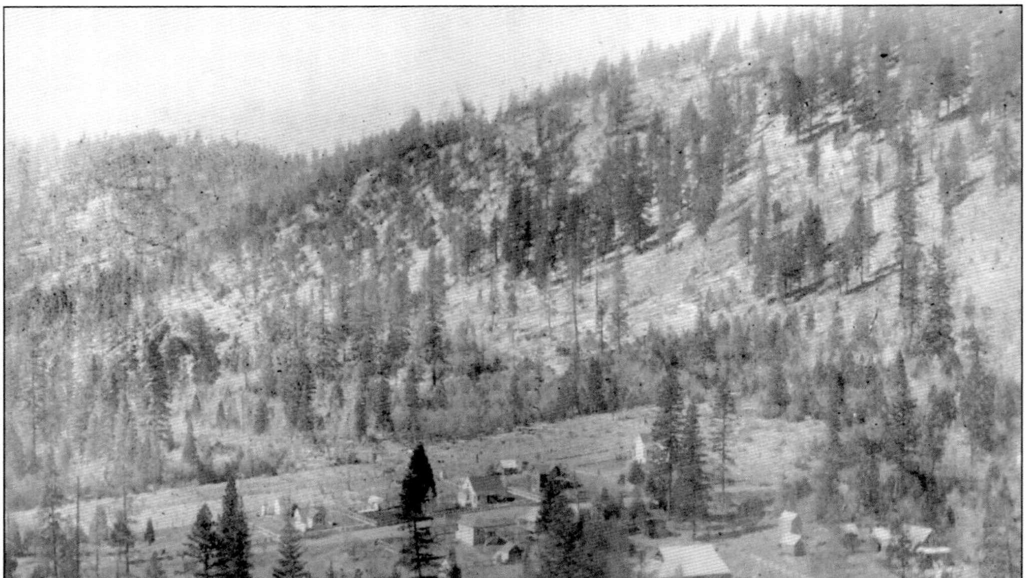

This is a view of the 148 acres homesteaded by Bob Martin around 1884, which was first known as Shoofly and later changed to its current name of Indian Falls. The town was like most in this area: it grew quickly, and when the mining faded, so did all the towns, but most are coming back now with new homes being built. Indian Falls is here to stay.

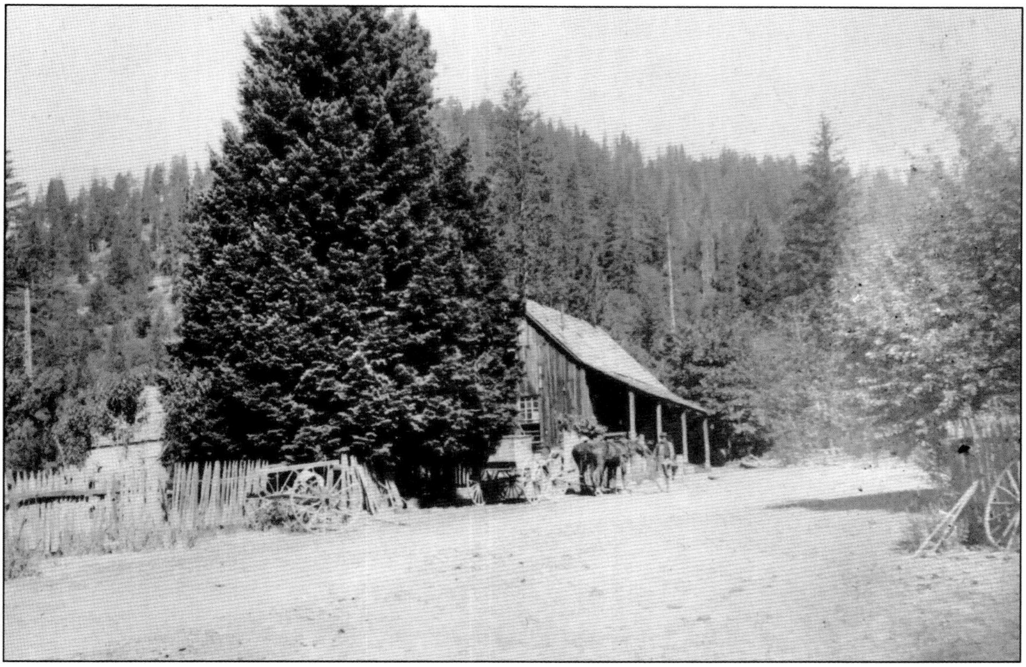

Pictured here is Bob Martin's house when the town was still called Shoofly. Bob Martin was one of the original homesteaders back in 1884. This house was along what is now Highway 89. At one time, Martin collected toll fees for traveling the road that ran down Indian Creek.

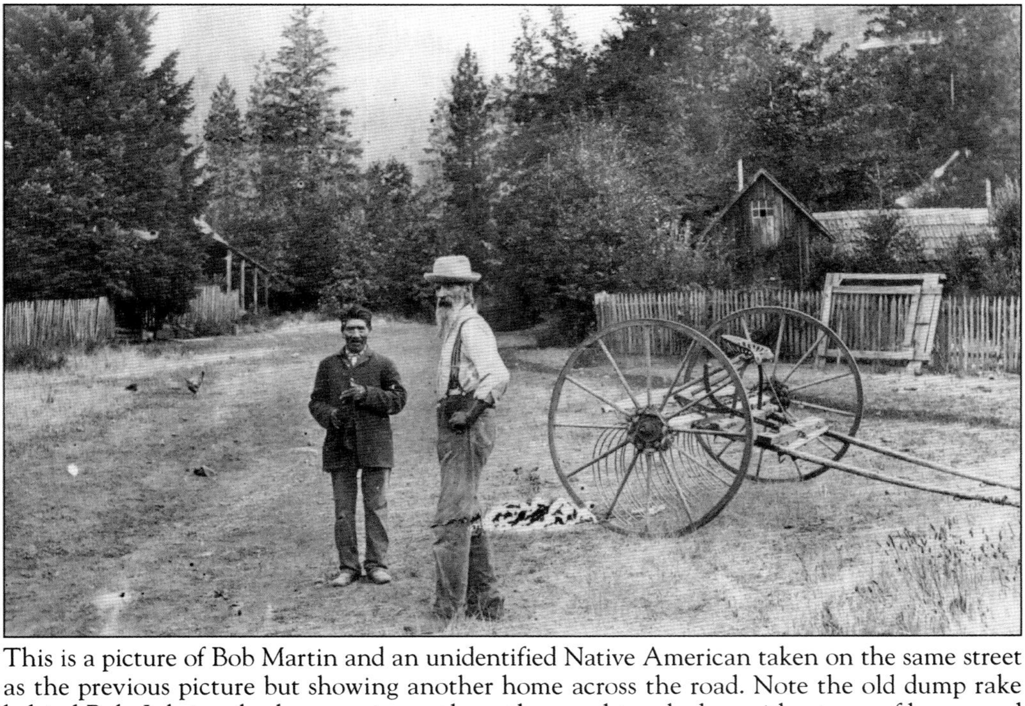

This is a picture of Bob Martin and an unidentified Native American taken on the same street as the previous picture but showing another home across the road. Note the old dump rake behind Bob. It brings back memories, as the author used to rake hay with a team of horses and a dump rake.

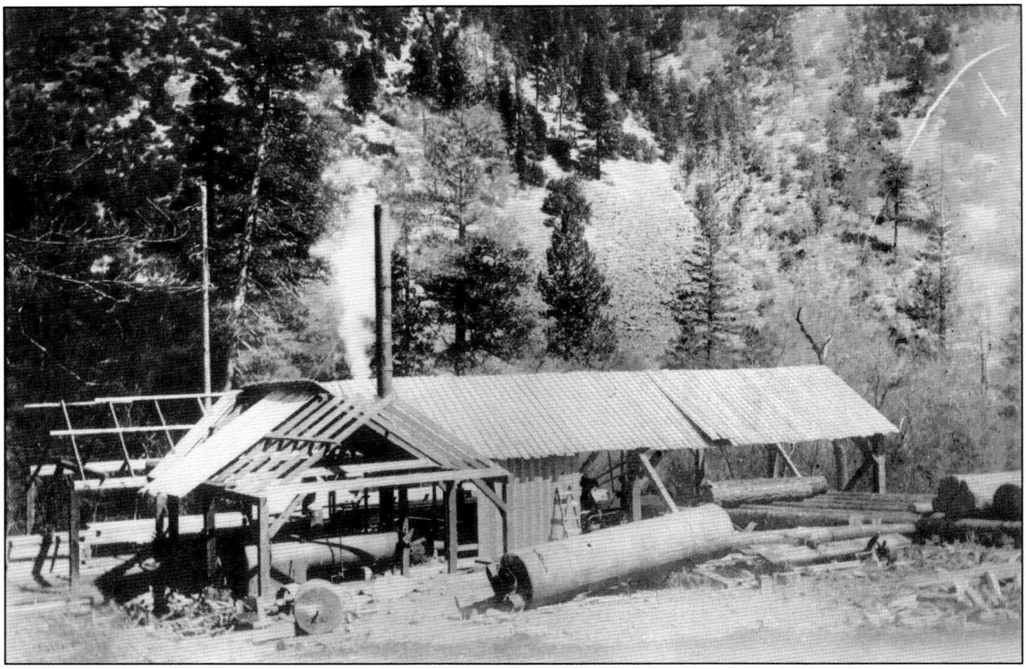

Pictured is the short-lived sawmill at Indian Falls. They built chutes to get the logs to the mill, but the first log down tore up the chutes, so they scrapped that idea and just logged the timber closer to the mill site. When that timber was logged, the mill closed down.

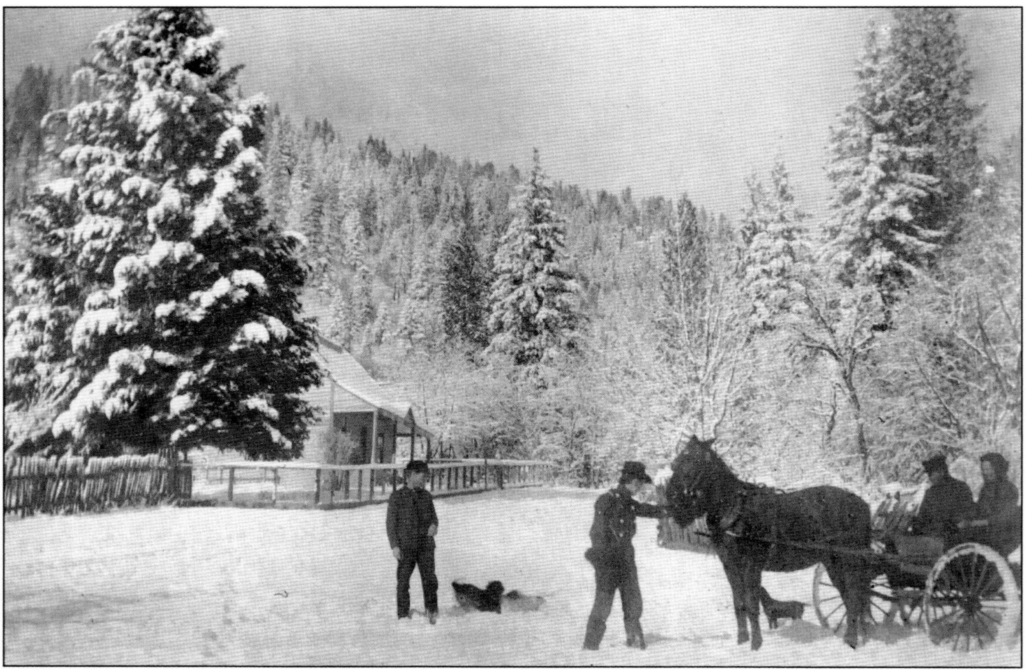

This is winter at Indian Falls. Indian Falls is a little lower in elevation then Indian Valley, so it does not get as much snow, but it does get some. This picture shows a horse and buggy with unidentified people.

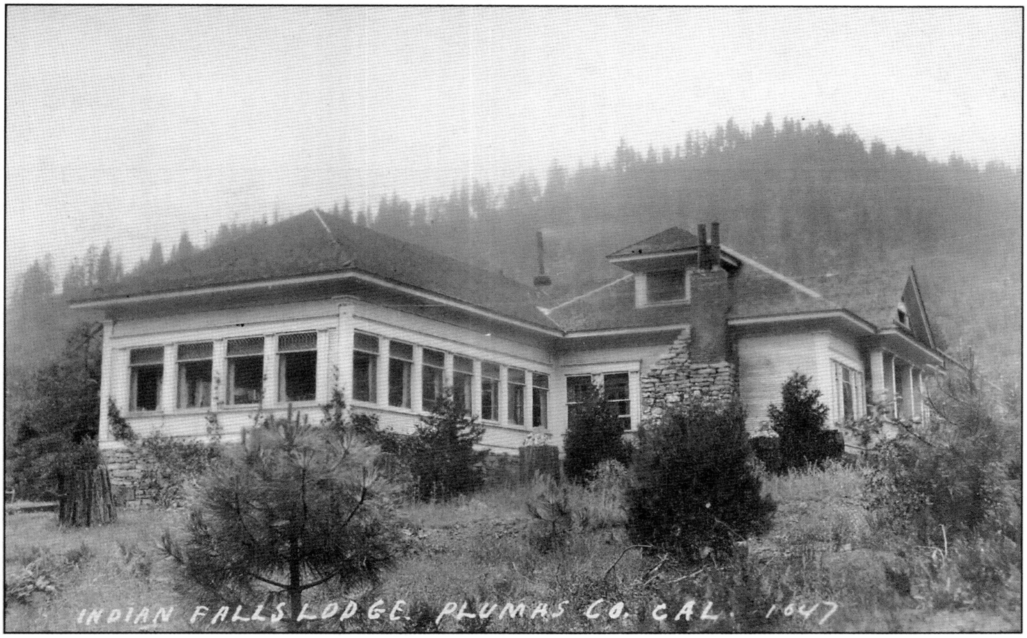

The lodge at Indian Falls is pictured here. When the mining was failing and the mill had no more timber, the town kept going because it was on the main route leading to many places. The lodge became very important, and the town promoted it to attract people to stop and stay the night.

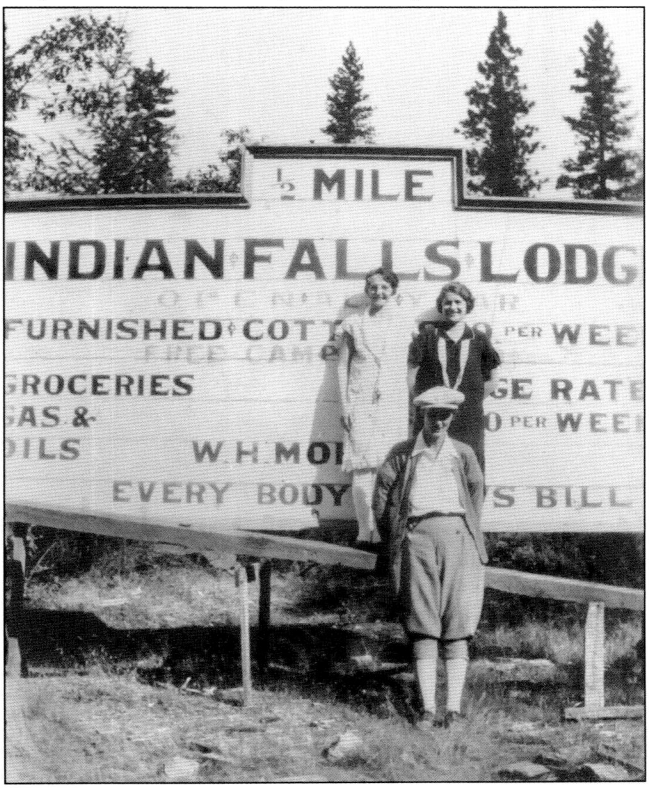

Just below Indian Falls was this sign promoting the lodging and groceries and such at Indian Falls. Another thing the town had going for it—and it still does today—was the falls. Indian Falls is visited by many people at all times of the year.

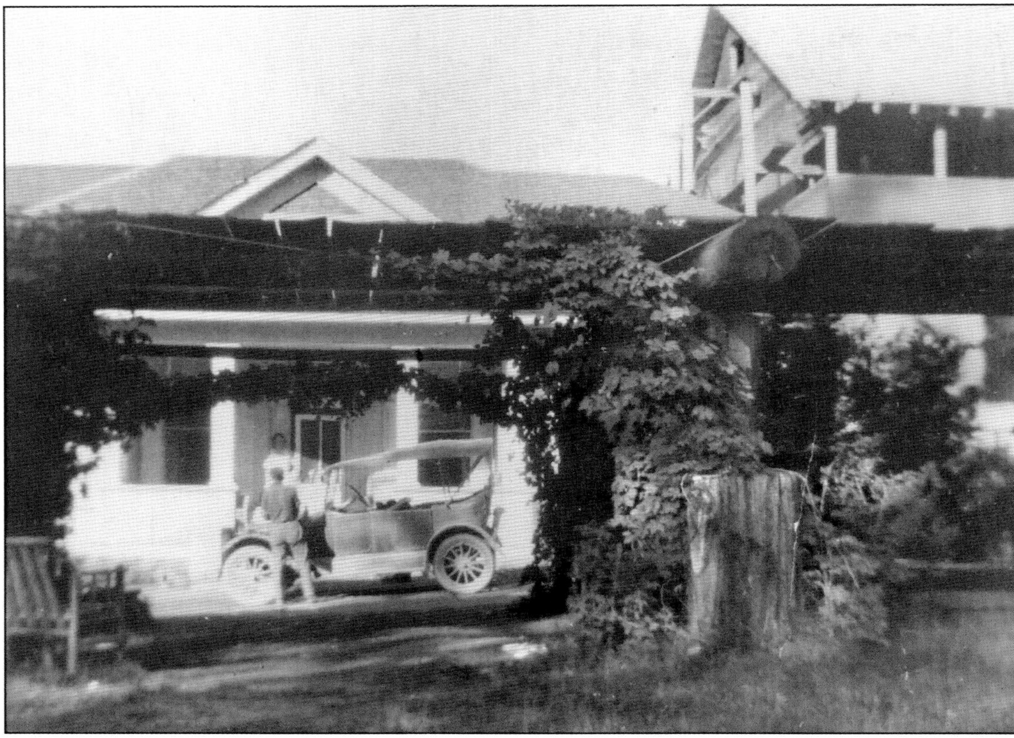

This is a closer look at the lodge building at Indian Falls, taken May 1, 1919. Neita Luzzadder was the operator, and Ralph Luzzadder is standing by the old automobile.

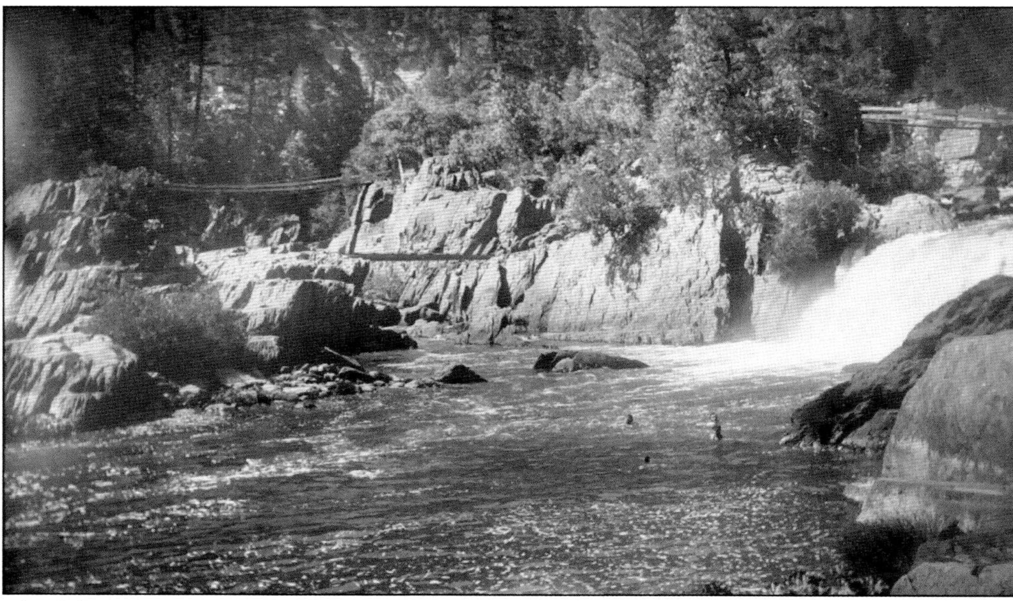

The falls were very high in the old days, but all the water that has passed over them has worn them down. The falls were a blessing for the Native Americans, as in the days before the dams were built in the Feather River, the salmon ran all the way to the falls. Now the salmon are stopped at a hatchery just north of Oroville.

Six

GENESEE

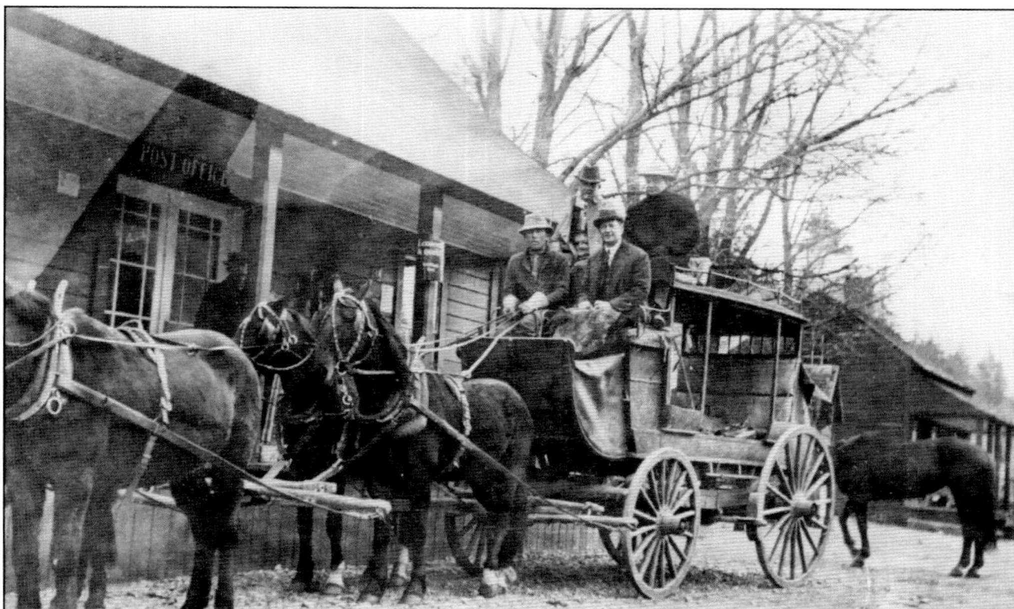

A stagecoach that ran from Reno to the Sacramento Valley stopped at the little town of Genesee located in Genesee Valley. The stage stopped here on every trip and is pictured in front of the old Genesee Store, which is still located in the same spot and open for business seasonally.

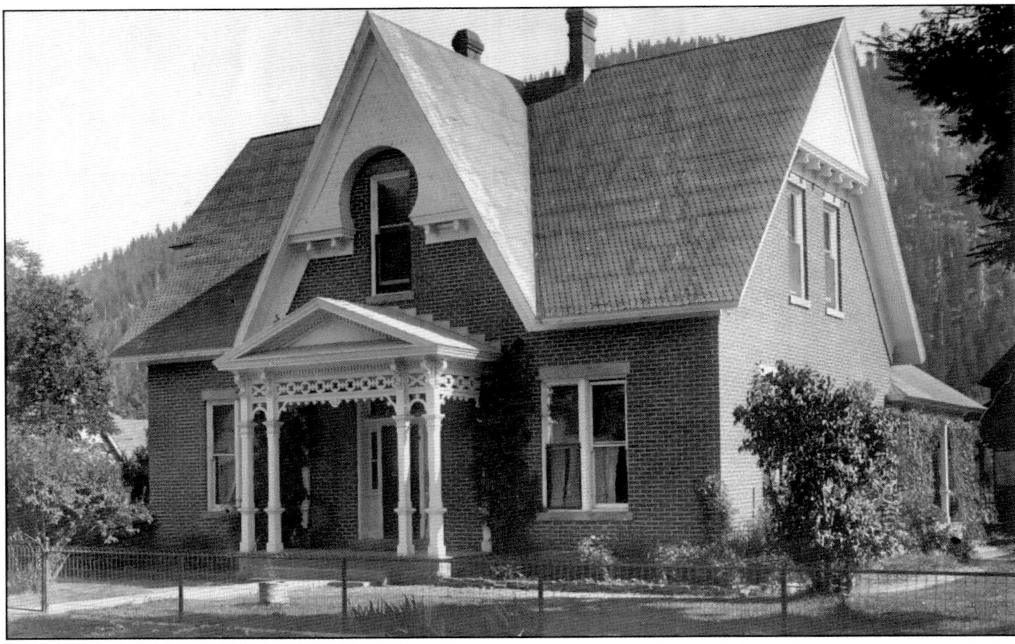

The old ranch house across the road from the store was bought by Edwin D. Hosselkus in 1862. It was built out of bricks that were made right in the valley. This ranch stayed in the Hosselkus family for many years, all the way up to the late 1940s. It is now owned by the Neff family. It is called Genesee Home and is used as a pastor's retreat.

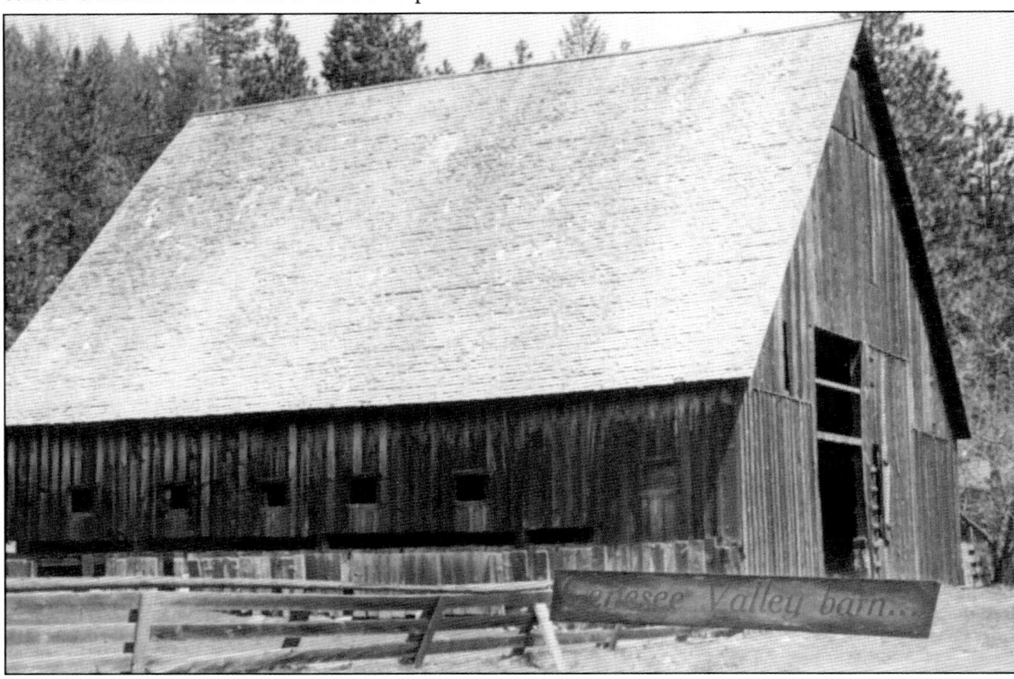

This old barn was on the Hosselkus Ranch up the road from the store. As with many barns in the area, the age and weather finally made it collapse. It is no longer in existence, but one can still see signs of it and where it stood.

Pictured here are Edna and Doug Hosselkus. They were the last Hosselkuses to own the ranch. In the early 1950s, they sold to the Grace family from Southern California. The Graces owned and operated a large candy factory in Southern California. The author can remember the Grace children bringing huge nut rolls to school for all to feast on. (Courtesy of Marie Brand.)

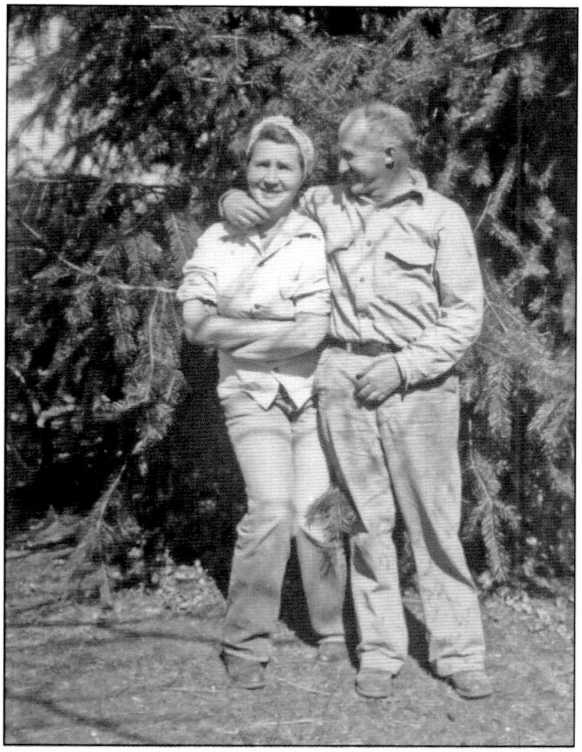

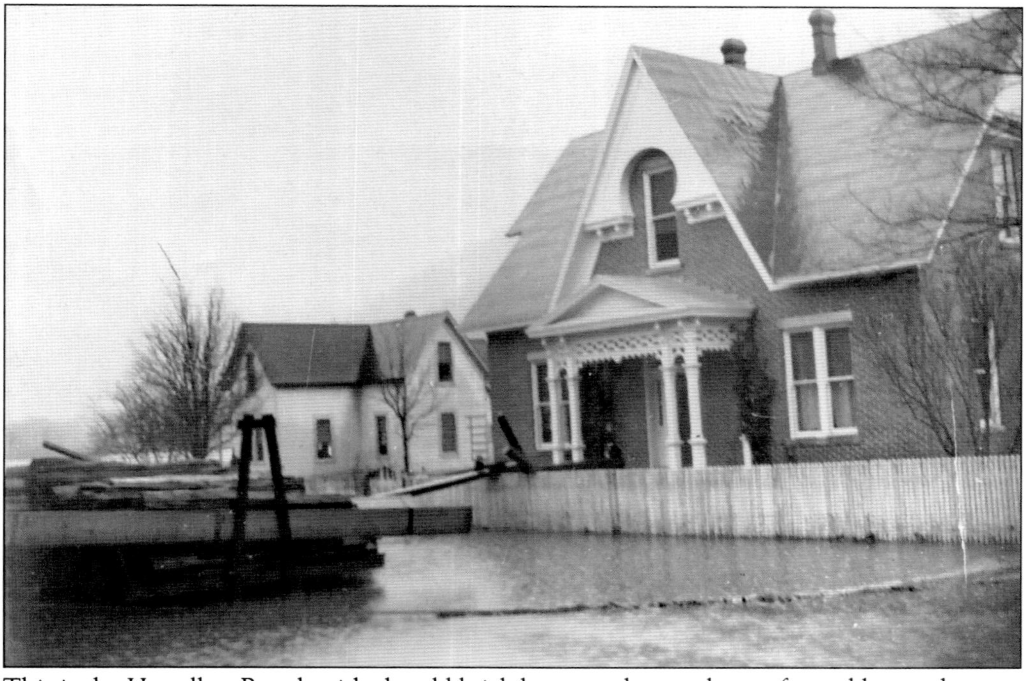

This is the Hosselkus Ranch with the old brick house and, next door, a framed house that was built later. It is flooded all around the ranch houses, which was not uncommon in those days. Flooding was quite frequent in winter and early spring.

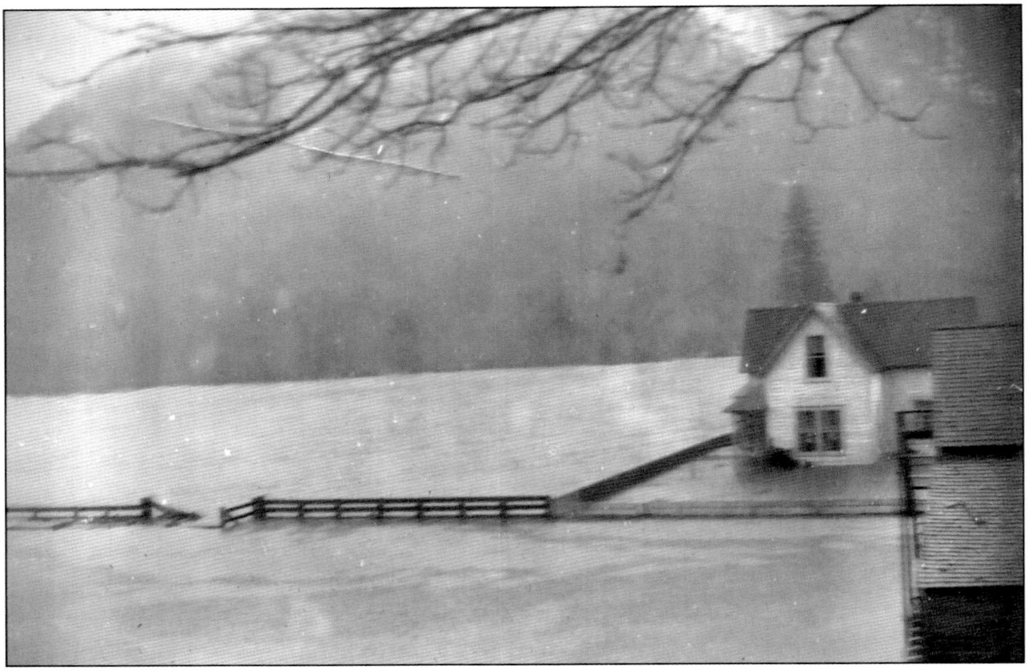

This pictured of a framed home shows just how deep the floodwaters would get in and around the houses. The floodwater was from Indian Creek, which has a large watershed with many streams feeding into it above the ranch.

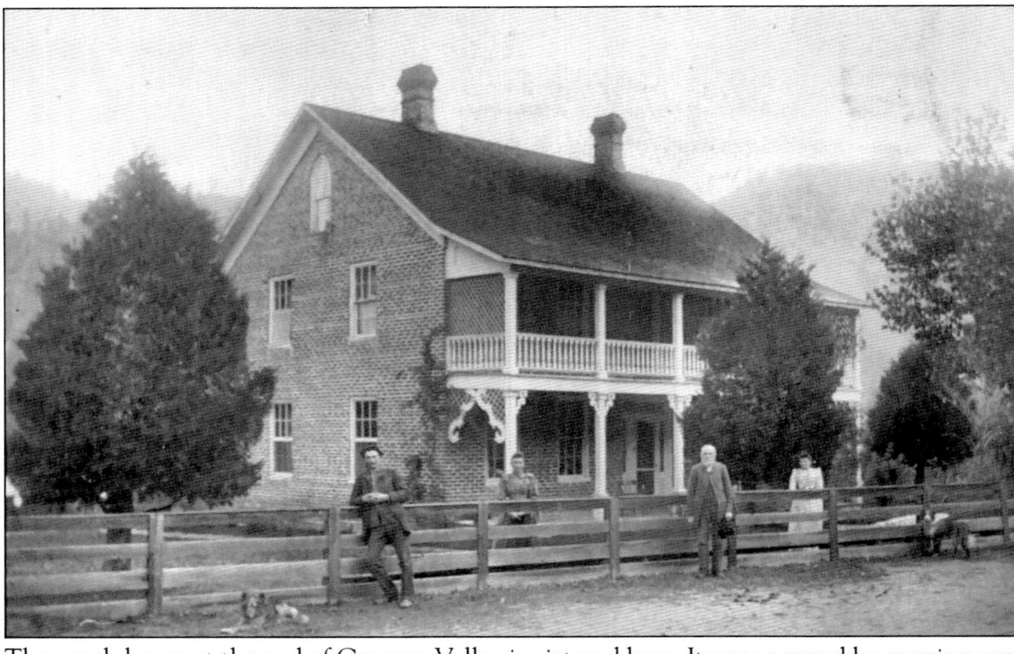

The ranch house at the end of Genesee Valley is pictured here. It was accessed by crossing over Indian Creek and turning on the old stagecoach road to Sierra Valley. This was the Flournoy Ranch. The Flournoys were relatives of Bob Cooke, a longtime resident of the valley. This home is no longer there, but there are a barn and buildings on the ranch site.

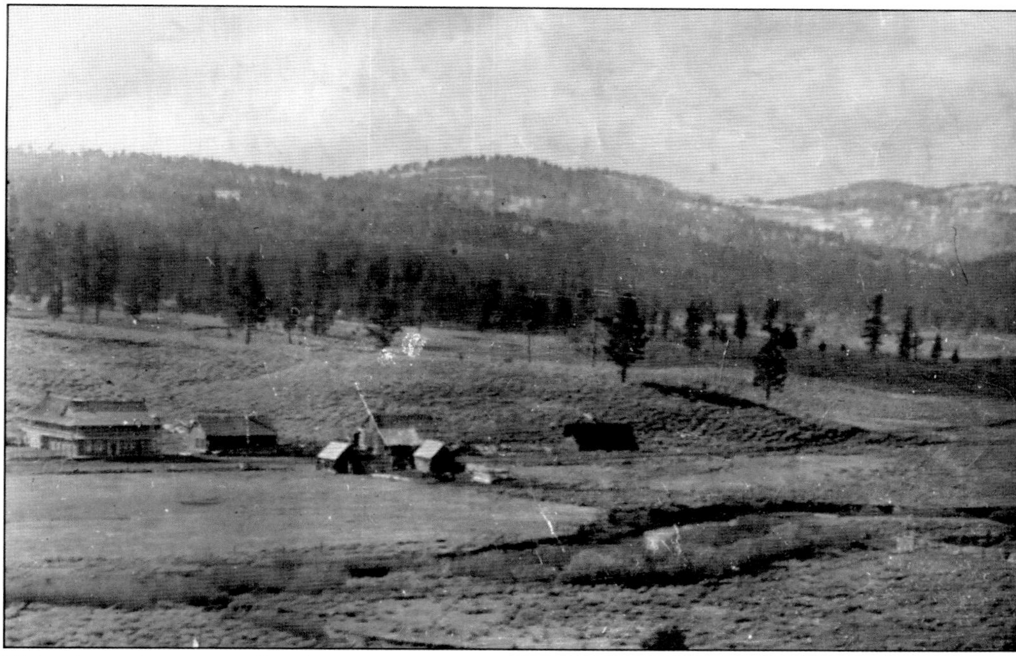

This picture is poor quality, but it was a must to have in this book as it is the only picture found of the old Chase Palace at the stage stop in the high country. This is the last stop before the stage came down into Genesee Valley. Visitors can still find many signs of it being there if they look around.

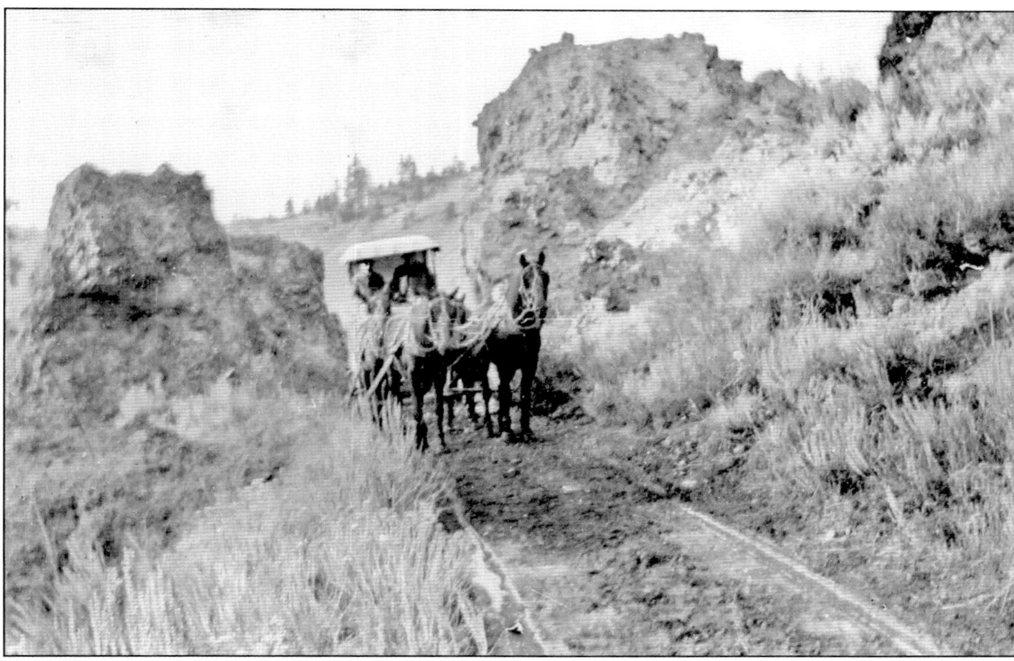

The stage, on its way to the old Chase place, is featured here. It shows how rough and primitive the stagecoach line roads were in the early days. Imagine how it looked in the winter. It was probably a welcome sight when travelers dropped into the pretty Genesee Valley.

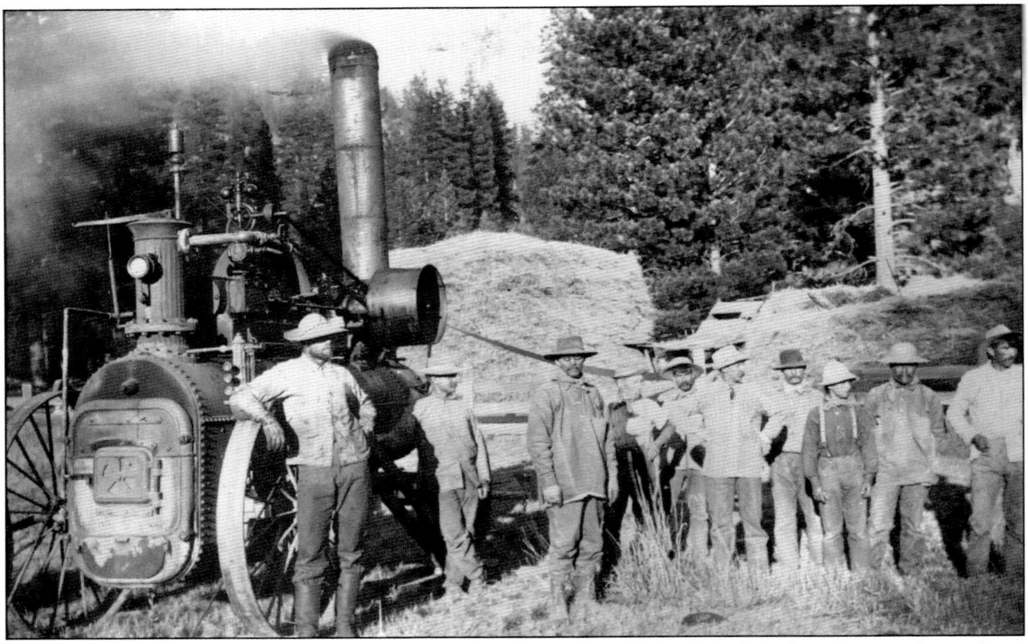

Here at the old Hosselkus Ranch in Genesee Valley, a crew works with a thrasher. In those days, a thrasher was pulled from ranch to ranch and used by many to thrash their grain. Among those shown in this picture are Frank Mead, John Hosselkus, and Pete Hosselkus.

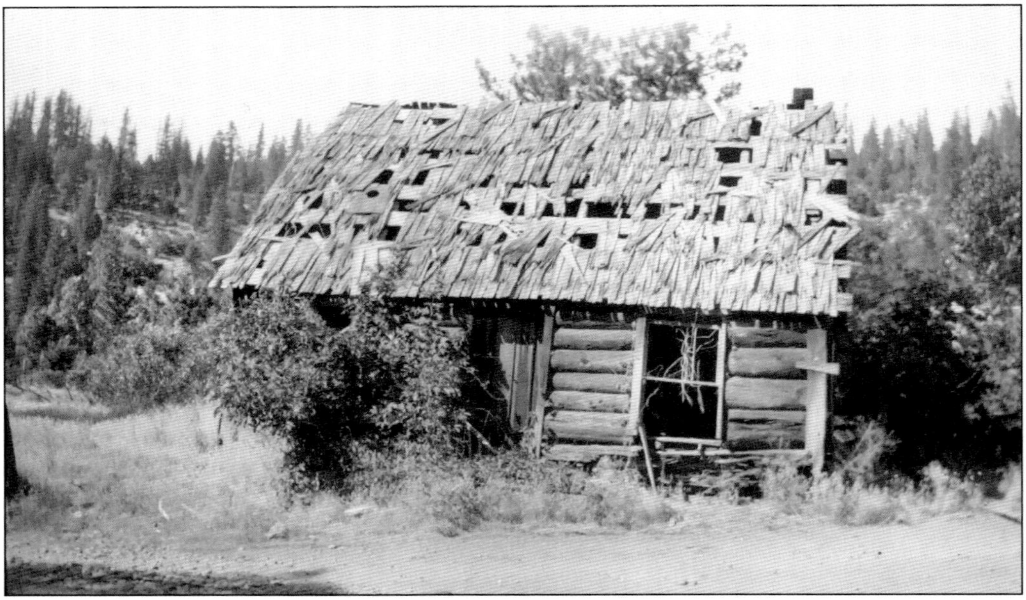

When people talk about Genesee, they have to mention the Sobrero family, who lived on Ward Creek, a feeder creek into Indian Creek. Pictured here is the Sobrero home, which is no longer there. (Courtesy of Marie Brand.)

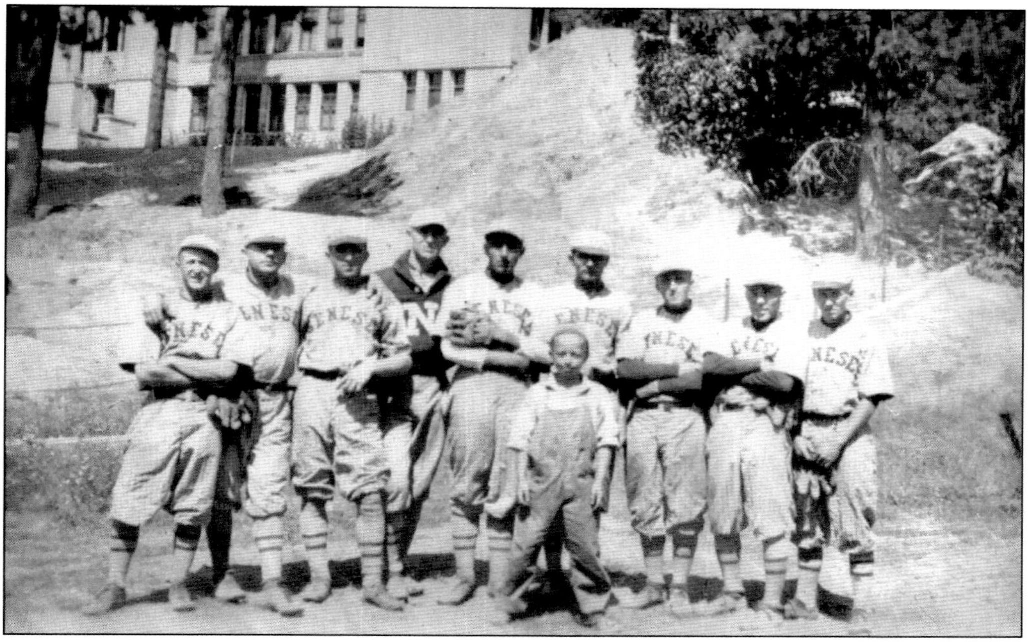

The Sobreros were very athletic and loved baseball. It was said they would walk for miles on the weekend to get to a baseball game. This photograph of the Plumas County League champs has three of the Sobrero brothers on the team. Second from the left is Frank Sobrero, second from the right is George Sobrero, and fourth from the right is John Sobrero. (Courtesy of Marie Brand.)

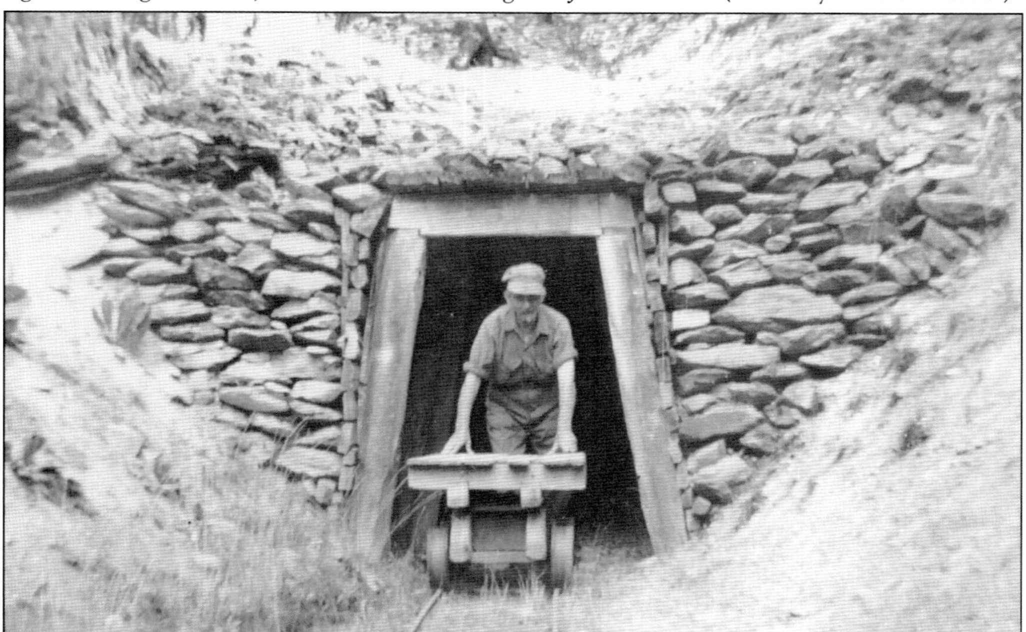

Across Ward Creek from the Sobrero home was another home and mine owned by the Goodhues, an old family from around the valley that started out in Indian Falls. This is Joe Goodhue coming out of his mine with a mine cart. Joe used to work on this mine daily. The author has been back into this mine as far as it was timbered, and that was far enough for him.

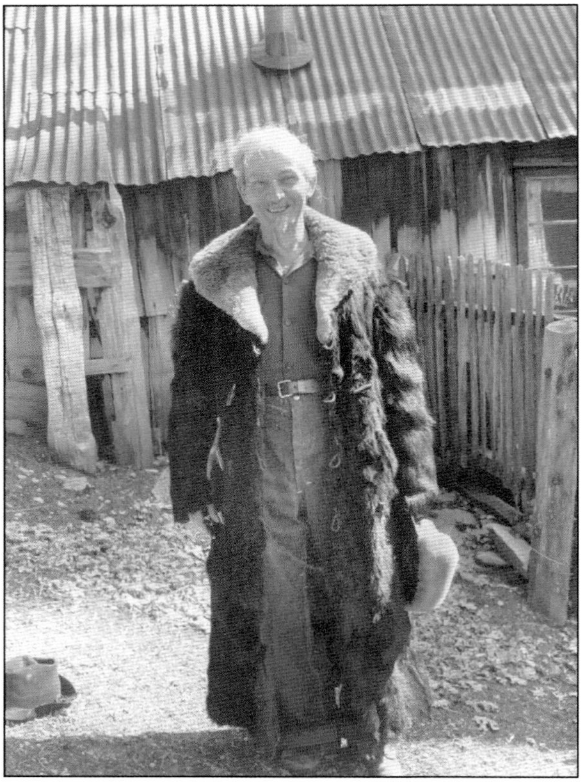

Joe Goodhue is pictured with his long fur coat made of bear skin with a sheepskin collar. It was purchased from Sears and Roebuck and is now on display in the Indian Valley Museum. Joe was nicknamed "Saturday Joe" and was known for his trips to town for supplies. He used to come into town in his open-air, 1920s Chevrolet with his bearskin coat on to keep warm.

Joe Goodhue was a shirttail relative of the author. In this picture is Joe with his nephew's family, who are all blood relations to Richard McCutcheon. From left to right are little Ricky Emmons, Ruth (Goodhue) Emmons, Harold Emmons, Mary Ann (Goodhue) McLean, Uncle Tommy, Claudia (Emmons) Gamaza, Robby Emmons, Joe Goodhue, Peggy Emmons, and Zelma (McCutcheon) Goodhue, also known as "Dutch." Zelma was the author's aunt.

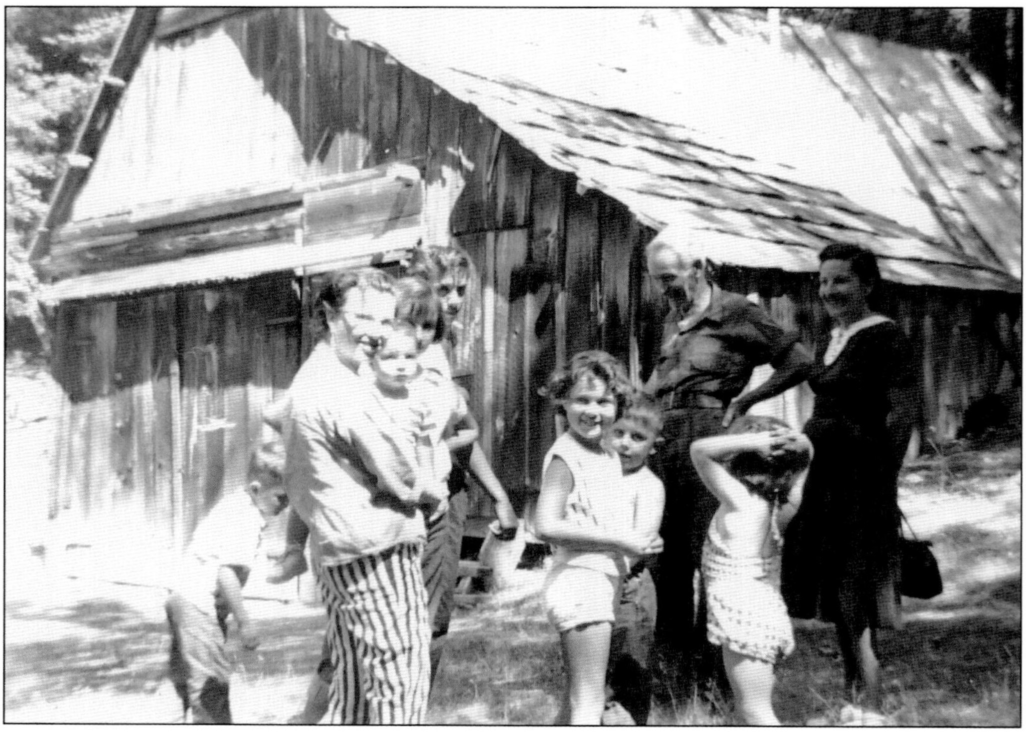

Seymour Smith was the most well-known Maidu in Indian Valley. Seymour was a boxer and a long-distance runner who placed fifth in a grueling run from San Francisco to Portland, Oregon. Citizens still hold the Seymour Smith Run from Taylorsville to Greenville in his memory. When Seymour passed on just shy of 95, his funeral was the largest ever seen in the valley.

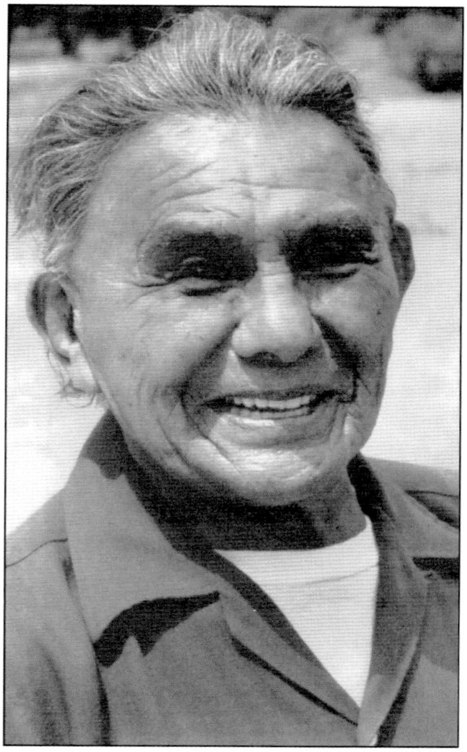

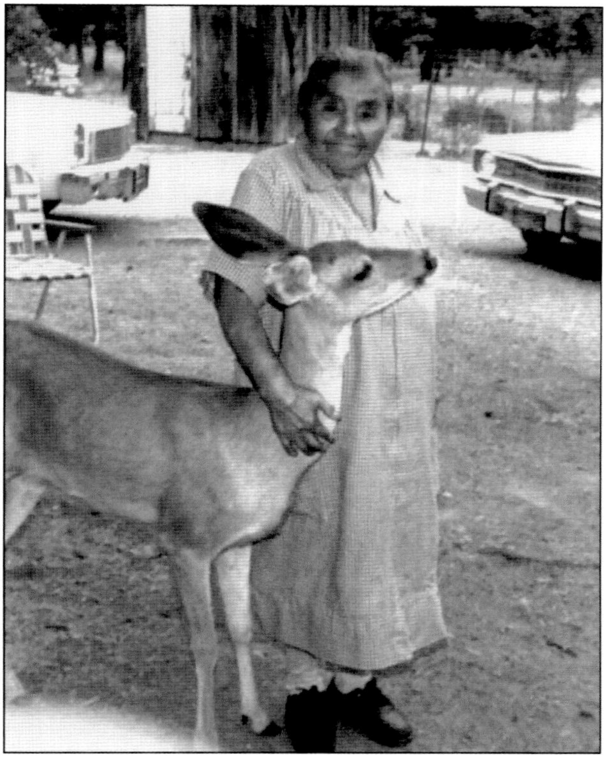

Pictured here is Louise Smith, wife of Seymour, with her pet deer, Bambi. Louise lived a very pleasant life with many kids, grandkids, and great-grandkids. The author can remember when Louise was 106, just before she passed on; she was at the county fair every night with some of her grandchildren. (Courtesy of Margaret Cooke.)

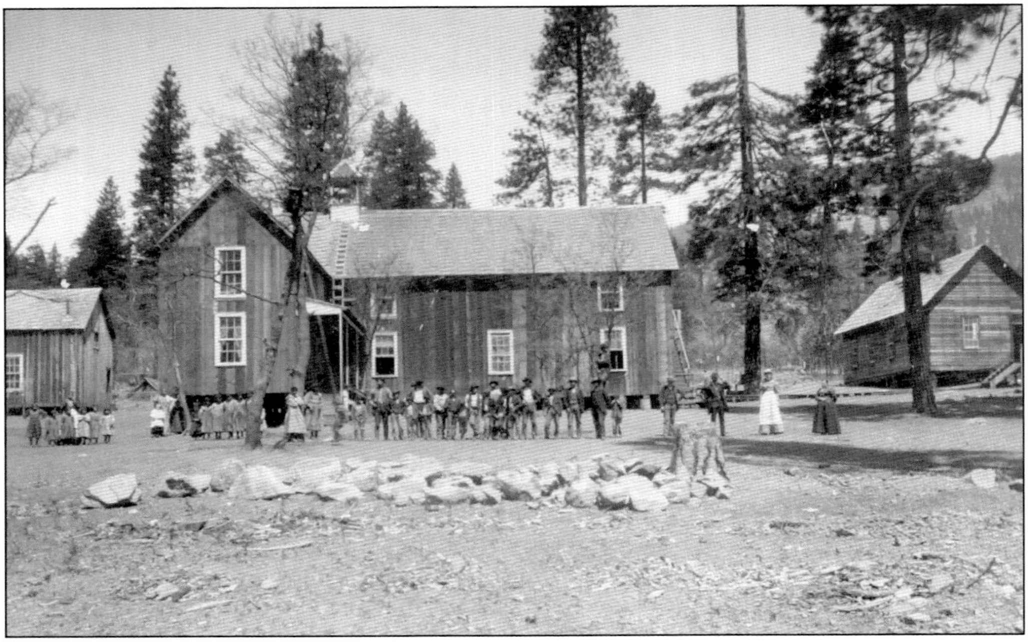

The Maidus had their own mission on the north side of the valley, which is still there today. In the earlier days, it was known as the Indian Mission; now it is called the Rancheria. Soon the mission had its own schools and many buildings on the site. This is a picture of the early school at the mission.

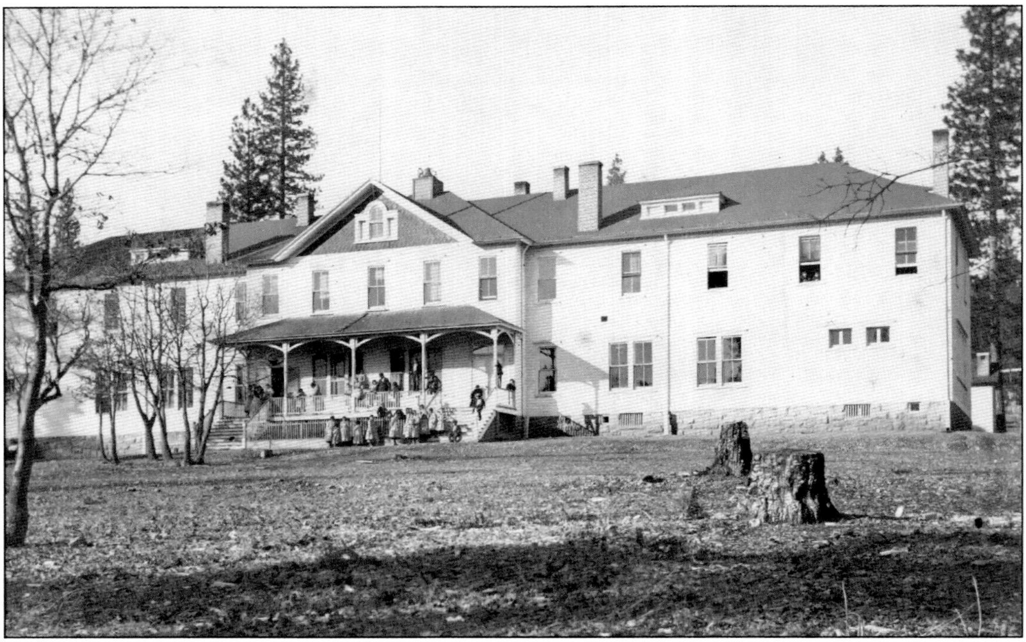

The main building of the school was built between 1889 and 1900 by the government. Built for the Maidus at the mission, the building had dorms, classrooms, a sewing room, indoor plumbing, and a kitchen with a huge stove. The school also had a small chapel down by the road. At one time, there were around 50 kids at the school. It later succumbed to fire.

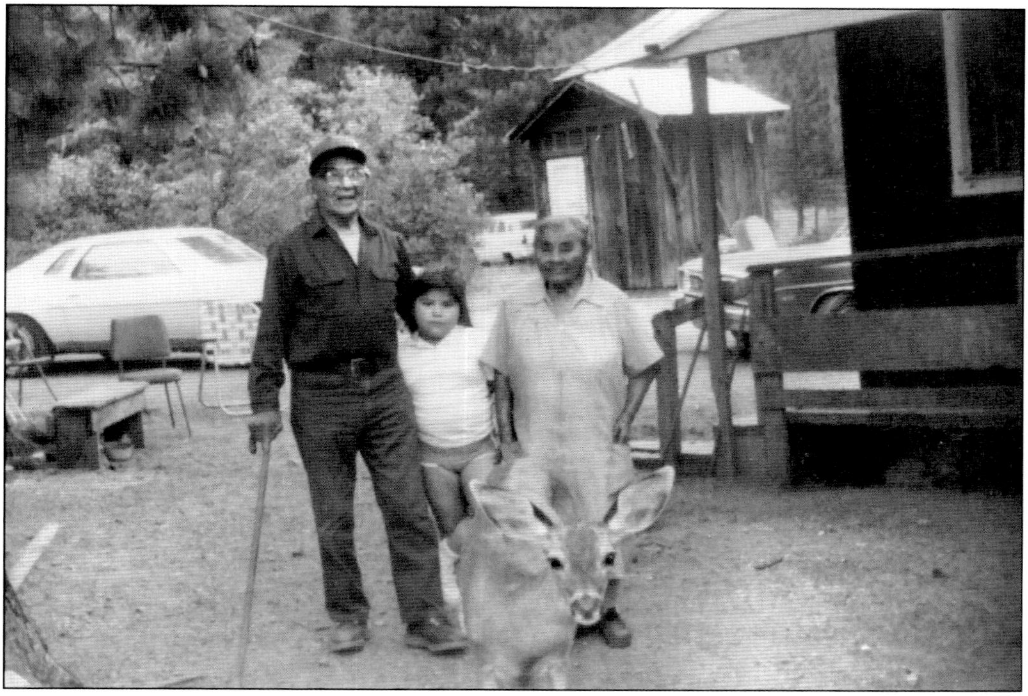

The Maidus soon adapted to the white man's ways and were very popular in the valley. One of the most popular large families was the Smith family. Pictured are Seymour and his wife, Louise, with one of their many granddaughters and Louise's pet deer, Bambi. (Courtesy of Margaret Cooke.)

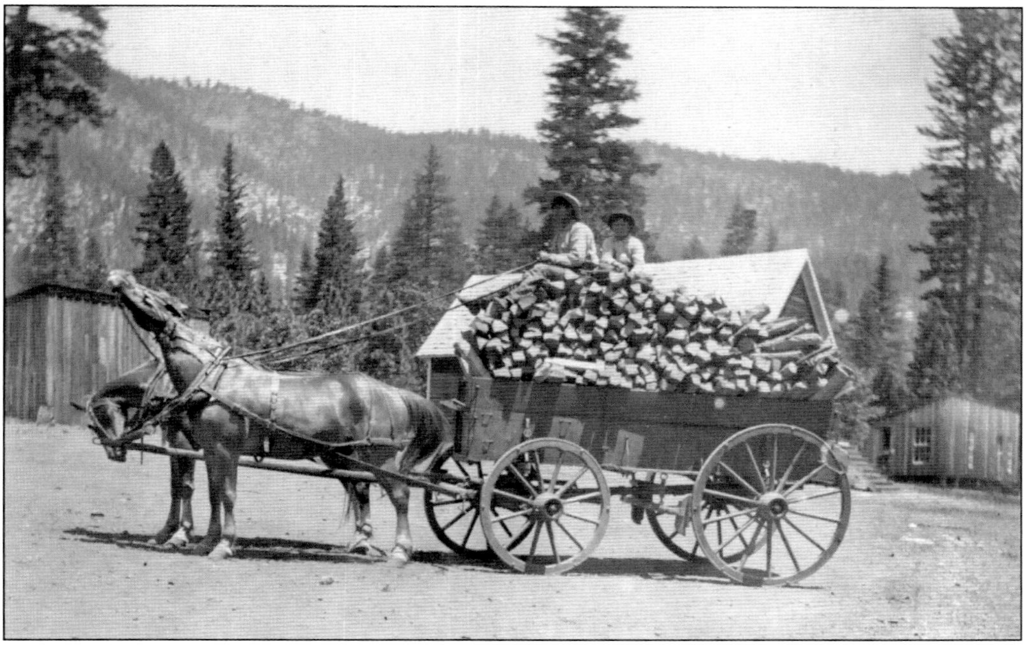

This image at the mission shows a team of horses pulling a wagon. It looks like it may not be fire wood but a wagonload of fence posts the two men must have split and hauled home for fence building.

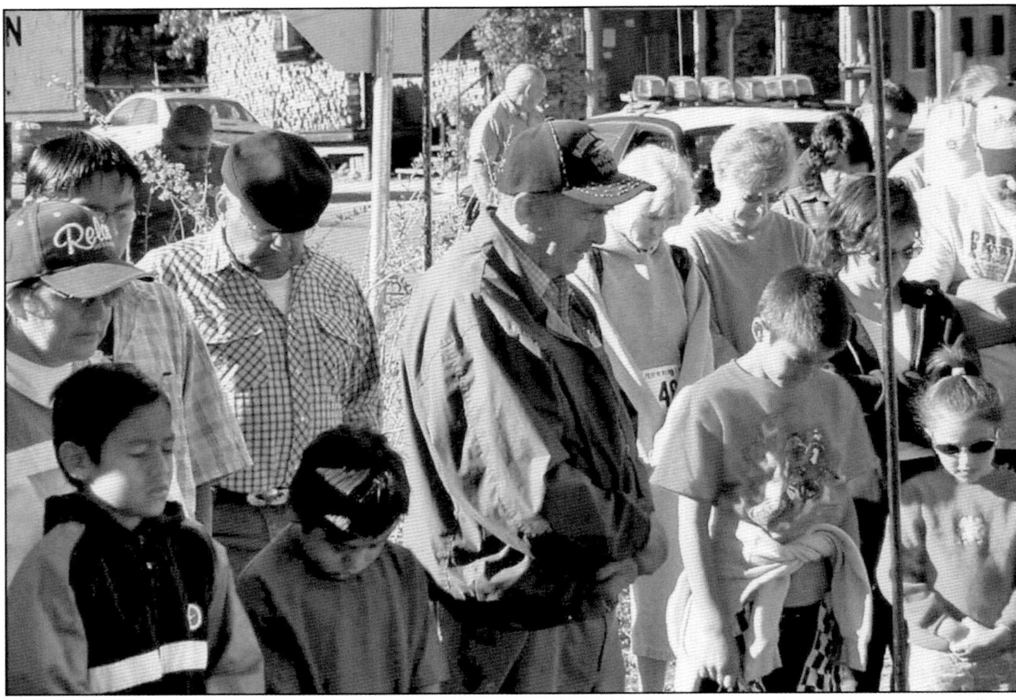

Pictured is Tom Merino, a Maidu, giving a prayer in the Maidu language for the beginning of the annual Seymour Smith Run from Taylorsville to Greenville. Tom has since passed on. To his left is Seymour Smith's son John Smith. The Seymour Smith Run still has many of Seymour's relatives in the run or walk. The race also includes a halfway run or walk covering half the distance to Greenville. (Courtesy of the author.)

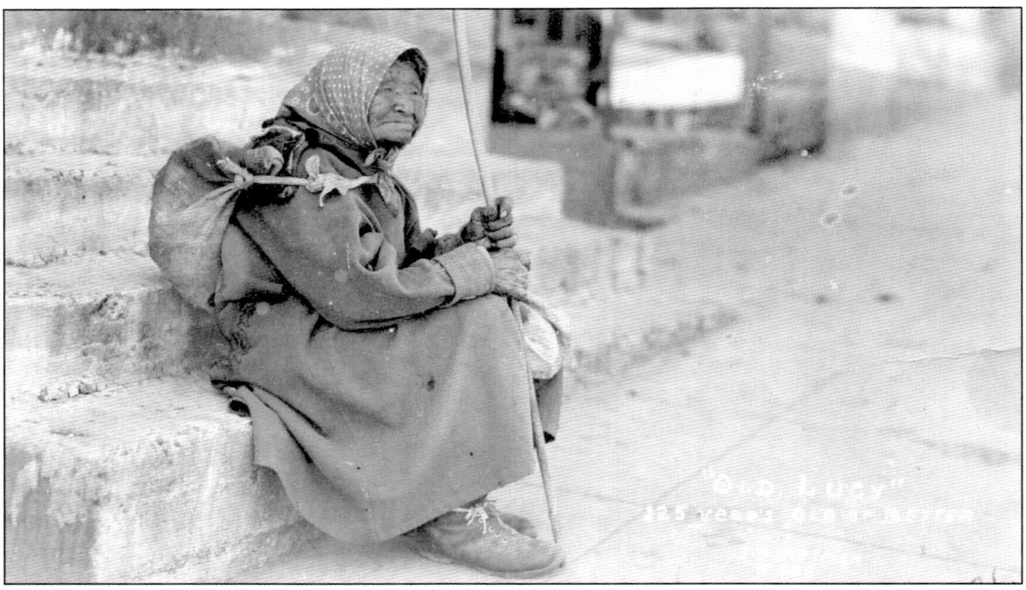

This is a picture of one of the older Maidus, known as "Lucy." It was said she was 125 years old. She was quite a woman, no matter her age. The oldest Maidu the author can remember was Louise Smith, who lived to 106.

Seven

LARGEST COPPER MINES

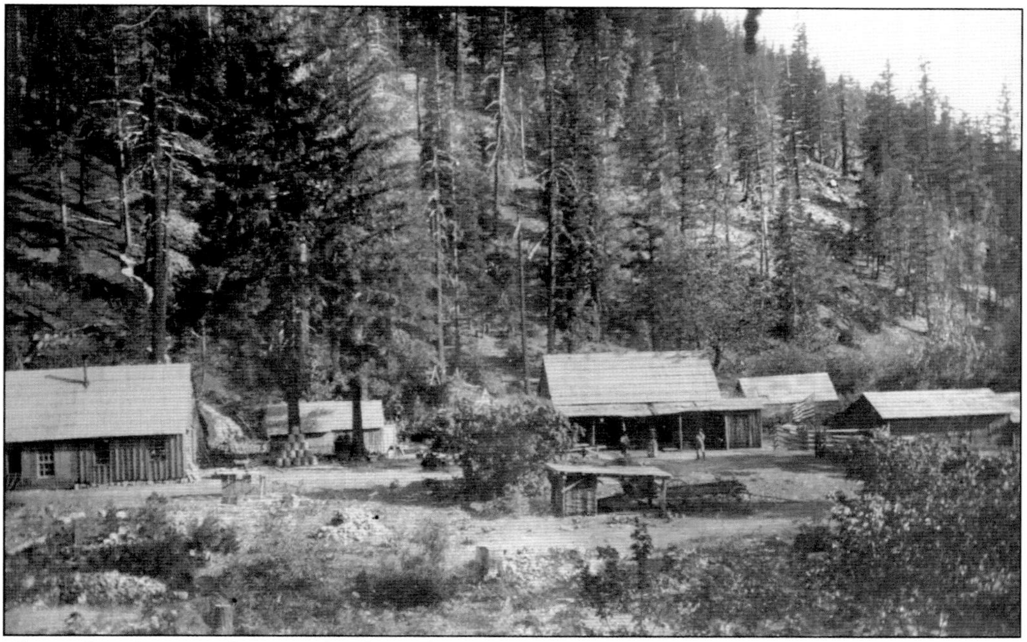

The earliest known photograph of Engels or Lower Camp along Lights Creek was taken in 1905. Henry A. Engels and his family settled here in 1880. Henry Engels Sr. was the manager of the Pacific Brass and Lock Foundry in San Francisco. His copper came from the Lake Superior region and cost him 35¢ to 60¢ a pound. He first came to the Plumas Copper Belt because of his interest in the metal from a manufacturer's standpoint. The photograph shows the Engels brothers, Charles and William, with their sister Emily Engels Cook standing in front of their parents' home. Note the butter firkins stacked outside their carpenter shop at left and the American flag at right. The Engels' butter firkins were their only means of support for many years. The picture was taken to facilitate the sale of shares of Engels Copper Mining Company for the construction of a 100-ton blast furnace to smelt medium-grade carbonate copper ores from the Engels Mine. The Engels brothers had incorporated the Engels Copper Mining Company in California on June 19, 1901. (Courtesy of Norm Lamb.)

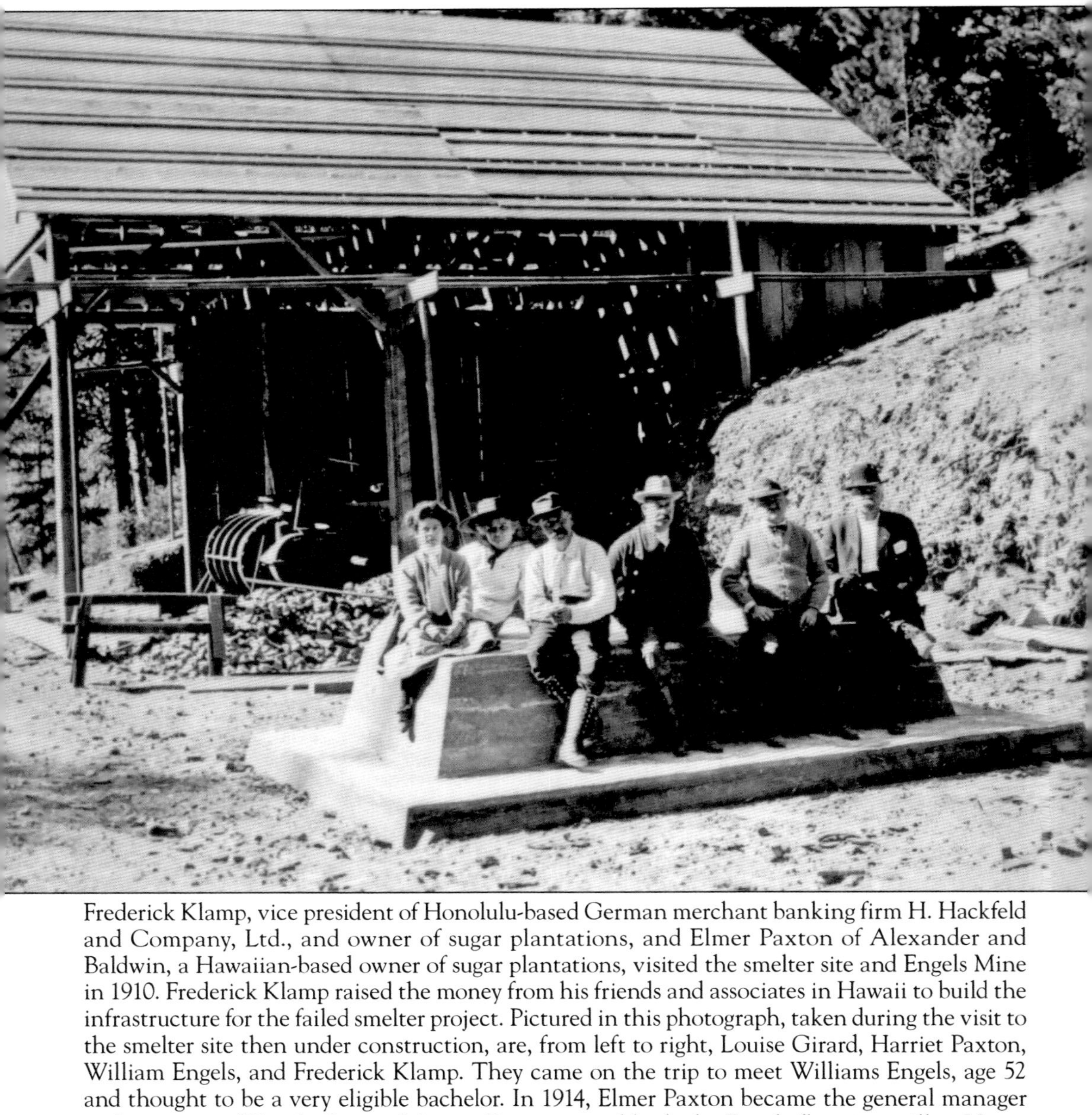

Frederick Klamp, vice president of Honolulu-based German merchant banking firm H. Hackfeld and Company, Ltd., and owner of sugar plantations, and Elmer Paxton of Alexander and Baldwin, a Hawaiian-based owner of sugar plantations, visited the smelter site and Engels Mine in 1910. Frederick Klamp raised the money from his friends and associates in Hawaii to build the infrastructure for the failed smelter project. Pictured in this photograph, taken during the visit to the smelter site then under construction, are, from left to right, Louise Girard, Harriet Paxton, William Engels, and Frederick Klamp. They came on the trip to meet Williams Engels, age 52 and thought to be a very eligible bachelor. In 1914, Elmer Paxton became the general manager and treasurer of Engels Copper Mining Company and built the Engels flotation mill at Upper Camp. Frederick Klamp became president of the company in 1922 after ousting Henry Engels in a proxy fight. (Courtesy of Norm Lamb.)

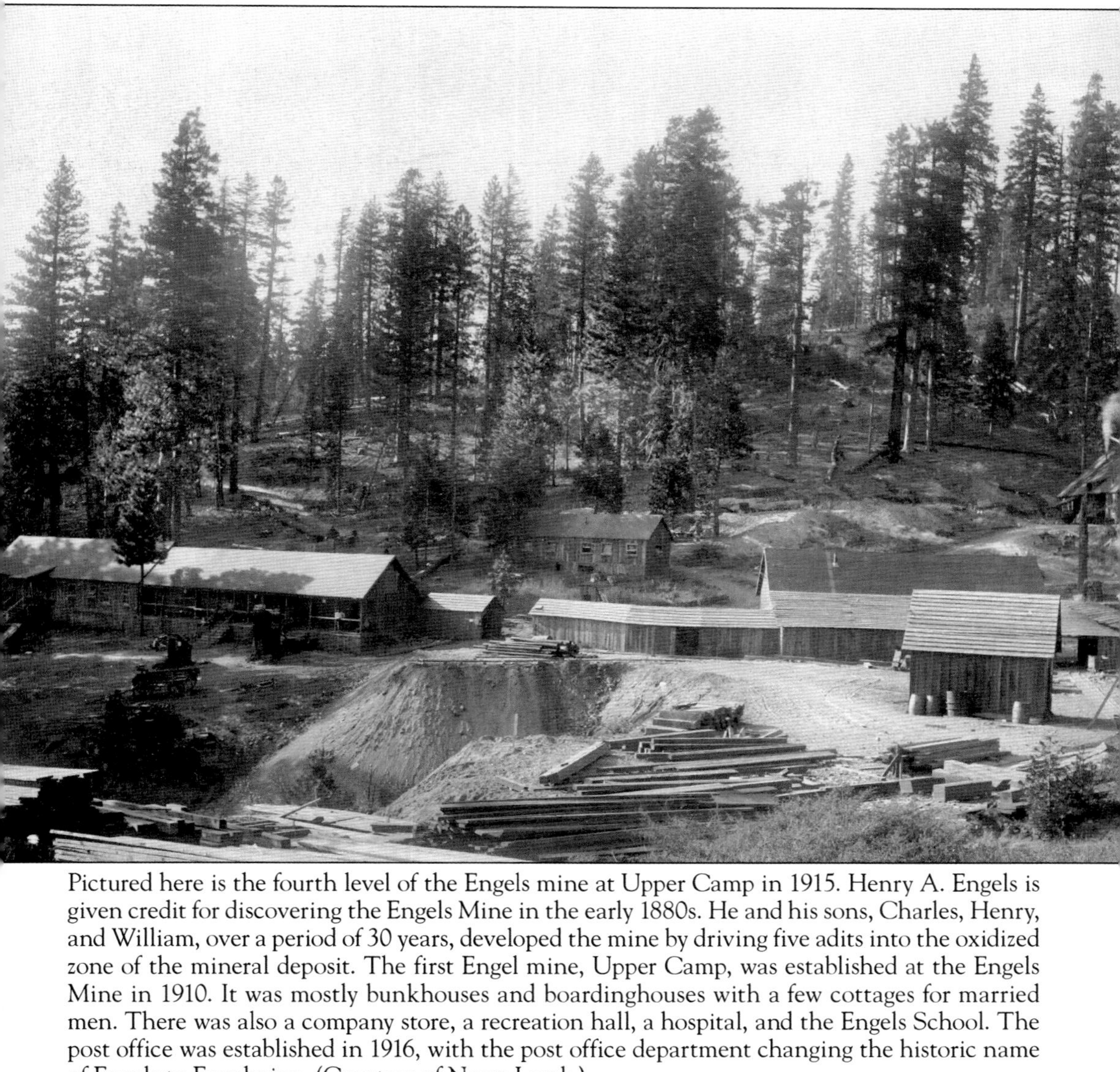

Pictured here is the fourth level of the Engels mine at Upper Camp in 1915. Henry A. Engels is given credit for discovering the Engels Mine in the early 1880s. He and his sons, Charles, Henry, and William, over a period of 30 years, developed the mine by driving five adits into the oxidized zone of the mineral deposit. The first Engel mine, Upper Camp, was established at the Engels Mine in 1910. It was mostly bunkhouses and boardinghouses with a few cottages for married men. There was also a company store, a recreation hall, a hospital, and the Engels School. The post office was established in 1916, with the post office department changing the historic name of Engels to Engelmine. (Courtesy of Norm Lamb.)

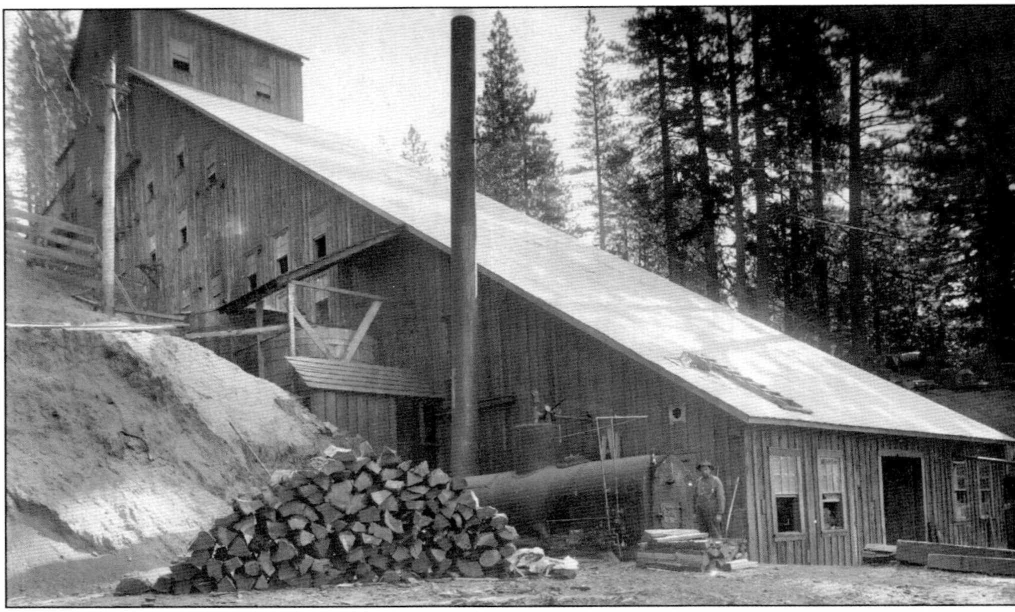

The first mill in the United States to use only the flotation process to concentrate its copper ore was completed in 1914 at the Engels Mine in Upper Camp. It was built by Minerals Separation American Syndicate, Ltd. The mill was designed to mill 150 tons per day and was milling 400 tons per day when it was closed on November 1, 1919, in lieu of the larger and more favorably located Superior Mill at Lower Camp. (Courtesy of Norm Lamb.)

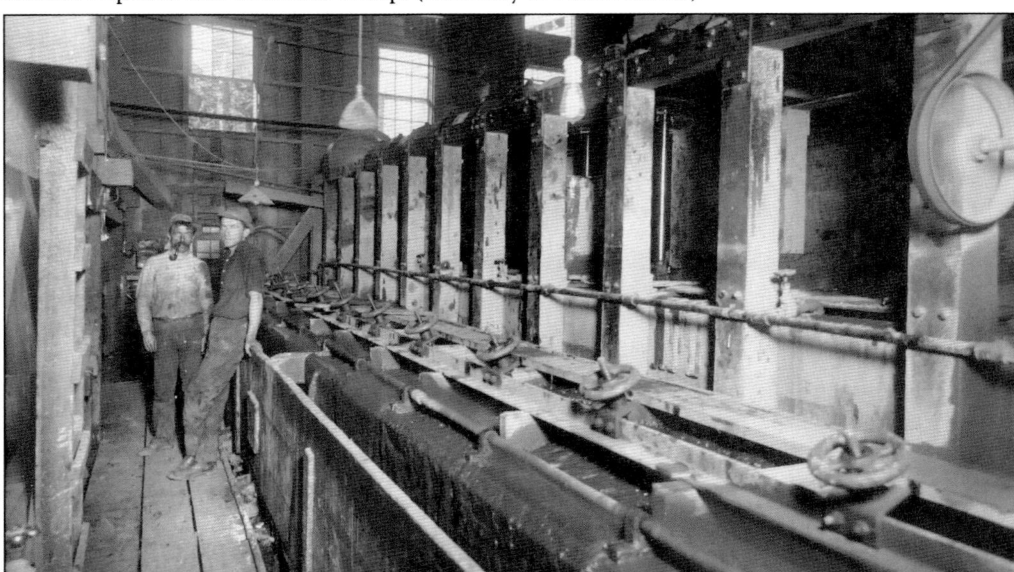

This shows the flotation cells at the Engels Mill at Upper Camp. Flotation was the most important development of the 20th century for the mining industry. It opened new mineral resources and averted an industrial crisis with the exhaustion of high-grade mineral deposits. Basically flotation "floats" the minerals on a water bath, where they are collected, dried, and sent to the smelter for final processing. Shown here are Will Gruss (left) and Charles Scott Haley. (Courtesy of Norm Lamb.)

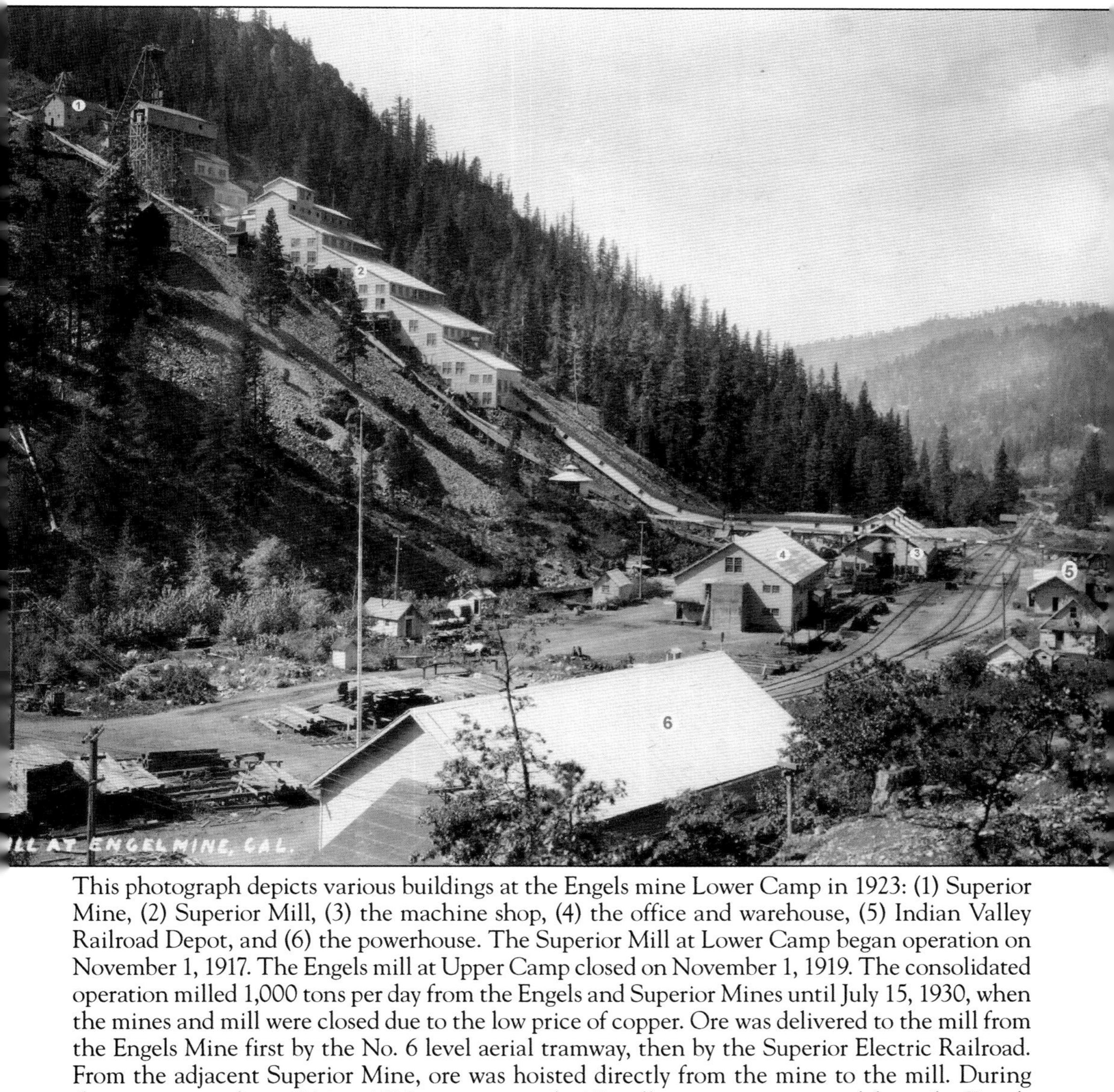

This photograph depicts various buildings at the Engels mine Lower Camp in 1923: (1) Superior Mine, (2) Superior Mill, (3) the machine shop, (4) the office and warehouse, (5) Indian Valley Railroad Depot, and (6) the powerhouse. The Superior Mill at Lower Camp began operation on November 1, 1917. The Engels mill at Upper Camp closed on November 1, 1919. The consolidated operation milled 1,000 tons per day from the Engels and Superior Mines until July 15, 1930, when the mines and mill were closed due to the low price of copper. Ore was delivered to the mill from the Engels Mine first by the No. 6 level aerial tramway, then by the Superior Electric Railroad. From the adjacent Superior Mine, ore was hoisted directly from the mine to the mill. During their operation from 1914 to 1930, approximately 4.7 million tons were mined from the Engels and Superior Mines and milling produced 160,170,000 pounds of copper and substantial values in gold and silver. Engels Copper Mining Company was a significant employer during World War I and the 1920s, supporting the local economy and paying dividends to its shareholders. (Courtesy of Norm Lamb.)

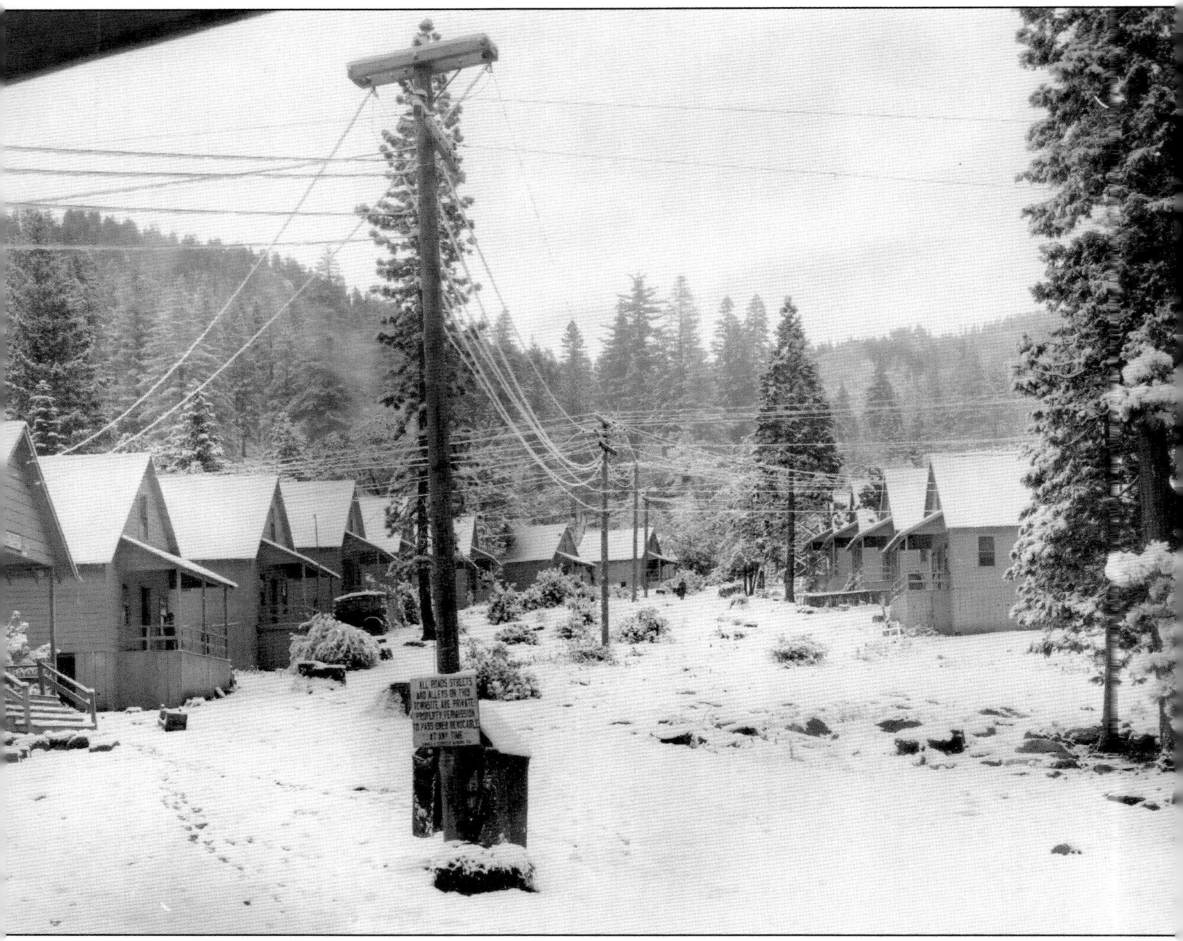

The Engel mine Lower Camp was for its day a modern company town, built on Lights Creek beginning in 1917 and completed in 1924. It was established to attract a stable workforce of married men and families. There were 154 well-built cottages of three to five rooms, 10 dormitories for single men, a boardinghouse for single men with a seating capacity of 368, a company store and hotel, a recreation hall, a hospital, the Superior School, and the post office. Cottages rented for $5 to $10 per month, and single men paid $1 per day for room and board. Health insurance was $1 per month. The town was divided into three parts: Engelmine, Hollywood, and Tijuana. The last two names undoubtedly were influenced by the silent movies shown weekly at the recreation hall. The company store sold goods at cost plus a handling charge. The Indian Valley Railroad provided access to the outside world, connecting with the Western Pacific Railroad at Paxton. San Francisco could be reached in eight hours by rail. (Courtesy of Norm Lamb.)

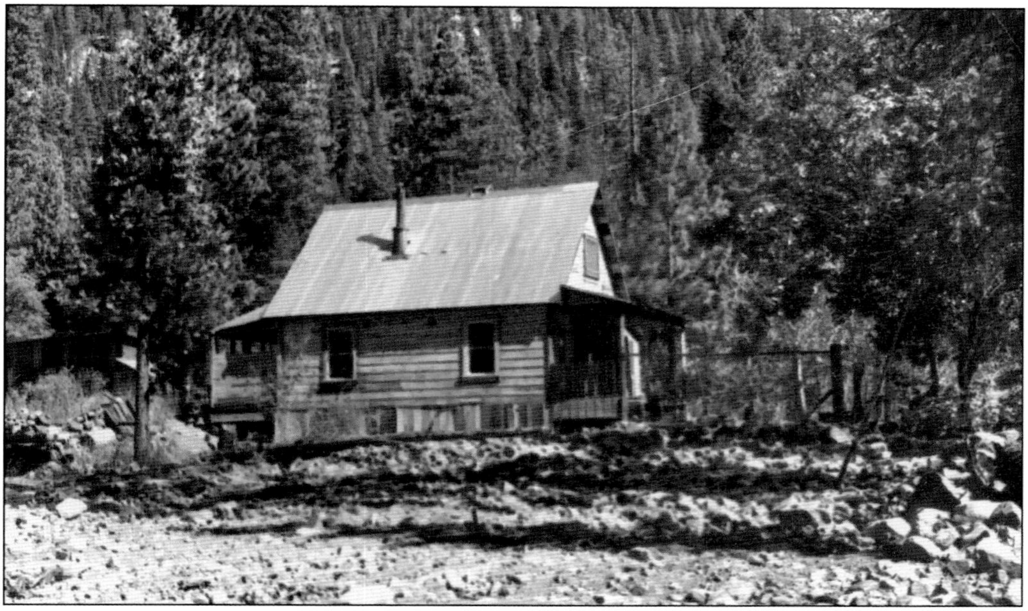

No mention of Engelmine would be complete without bringing up the Downeys. They had a claim on Lights Creek and, at one time, had a bridge over the creek and a couple of homes built there. This is Dave Downey's home across Lights Creek. One home burned, but they replaced it. Engelmine had been shut down many years before the Downeys left. (Courtesy of Alice Williams.)

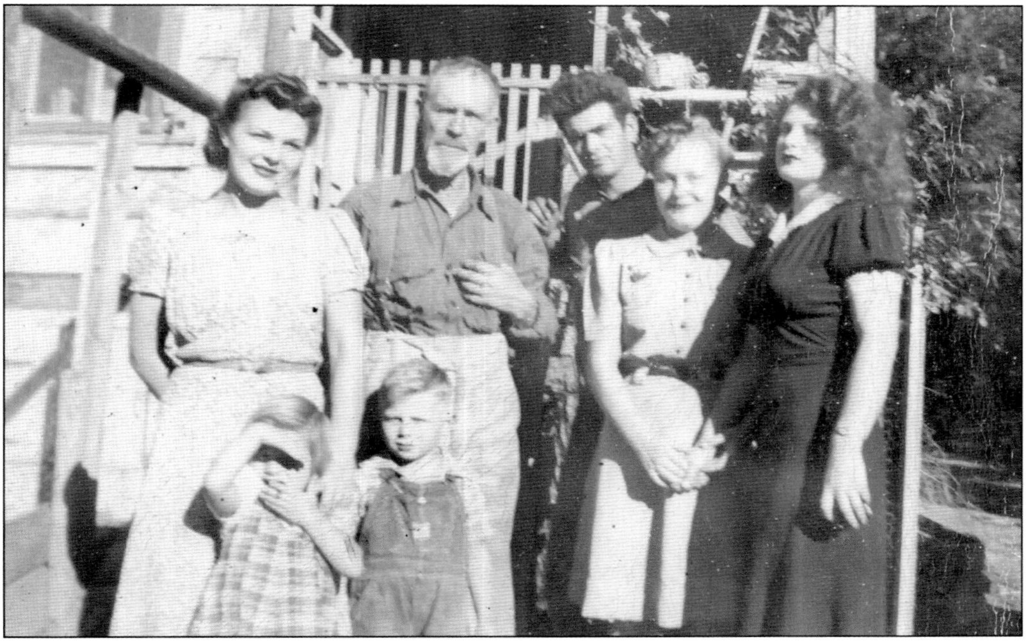

Alexander Downey and his family are shown in front of their house. From left to right are the oldest daughter, Susan (Eveland) Downey, Alexander (known as Alex), son-in-law Allan Eveland, daughter Alice (Williams) Downey, daughter Helen Downey, and (in front) Susan's two children, Carol and Allen Kelley Eveland. Alex's son William Downey (not pictured) was in the military at the time. William later became the author's step-father. (Courtesy of Alice Williams.)

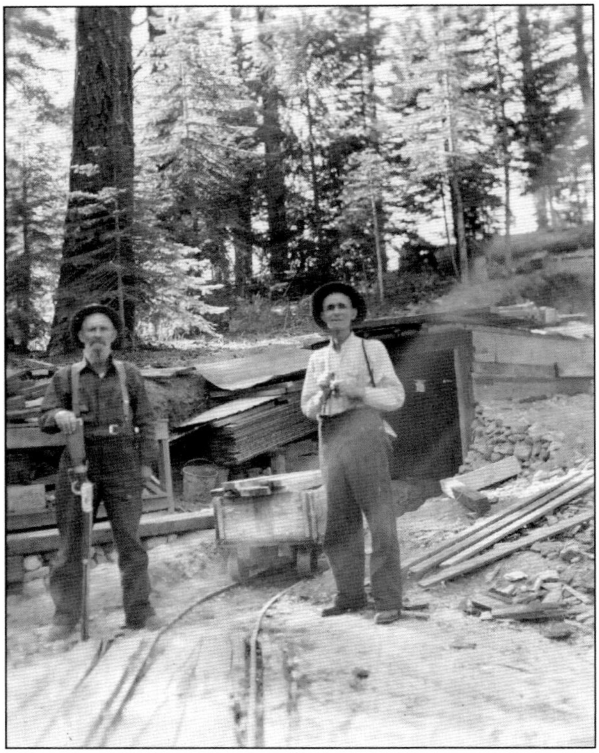

This is one of the mine shafts near the Upper Camp of Engelmine. It belonged to the Downey family. On the left is Alex Downey, and on the right is his brother Dave Downey. They also had a brother Charlie who was a frequent visitor at the mine. (Courtesy of Alice Williams.)

The Indian Valley Railroad Company was incorporated on June 30, 1916, by the Engels Copper Mining Company. The purpose was to build a standard-gauge railroad from a connection on the Western Pacific Railroad at Paxton to Engels, a distance of 21.6 miles. This would facilitate the movement of ore concentrates, freight, and passengers. In this photograph, Baldwin locomotive No. 2 is crossing Indian Creek with gondola and passenger cars. (Courtesy of Bob Cooke.)

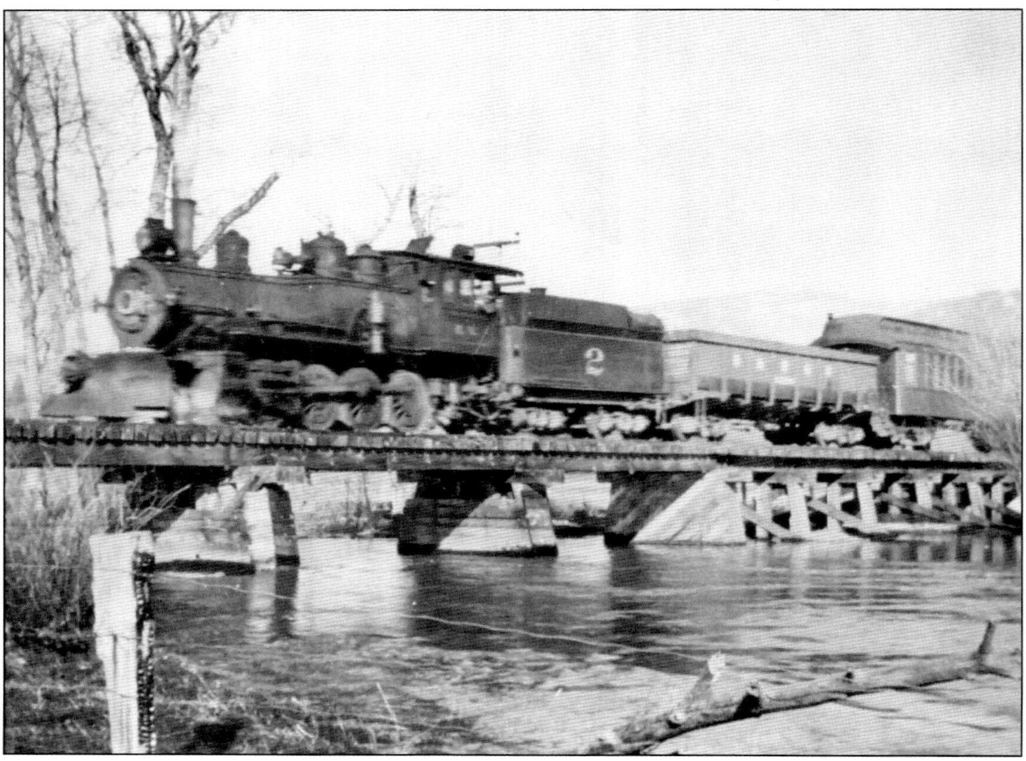

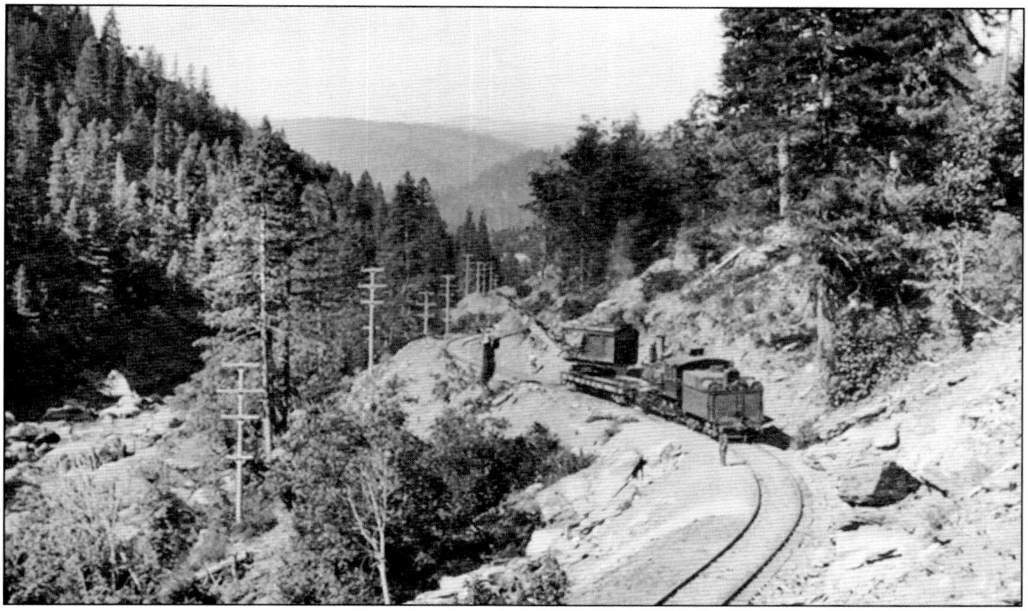

Utah Construction Company began grading for the Indian Valley Railroad on July 31, 1916, and finished by November. This photograph shows the ditcher working on the railroad bed between Dixie Canyon and Indian Falls. This section of the railroad between today's Greenville "Y" and Arlington became Highway 89 in 1938, after the right-of-way was sold to the State of California upon approval of abandonment of the rail line.

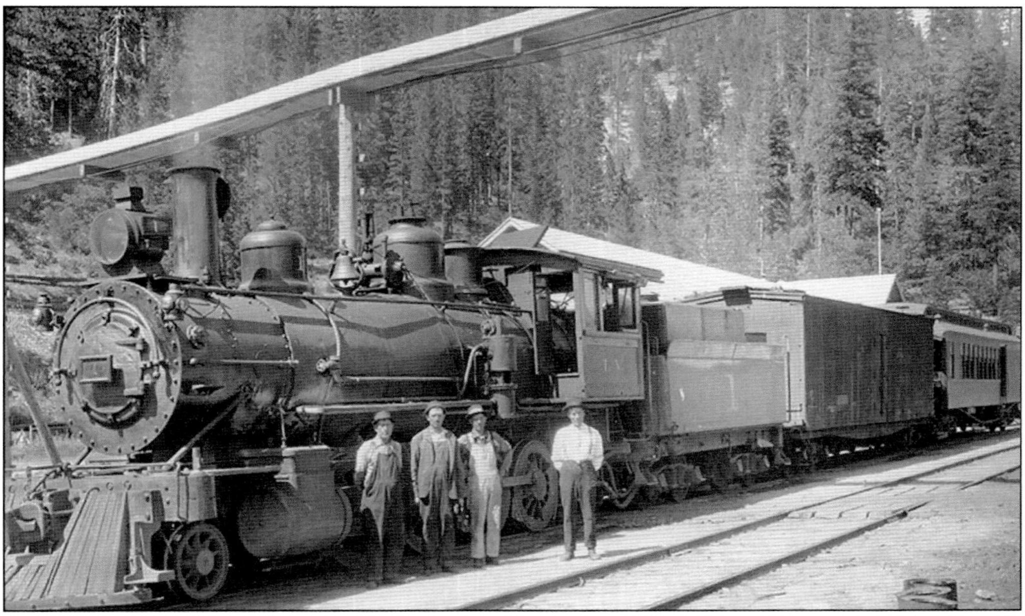

Indian Valley Railroad Baldwin locomotive No. 1 pulls freight and passenger cars in front of the Engels depot at the Engels mine Lower Camp, westbound for Paxton to connect with the Western Pacific Railroad. The overhead trestle in the photograph carried steam from the heating plant to the Superior Mill on the hillside to the right. Note the carbide cans in lower right corner of the photograph being recycled as trash cans.

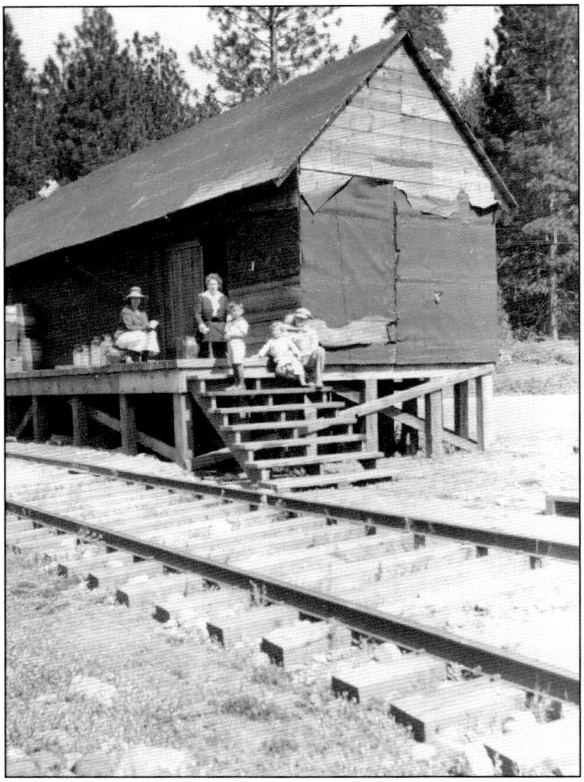

Veramont was the station at Taylorsville. It was located near the intersection of North Arm Road and Deadfall Lane. It was originally called Red Hog Siding after the numerous red hogs on the H. M. Barngrover Ranch. Red Hog Siding was not a very stately name, so it was renamed Veramont after the farmer's daughter, Vera Barngrover. The station in this photograph burned to the ground on December 31, 1919.

Pictured is the new Veramont station on the Indian Valley Railroad at the corner of Deadfall Lane (in the foreground) and North Arm Road. A full train of freight, gondola, and passenger cars heads up the North Arm of Indian Valley toward Engelmine.

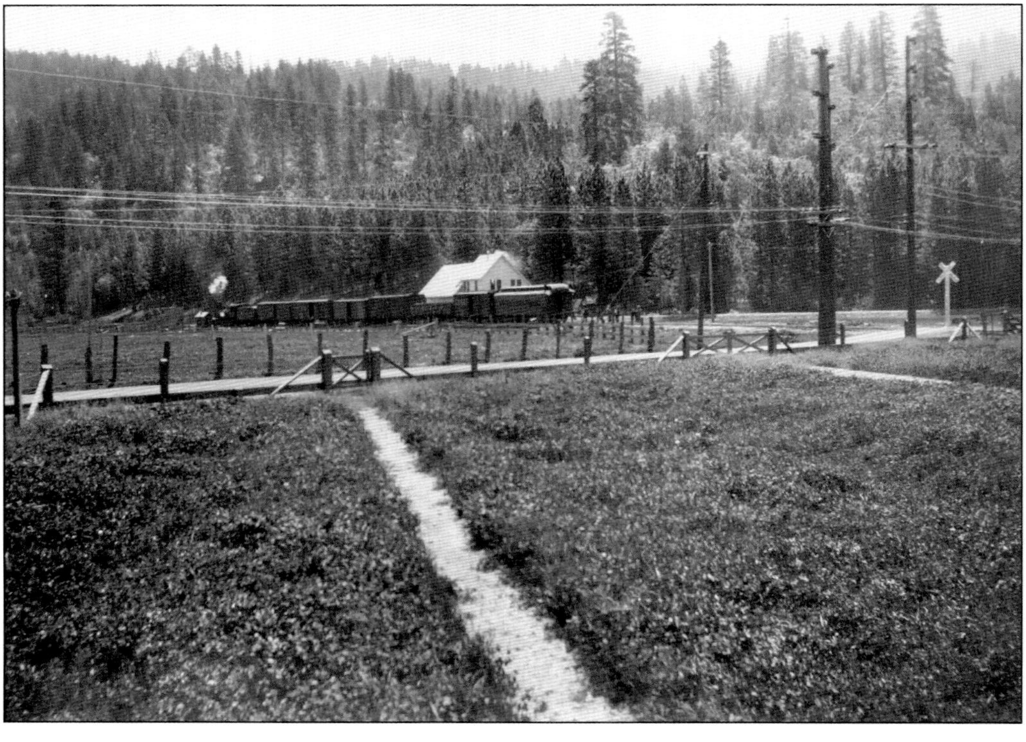

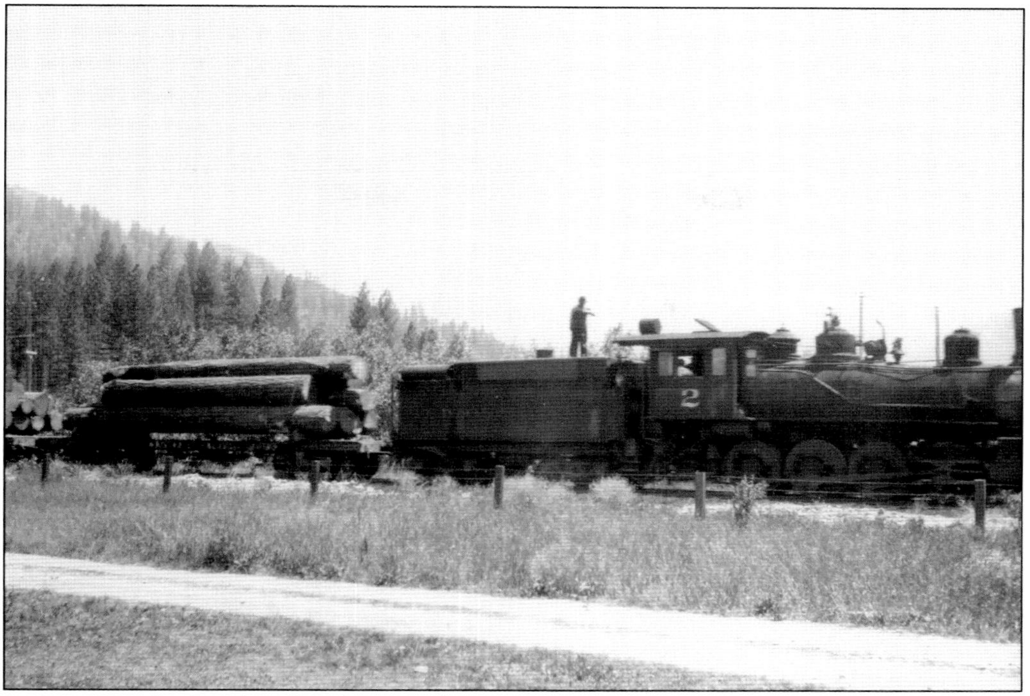

In the 1930s, the Taresh and Awbrey Lumber Company loaded logs on the Indian Valley Railroad at Veramont for delivery to the Frizzie Mill in Dixie Canyon for rough cutting. The lumber was then shipped on the railroad to a planing mill in Crescent Mills for finishing.

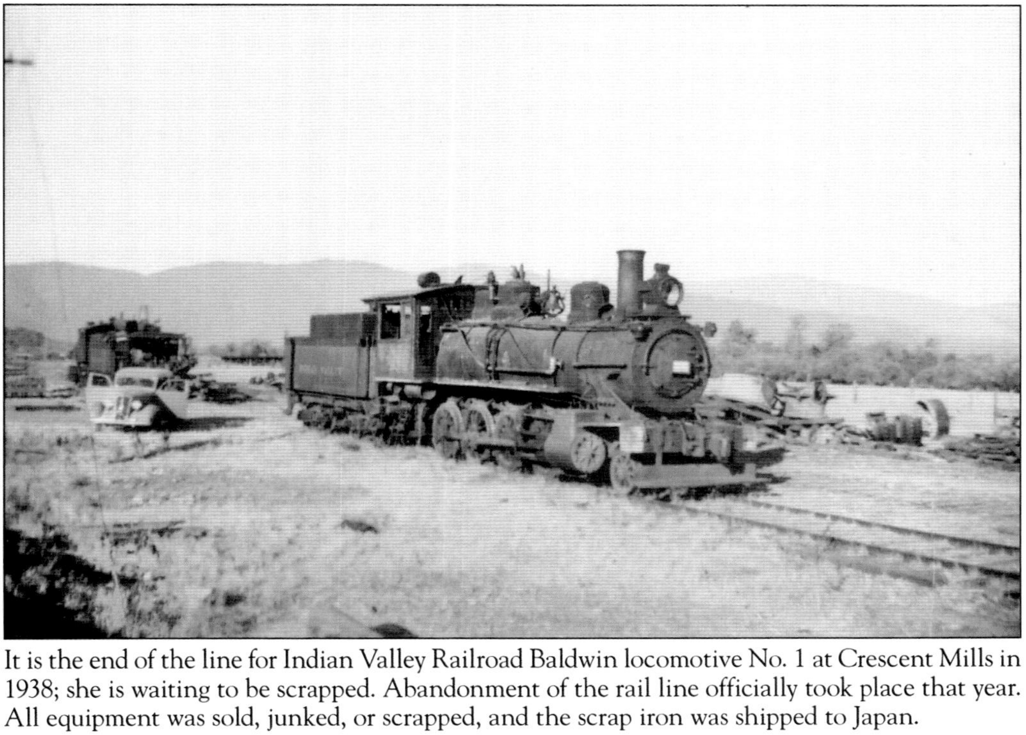

It is the end of the line for Indian Valley Railroad Baldwin locomotive No. 1 at Crescent Mills in 1938; she is waiting to be scrapped. Abandonment of the rail line officially took place that year. All equipment was sold, junked, or scrapped, and the scrap iron was shipped to Japan.

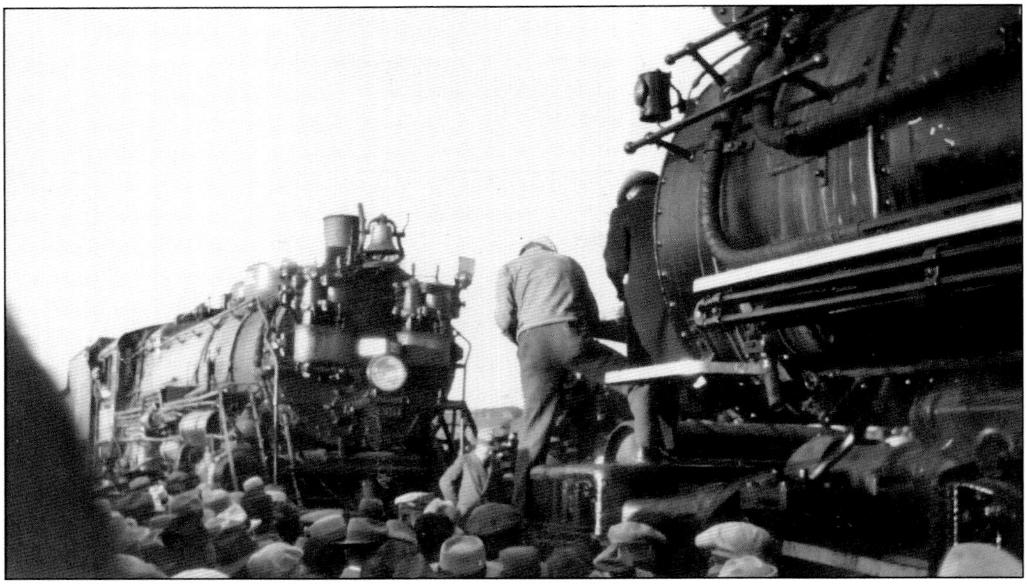

The Western Pacific Railroad began construction of the 112-mile HiLine from Keddie to Bieber in 1930, thus guaranteeing the demise of the Indian Valley Railroad. Stations were established at Crescent Mills and Greenville. At completion, seen here, the Western Pacific met the Great Northern Railway at Bieber on November 10, 1931.

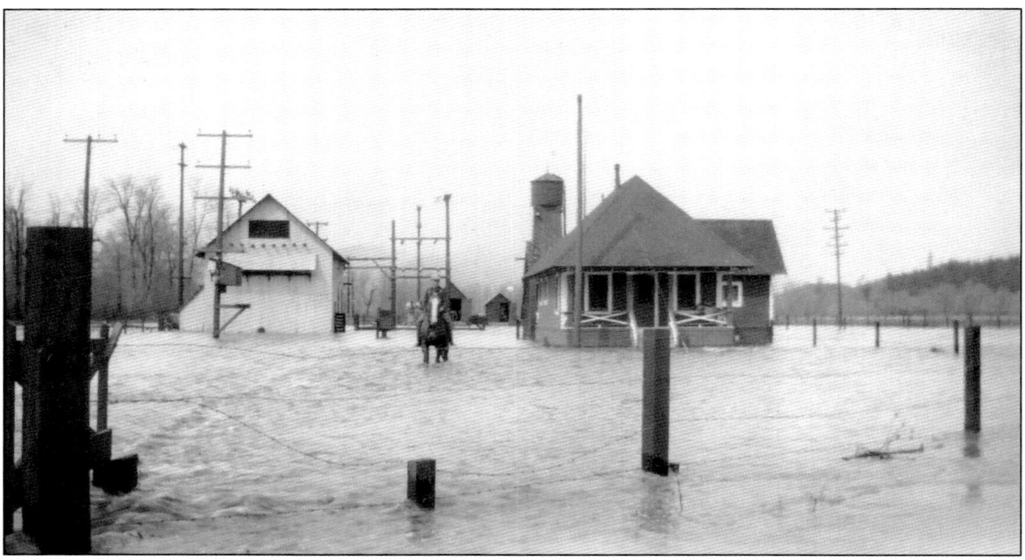

Flooding was not uncommon here. Pictured in 1926 or 1927 is the Veramont PG&E substation across the road from the Veramont Depot. The author and his family lived in this house beginning in 1941 or 1942 for around five or six years, and it flooded many times.

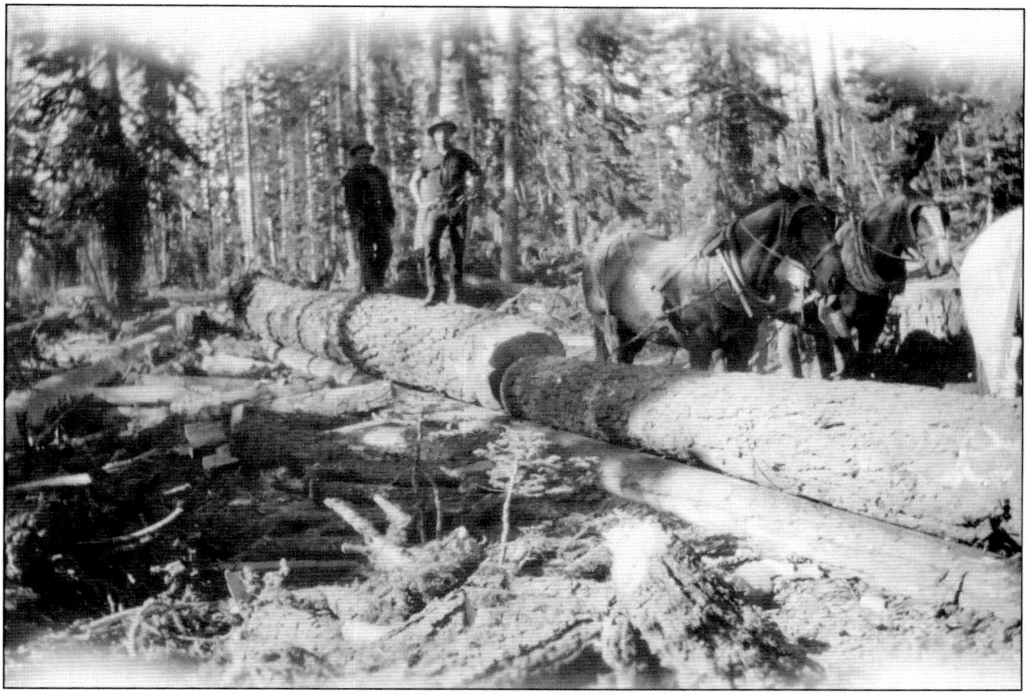

This is one of the earlier pictures showing activity at Walker Mine. As in most cases, as soon as there was construction, logging started and a mill popped up to get the lumber to build with. This shows some of the first logging at Walker Mine, with logs being skidded by horses.

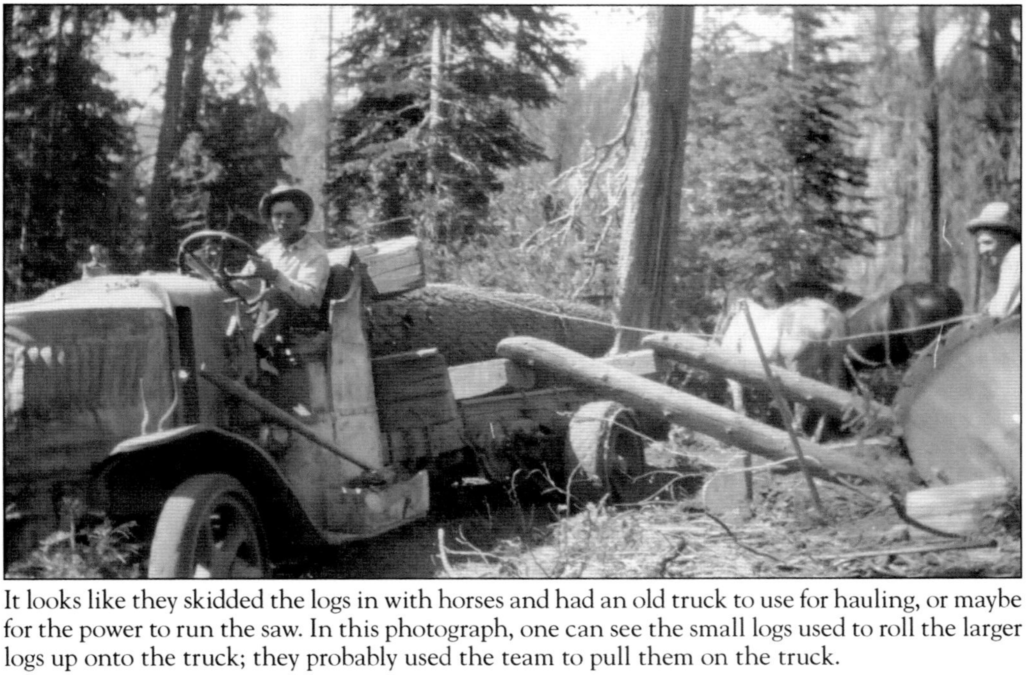

It looks like they skidded the logs in with horses and had an old truck to use for hauling, or maybe for the power to run the saw. In this photograph, one can see the small logs used to roll the larger logs up onto the truck; they probably used the team to pull them on the truck.

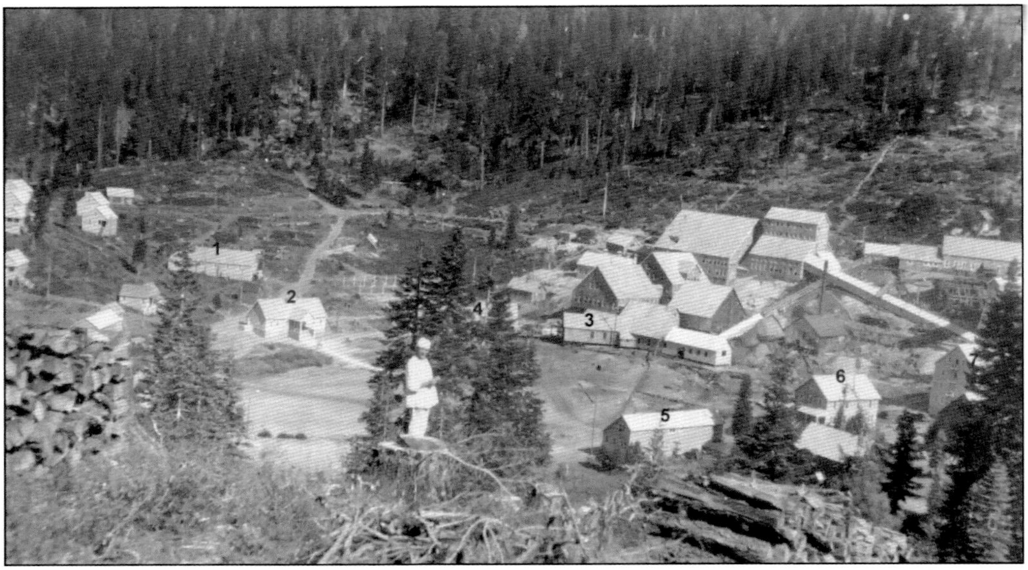

Here is the cook from the cookhouse standing on a stump and looking down over the town. This photograph points out the structures at Walker: No. 1 is the theater and schoolhouse, which was also used for dances; No. 2 is the main office; No. 3 is the tram house, No. 4 is the grocery store, No. 5 is the hospital, and No. 6 is one of the bunkhouses that the company had for its employees.

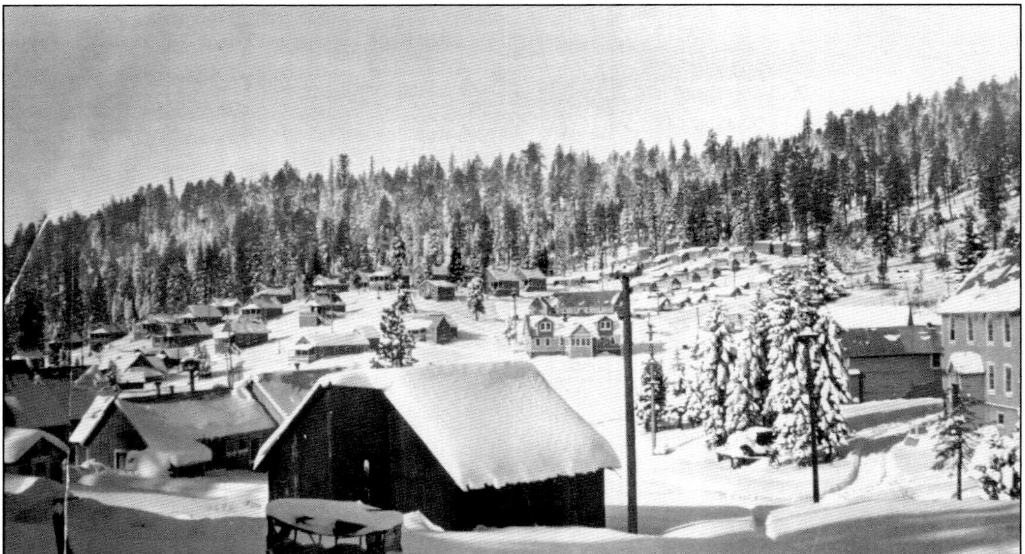

Walker Mine was soon growing by leaps and bounds. It was one of the largest copper mines in the state, second only to Engelmine. The only difference between Walker and Engels is that Walker was higher in elevation and had quite severe winters. Soon it was a large town, with schools and other businesses.

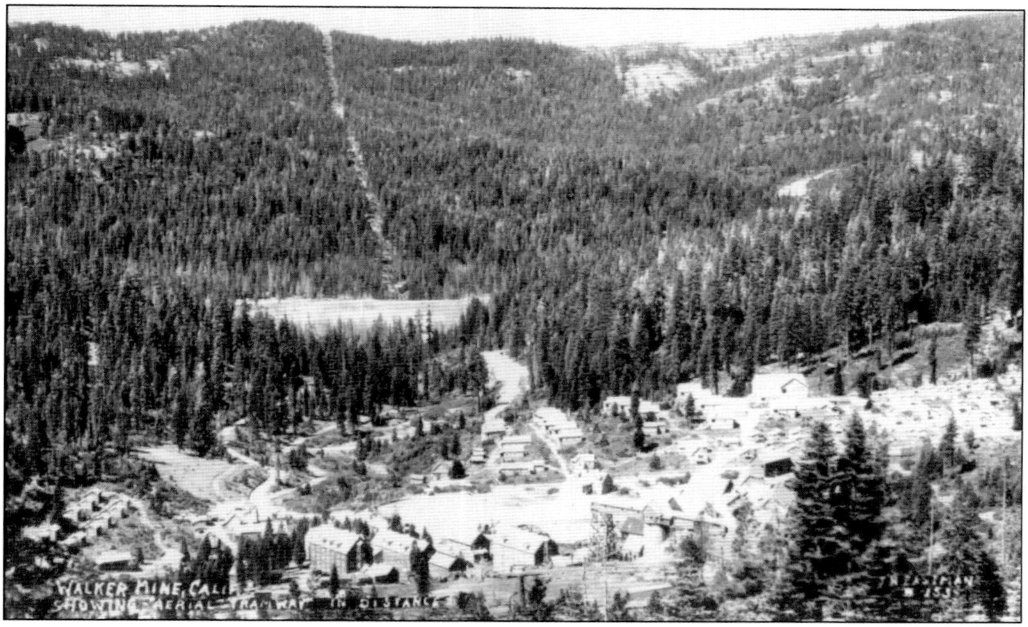

Walker Mine was discovered in 1904 by George Bemis. He and Joseph R. Walker incorporated Walker Mining Company in 1909. The first flotation mill was built in 1916 and control of the company was acquired by the Anaconda Copper Mining Company in 1918. A 9-mile-long aerial tramway was built to Spring Garden to connect with the Western Pacific Railroad that year. Thus began a 23-year period of expansion and production. In the top photograph, the aerial tramway is in the background, the tailings dam is in the center, and in the foreground are the Walker Mine town site and mill. In the bottom photograph is a close up of the mill and bunkhouses. By the time the mine closed in 1941, it had produced 167,788,000 pounds of copper and substantial values in gold and silver.

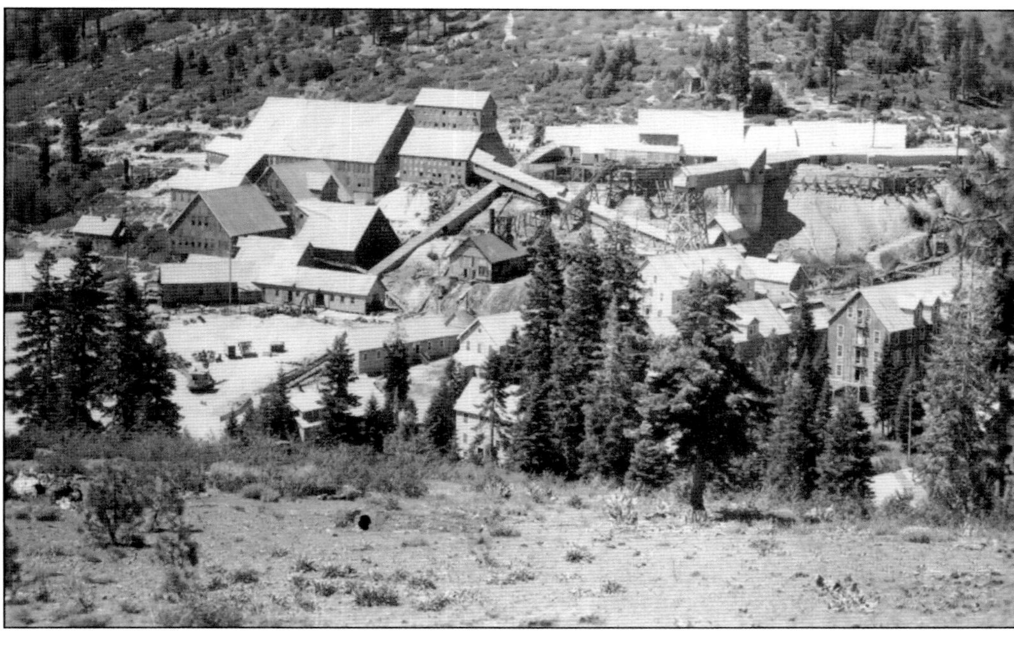

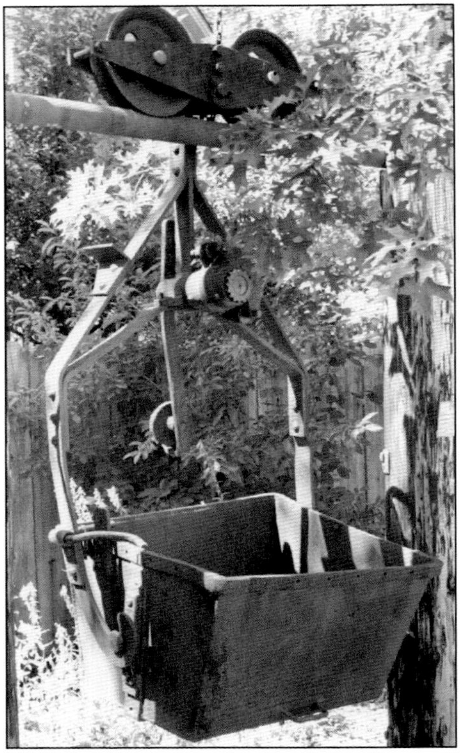

This is one of the tram buckets used to transport the ore and people out to Spring Garden. The author's aunt and uncle, Zelma McCutcheon Goodhue (known as Dutch) and Leroy Goodhue (known as Buster) used to live at Walker Mine. On a chilly November day when Dutch went into labor with her first child, they sent her out on the tram line.

The town slowly disappeared, and now, not much remains of Walker Mine. Slowly everything was either moved or torn down, and electricity was no longer available to the area. Today one can see where the town and mine and the tailing pile below once were, but visitors would never believe what it was at one time.

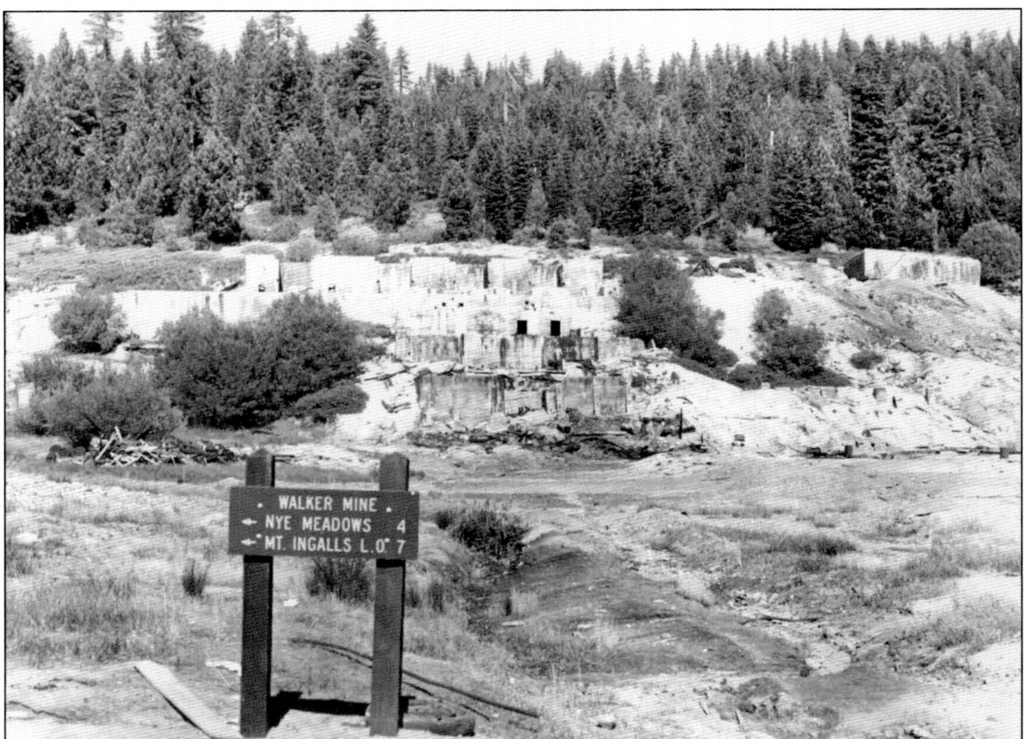

Eight

After the Mines Weakened Logging and Ranching

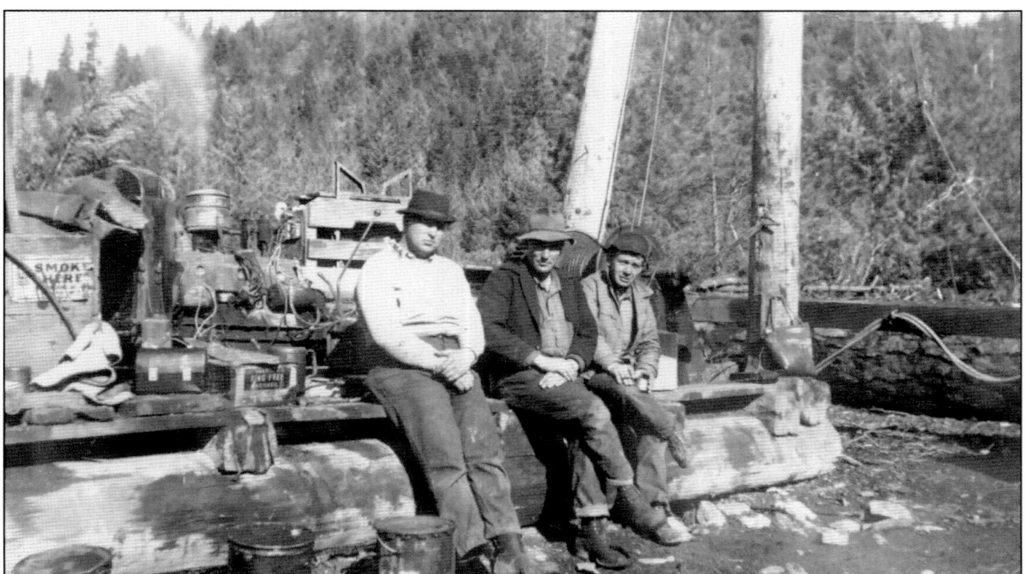

These are the three original men who started the Trio Logging Company. From left to right sitting in a landing on their loader are Rip Stead, Bert Wilson, and Al Olds. The mines were fading but logging and ranching were still booming, so these men organized a logging company. (Courtesy of Carl Stead.)

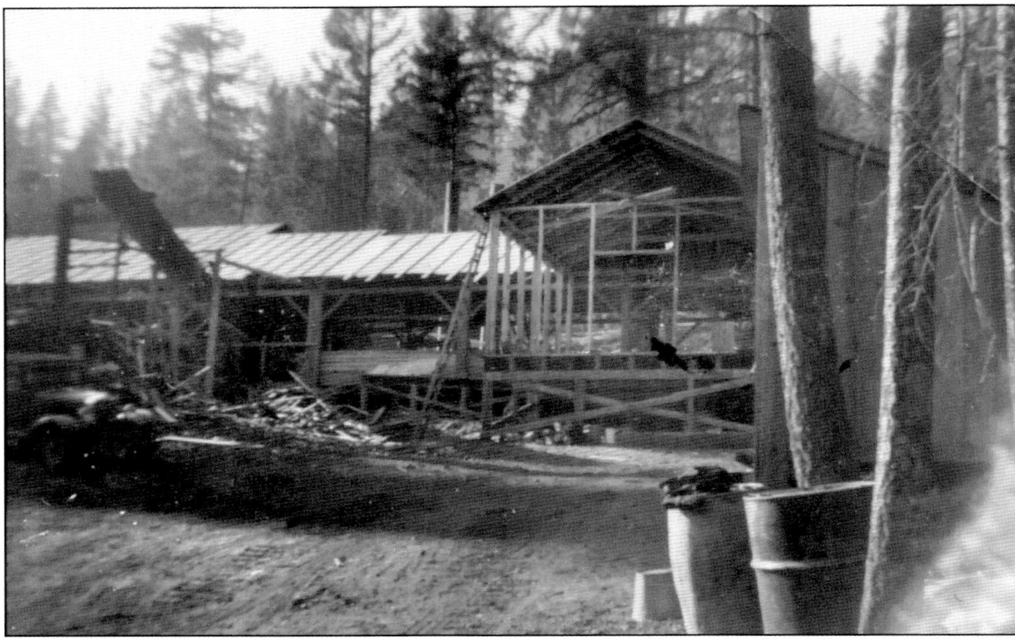

Many mills were being built because of the demand for lumber. This little mill was built just above Genesee Valley and was close to the timber they were logging. By being close to the timber, they were able to haul 10-foot-wide loads into the mill. If on the highway, they would be restricted to an 8-foot width. This was the beginning of Plumas Lumber. (Courtesy of Nansi Bohne.)

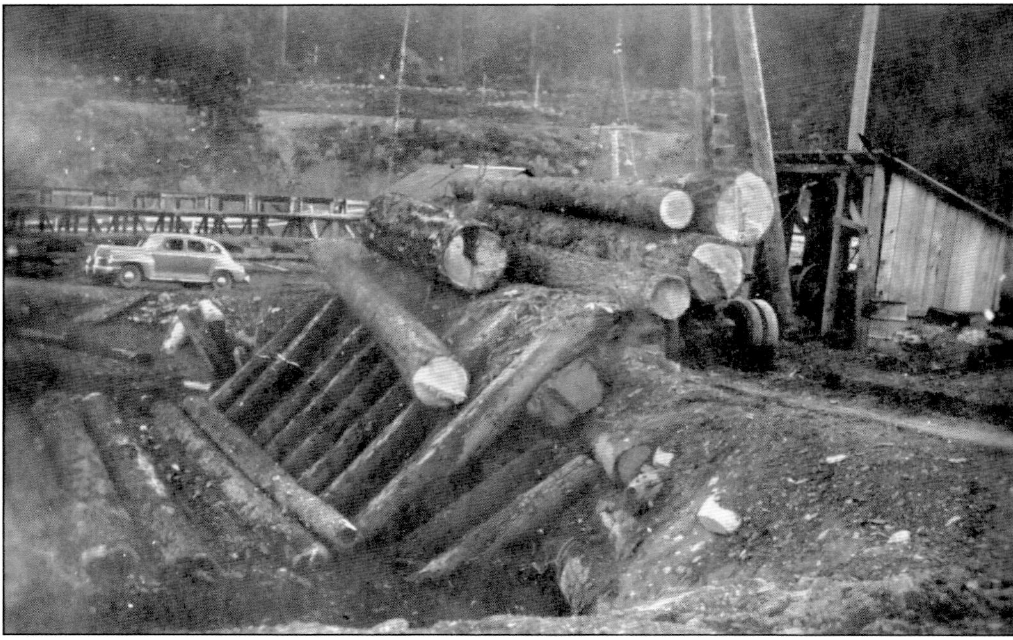

This mill was on the outskirts of Greenville on Highway 89. It was mainly a stud mill, which cut only 8-foot to 9-foot studs for framing, but did cut many railroad ties in its day. Many military people said it made them feel at home to be all the way around the world and see a stud stamped on the end with "Cheney Stud." (Courtesy of Nansi Bohne.)

One of the early logging trucks is pictured here. The man hanging out the window is Rip Stead, part-owner of the company. In those days, one could not tell the boss from any other worker; they all worked side by side. Note the front tires with no fenders around them. (Courtesy of Carl Stead.)

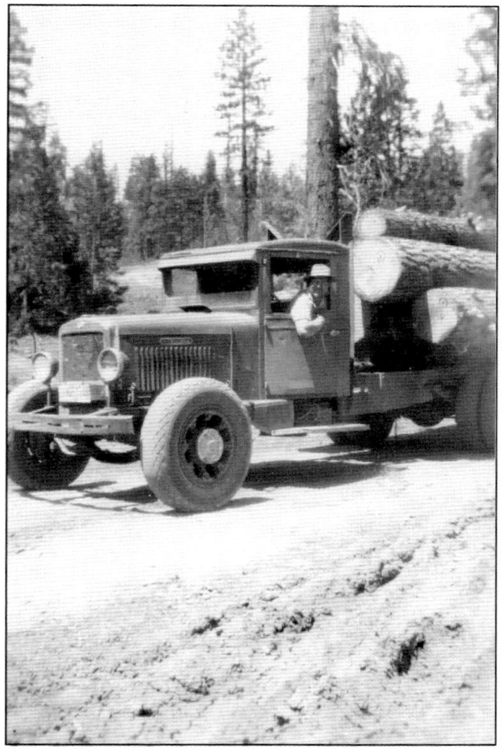

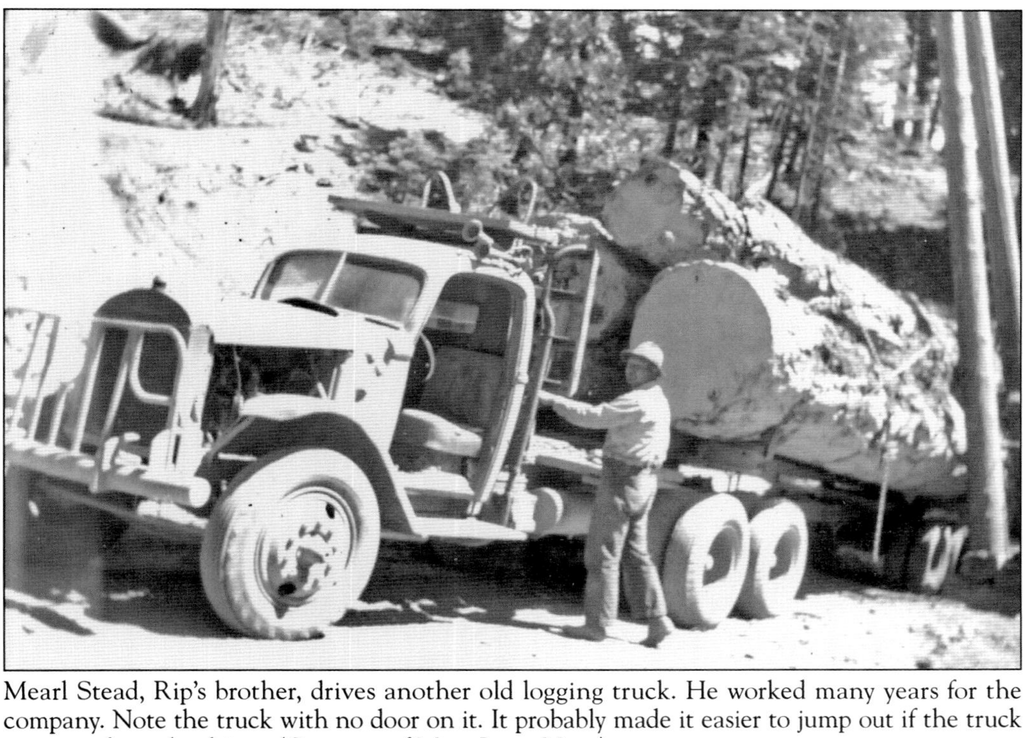

Mearl Stead, Rip's brother, drives another old logging truck. He worked many years for the company. Note the truck with no door on it. It probably made it easier to jump out if the truck got away from the driver. (Courtesy of Mary Lynn Neer.)

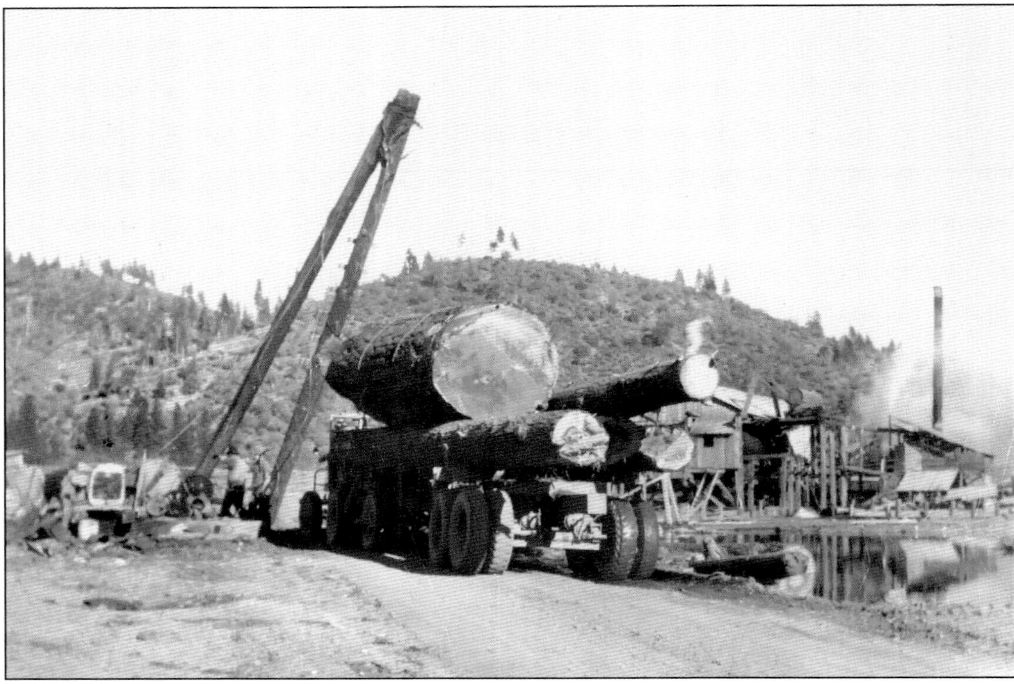

This is one of the first sawmills. It was called the Taresh and Awbrey Company. It was started by the Taresh brothers—Joe, Charlie, and Arnold—and Bert Awbrey. It was a circle sawmill and did not produce as many board feet as mills do today. Note the size of the log they are dumping into their millpond. (Courtesy of Mary Lynn Neer.)

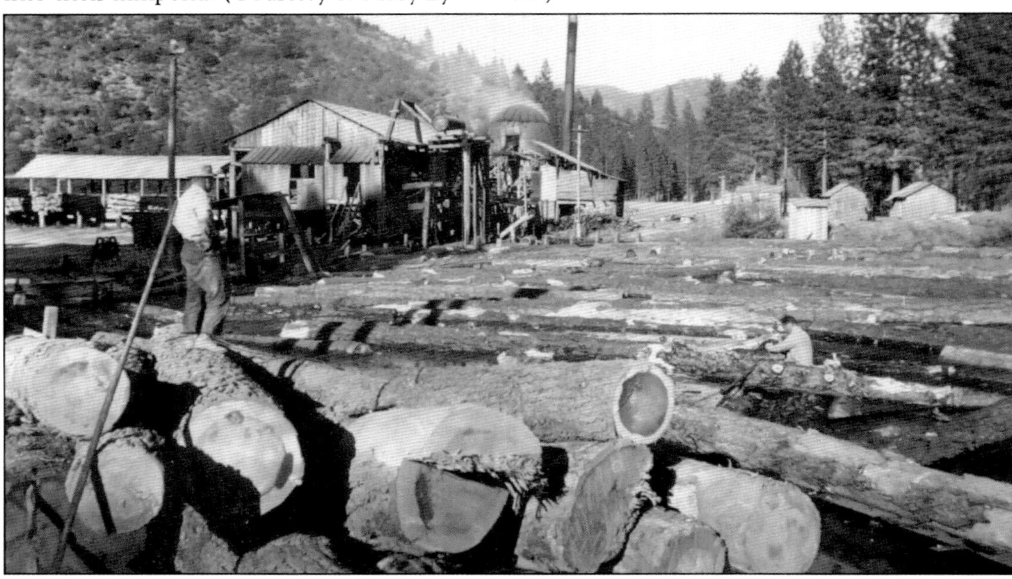

Taresh's millpond is pictured here. In those days, millponds were very popular. It was an easy way to move the logs to get them to the mill. Mills had what they called a slip coming up out of the pond to bring the logs into the mill. They also usually had a water spray to wash the dirt off of the logs as well as a man they called a rock picker, who looked for rocks before the logs got in the mill and into the saw. (Courtesy of Carl Stead.)

Pictured here is an older mill site along Highway 89. It was called the Frizzie Mill, named after Frizzie, who started it. It was on the creek side of the highway. Here Al Olds is getting ready to unload his truck. The highway was above the old store that used to operate at the base of Dixie Creek. (Courtesy of Mary Lynn Neer.)

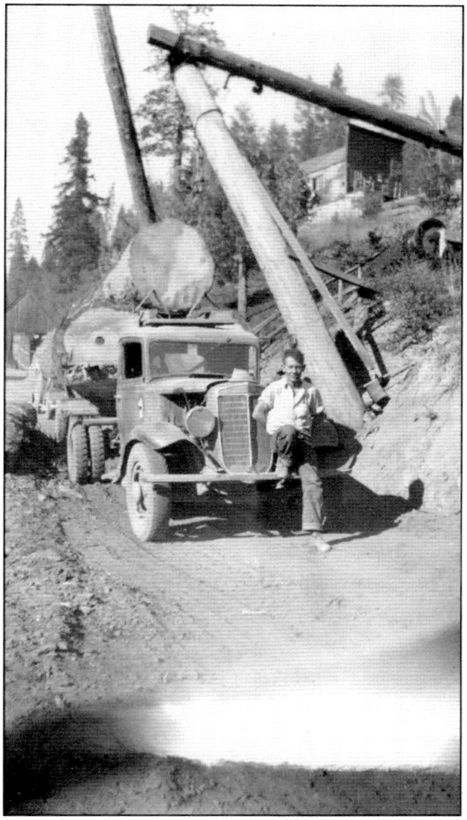

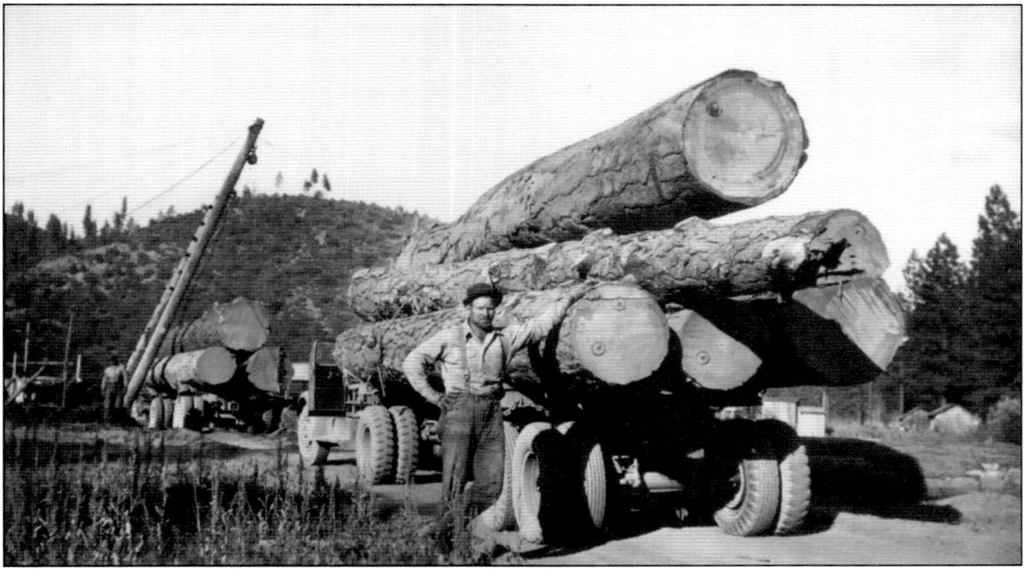

These are Trio Logging trucks coming into the Taresh Mill. Rip is driving one again and is waiting for truck ahead of him to unload. The A-frame built with poles is anchored behind, and they have a winch with cables that goes under the logs and moves them into the log pond. (Courtesy of Carl Stead.)

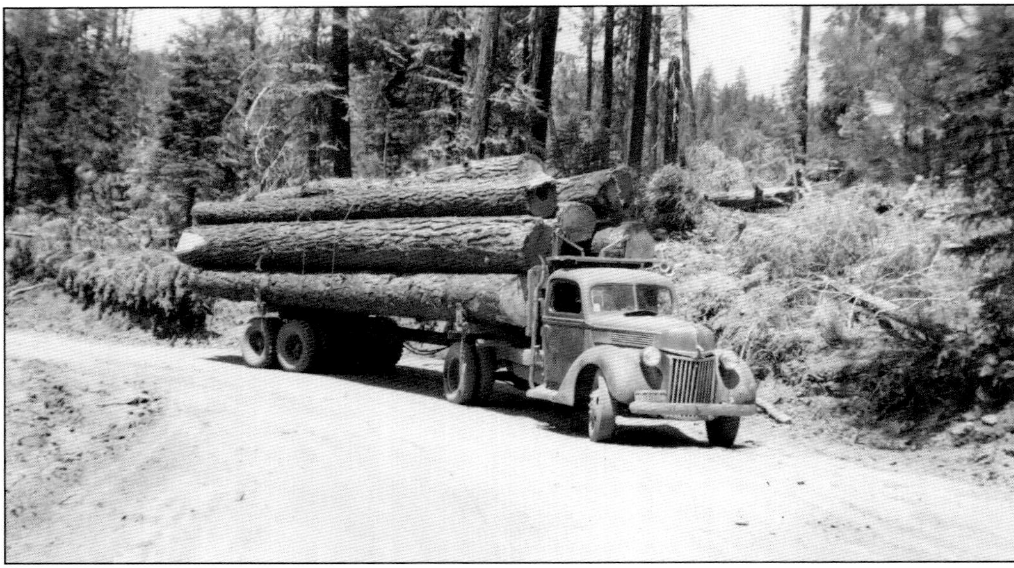

The trucks were getting better all the time. This is one of the newer models, but it's hard to imagine coming off the hill with mechanical brakes with that huge load. It is no wonder they took the driver door off. That is one large load of logs. (Courtesy of Carl Stead.)

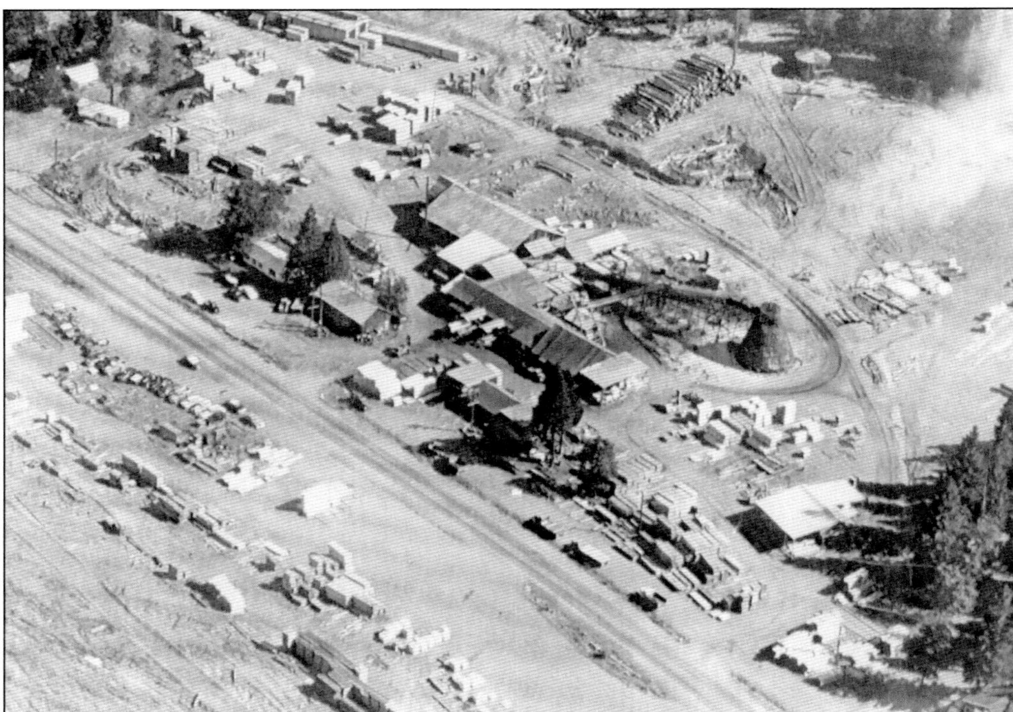

This is a picture from above showing how large a mill site this was. It was called Almanor Lumber Company and was run by Stanley Nagler. It was like the Setzer Mill, a full operation with a box factory and their own logging and lumber trucks. This mill employed many people and was located across the road from the Cheney Mill on Highway 89. (Courtesy of Lona Barham.)

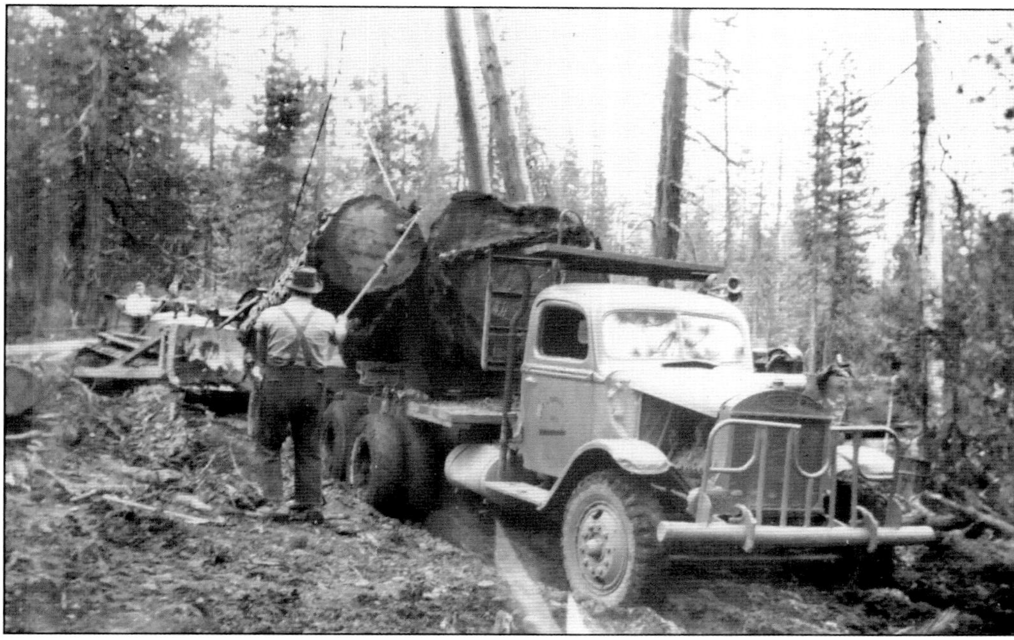

Rip Stead helps load a truck in the photograph; he is guiding a log with the hook. There were two hookers, one on each end of the log, and here the caterpillar is coming in toward the large log. Sometimes they had to get help from the cat skinner by pushing the blade into the log to help lift it up. (Courtesy of Mary Lynn Neer.)

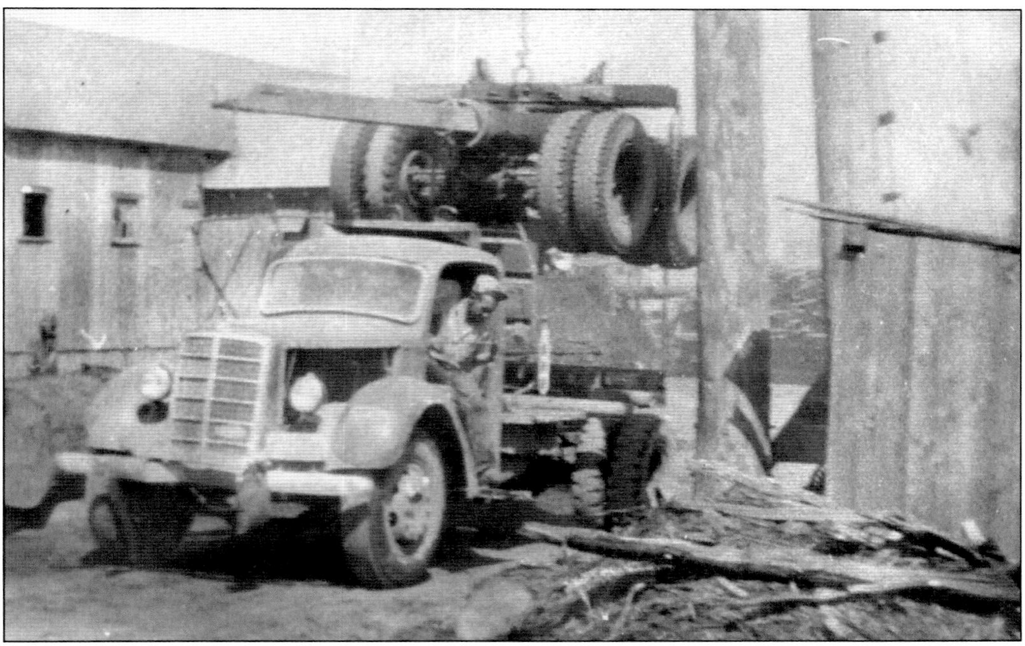

This picture shows the same thing as in the landings, but this is at the mill, and they usually had a winch they pulled under the A-frame to hook the cable to the eyelet. They then unhooked the trailer, raised it into the air, and backed under it to set it on the truck. Al Olds backs under his trailer to put it on the truck. (Courtesy of Mary Lynn Neer.)

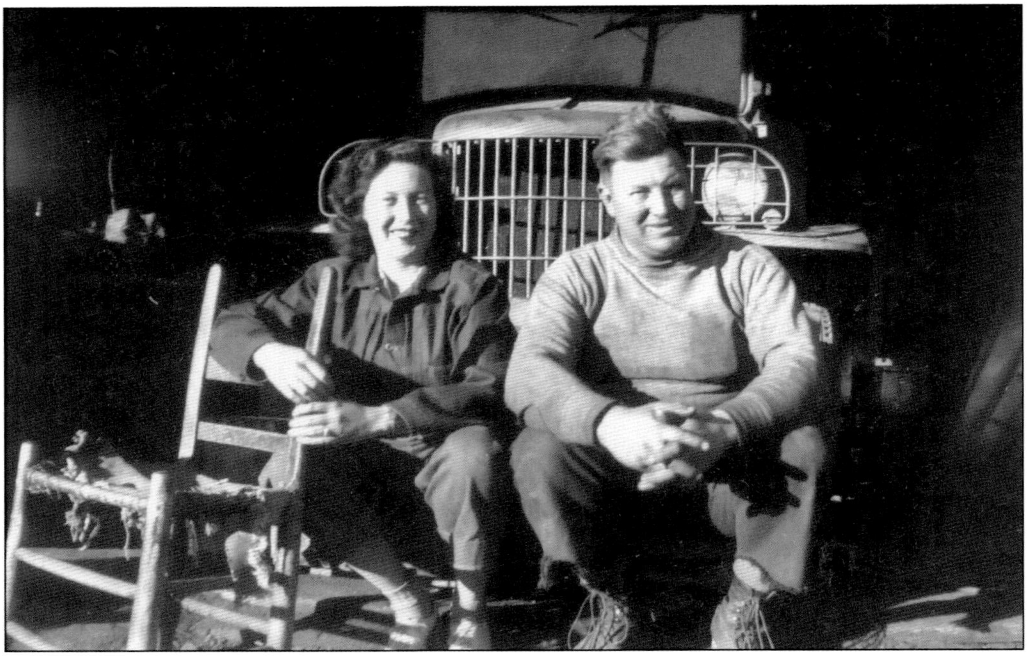

Trio dissolved the partnership, and the last owners of Trio Logging Company, Rip and Ruth Stead, are shown here. Rip Stead was later killed in a grader accident. His wife, Ruth, continued to run Trio until its closing. Ruth had a lot of qualified help from her brother, Grobner, and her brother-in-law, Mearl, to help her run the operation. (Courtesy of Carl Stead.)

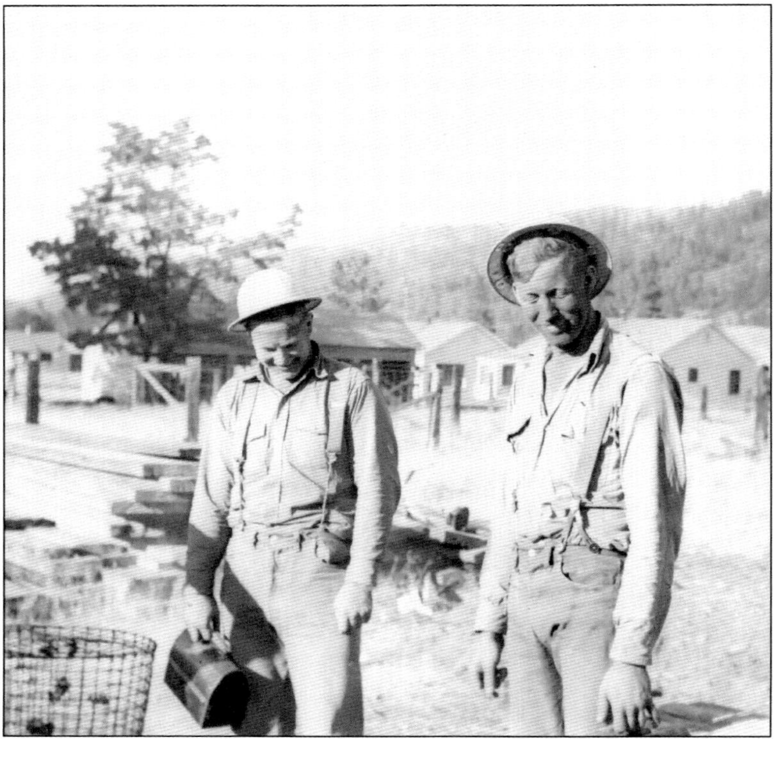

This is a more recent picture with Mearl Stead, left, and Grobner Williams, right, also known as "Grobe" or "the Cheese." Maybe they thought he was the head cheese. Grobe was a brother to Ruth Stead and ran the operation for her for many years. The author worked for Trio when Grobe was the boss back in 1955. They were very nice to work for, and in later years, the author became a shirttail relation of Grobe. (Courtesy of Carl Stead.)

One gypo logger (an independent logging outfit or truck driver/owner) in the area was a man by the name of Jack Hopkins. He and his brother-in-law Lloyd Wheeler started what was called Wheeler and Hopkins Logging Company, later changed to Hopkins Logging Company. Jack married into a local family here in the valley. This is Jack and his wife, Evelyn (Wheeler) Hopkins. The old Wheeler Ranch is still on North Valley Road. (Courtesy of William Hopkins.)

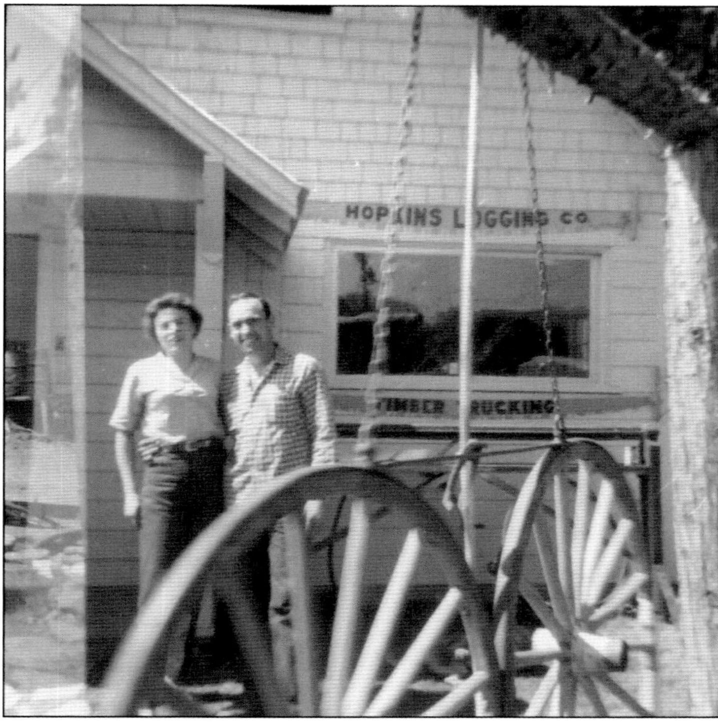

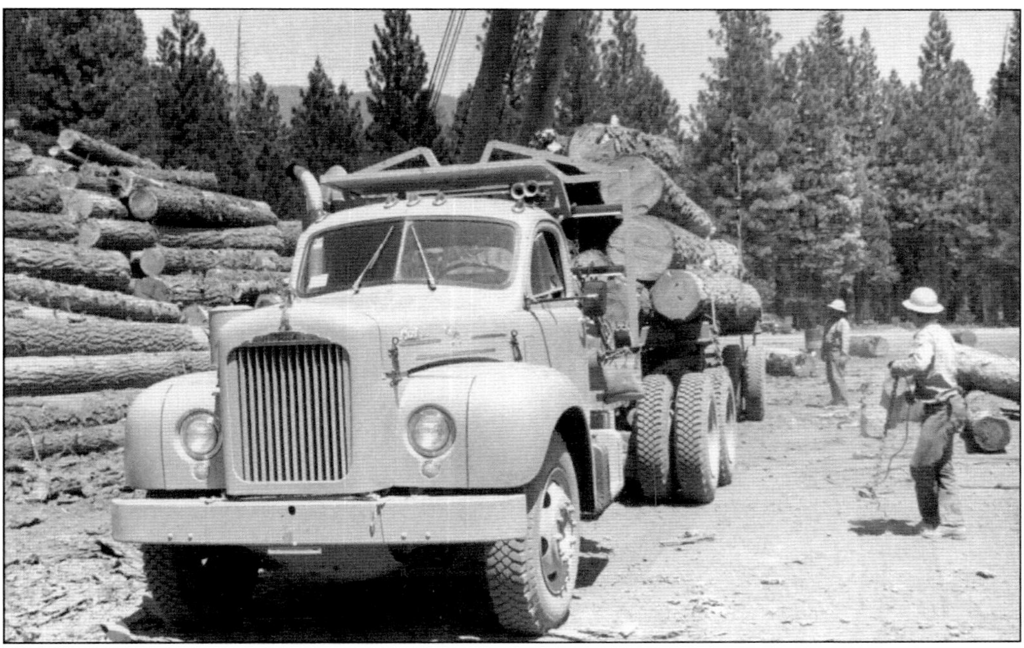

This is one of the Hopkinses' trucks unloading at the old Calvada Mill just north of Greenville. The road was known as Setzer Road when it ran through what was known as Oakie Flat. This mill was one of the last ones built and was a very modern electric mill. It was built by a company from Quincy but was only a sawmill, so all lumber had to be trucked to Quincy. (Courtesy of William Hopkins.)

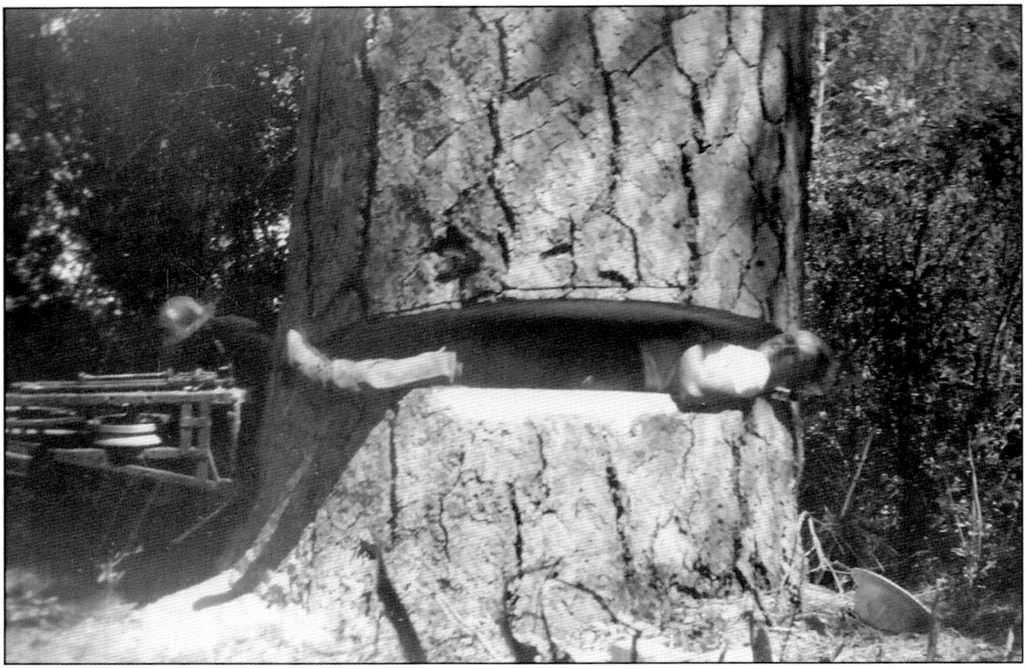

This is a great picture of Jack Hopkins's brother-in-law Lloyd Wheeler lying in the undercut of a big ponderosa pine in the Genesee Valley in 1950. On the left, Jack Hopkins is setting up the Woodsman gypo drag saw for the back cut. It was not uncommon in the early logging days to see such huge trees being logged. (Courtesy of William Hopkins.)

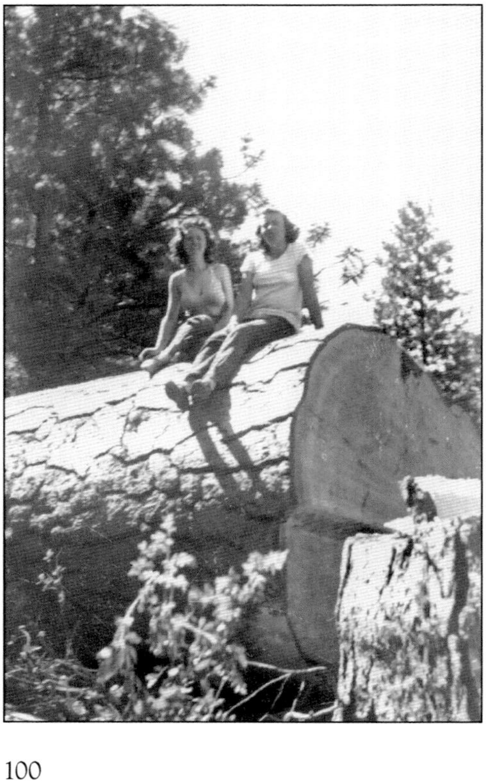

This huge ponderosa tree is shown after it was felled by Lloyd and Jack. Sitting on top of it are their wives, Juanita (Van Ronck) Wheeler and Evelyn (Wheeler) Hopkins. They used the Woodsman gypo drag saw to fell it; the saw is on display at the Taylorsville Museum today. They are not used anymore, as loggers have modern chain saws to fell timber with now. (Courtesy of William Hopkins.)

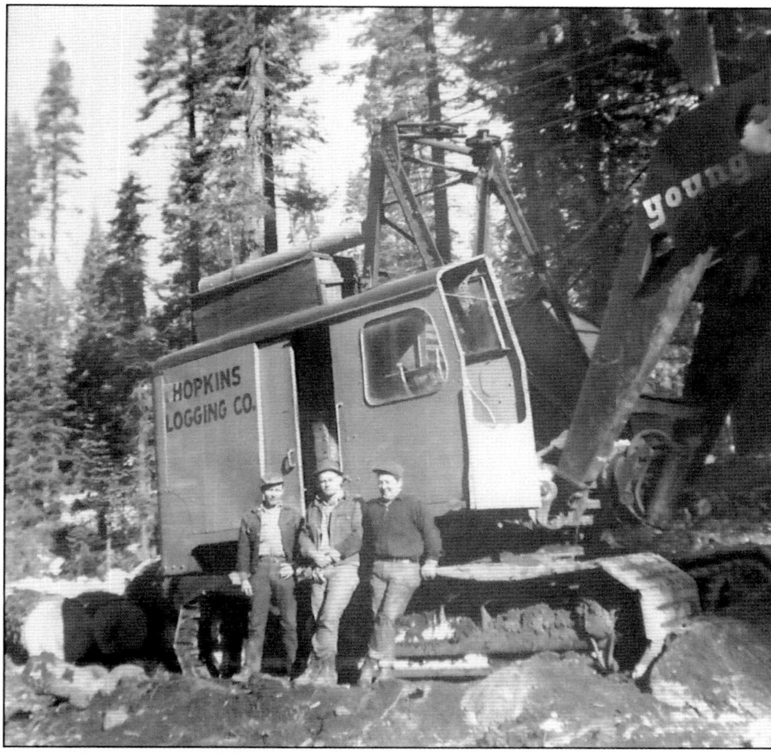

This image shows the more modern loaders that were used after the A-frames on skids were obsolete. This is Jack Hopkins's new Model 6 Northwest shovel used for loading in the landings. It had a Young heel boom and log grapples, which were designed to grab the logs and hold on until released by the operator. This picture was taken at the Swain Mountain Timber Sale in 1965. (Courtesy of William Hopkins.)

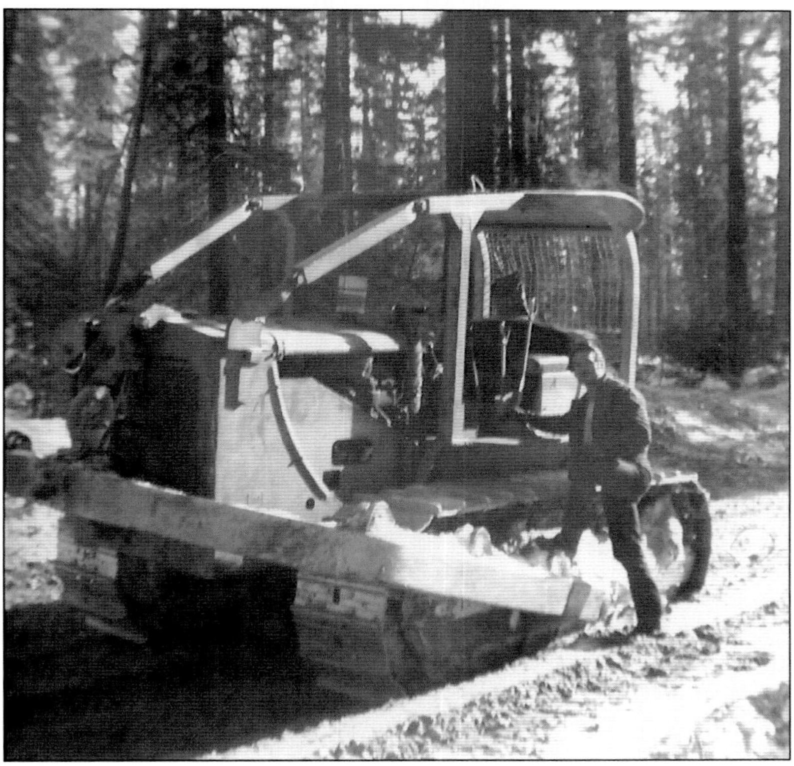

This is Jack Hopkins's D-7 Caterpillar, used for skidding logs into the landing. An unidentified cat skinner poses beside it. Note that the blade is not on the Cat, but the yoke is still there where the blade attaches. That yoke is very important to move things in the skid trail when the blade is off and being worked on. One feels helpless when neither is up front on a Cat. (Courtesy of William Hopkins.)

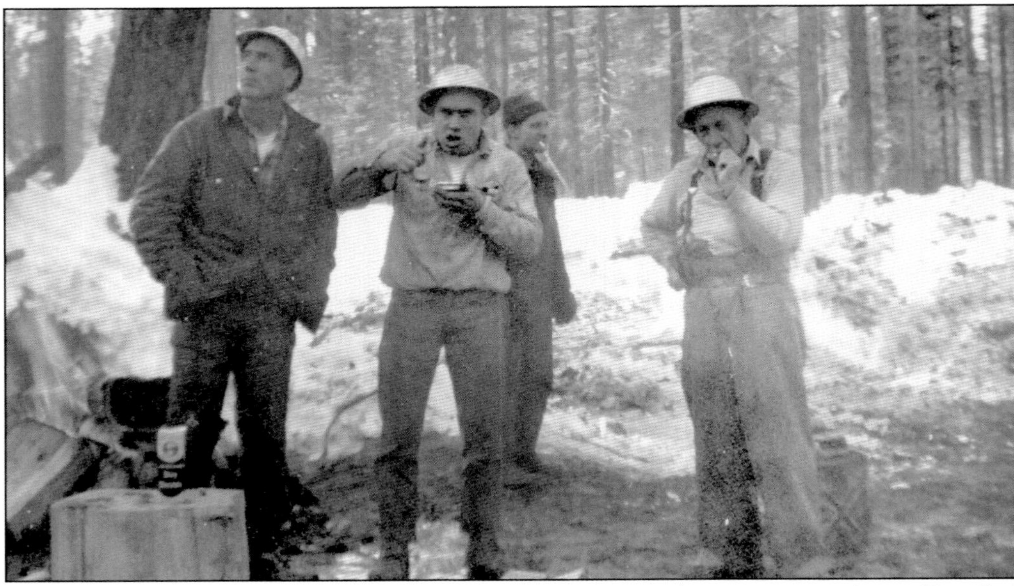

During lunchtime in the woods, there is "no time for tea" and no time to sit down. Here Jack Hopkins has lunch with some of his crew. On the right is timber feller Ben Jasper, behind Jack is cat skinner Maurice Olson, and on the far left is (possibly) timber faller Sox Stevens. Note the lunch pail on the ground and the carton of cream on the block of wood. This picture is from the Swain Mountain Timber Sale in 1965. (Courtesy of William Hopkins.)

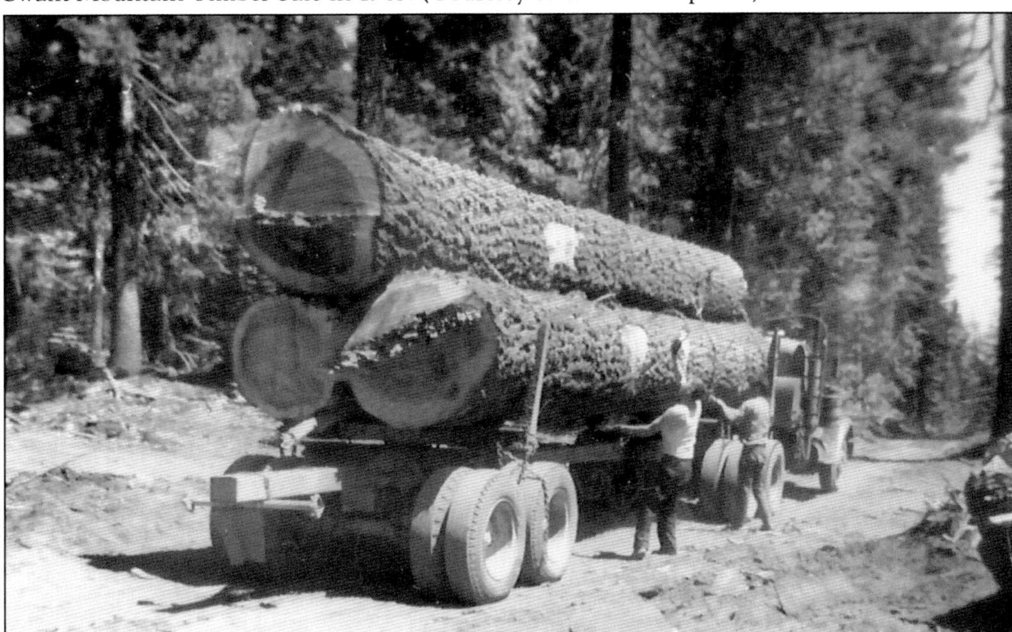

This is a three-log load of old growth white fir, which was not uncommon in those days. The man on the rear of the truck, driver Jess Miller of Greenville, is binding down the after end as Jack Hopkins helps bind the front end of the load. These were logs out of the Homer Lake Timber Sale back in 1967. Homer Lake is up on Keddie Ridge, which is also known as Indian Head. (Courtesy of William Hopkins.)

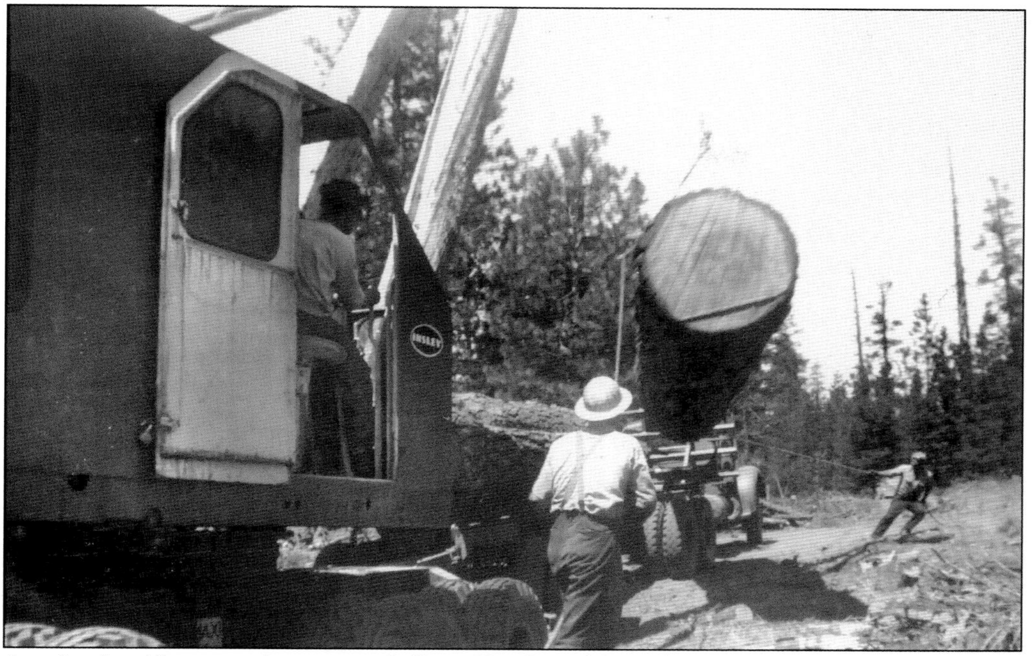

Another local logger in the area was Lilburn Hue Brand from the L. H. Brand Logging Company. Lilburn was better known as Si Brand. Pictured here is Elephants Playground. Men are loading a huge log onto a truck, with Loren Kingdon on the hook rope in the foreground and Si Brand on the back hook guiding the log to where they want it placed on the truck. (Courtesy of Loren Kingdon.)

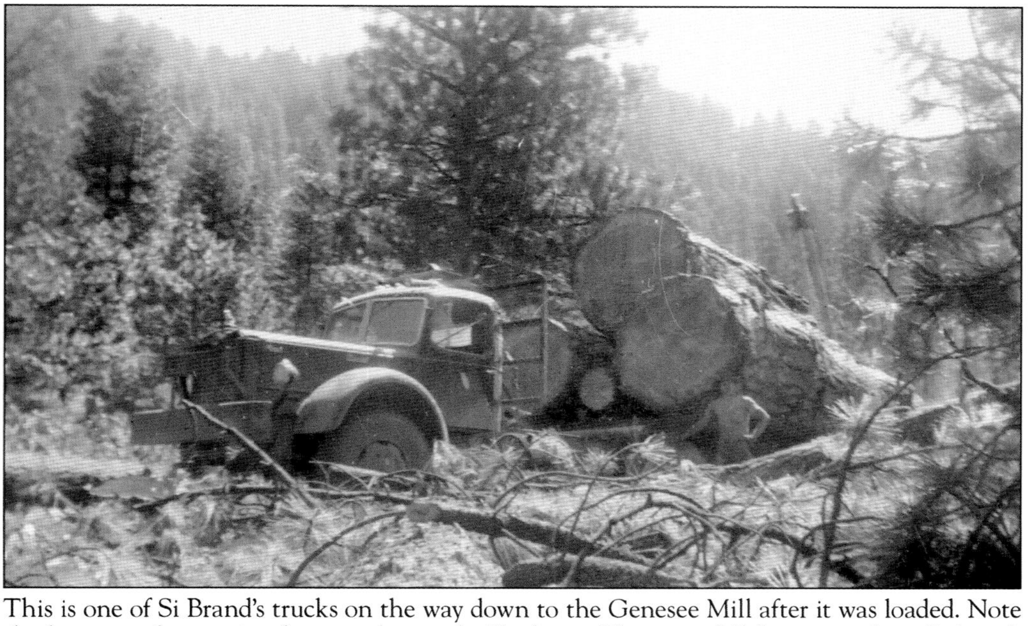

This is one of Si Brand's trucks on the way down to the Genesee Mill after it was loaded. Note the huge ponderosa pine logs on the truck. Elephants Playground Sale was up from Babcock Crossing, which crossed over Indian Creek. Back then it was a dirt road all the way to the mill. (Courtesy of Loren Kingdon.)

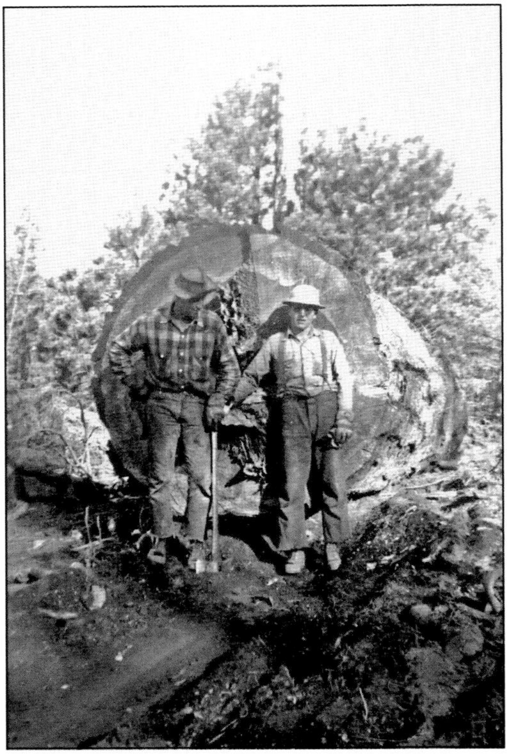

Spike Edgeman, left, and Loren Kingdon, right, are standing beside a huge log to show how large it really was. It was not uncommon then to see such huge logs. The most mature trees were harvested before they got overripe. (Courtesy of Loren Kingdon.)

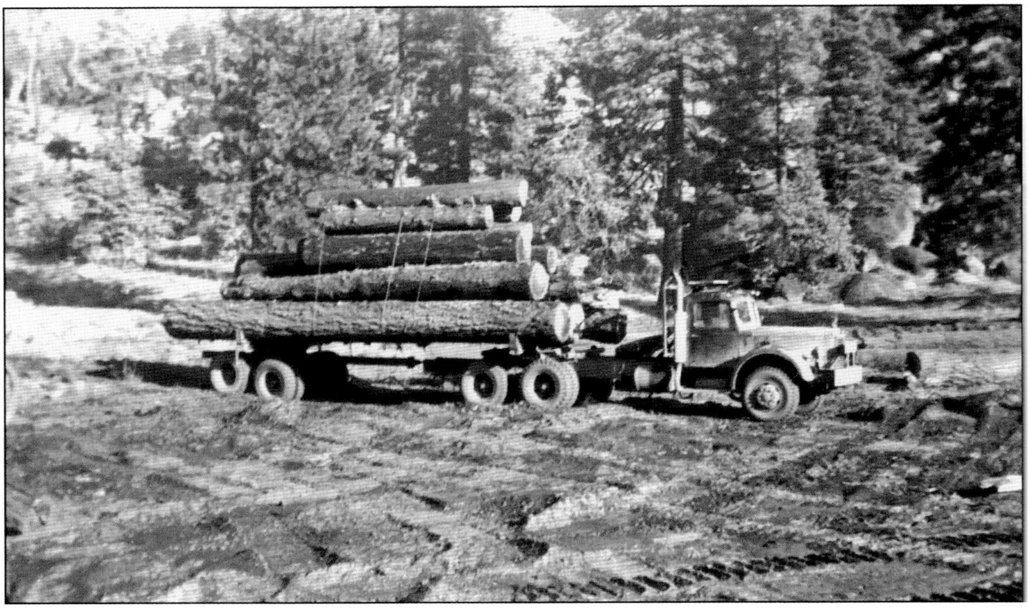

Another load of logs is shown on one of Si Brand's trucks. This picture shows how large a load they hauled out of Elephants Playground. Si hauled them to a mill at the bottom of the hill, Plumas Lumber Company. It was all off-road hauling, so he was able to haul 10-foot-wide loads rather than the highway-legal width of only 8 feet. Needless to say, the loads were huge. (Courtesy of Loren Kingdon.)

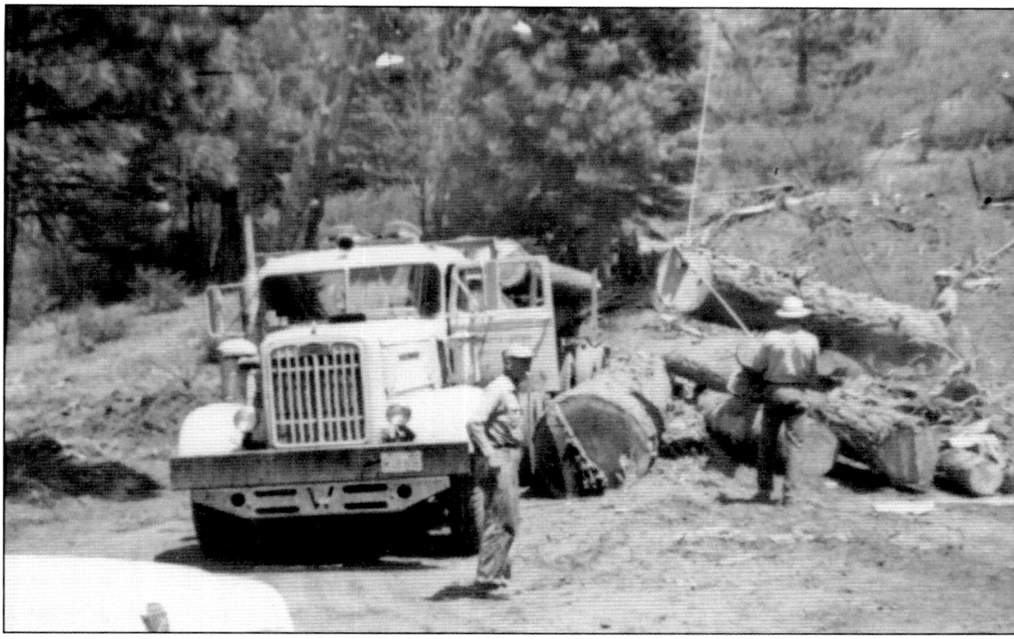

The truck being loaded belongs to another gypo logger named Bill Wattenburg, better known as Pops. Here the hooker guides the log as it swings up on the load. The first thing hookers were taught was to let go of the rope if the hook pulled, which many times it did. But they did have to try to slow the hook down so it did not hit their partner on the other end. (Courtesy of Nansi Bohne.)

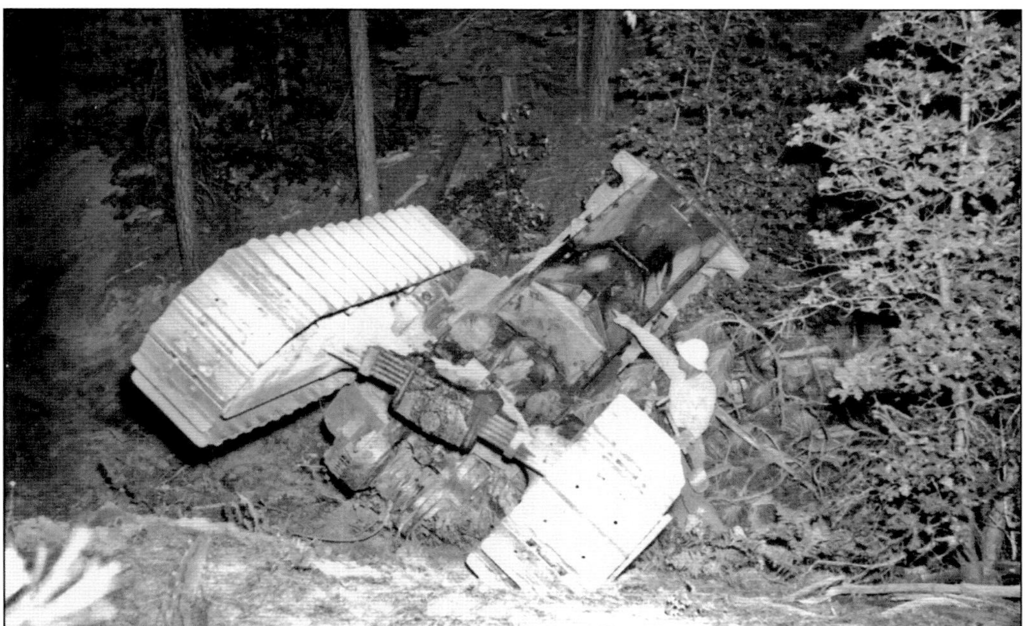

This is Bill Wattenburg's Caterpillar. The Cats, as they call them, do not always stay right side up. Skinning cat is a very dangerous job. They go through some very steep and rough ground trying to get the logs hooked up and skidded out of the woods. (Courtesy of Nansi Bohne.)

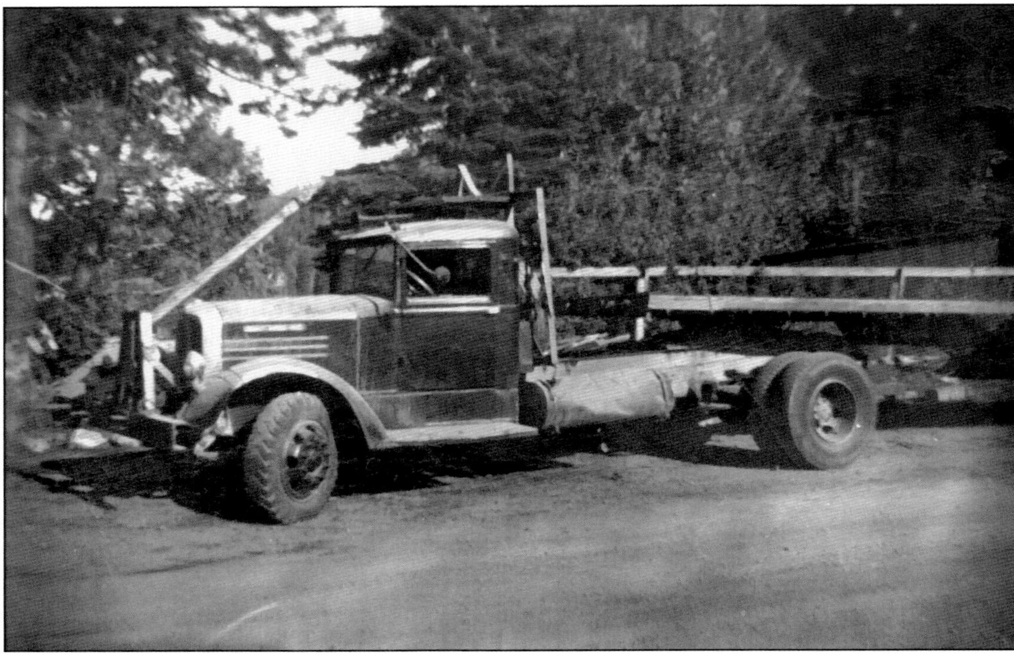

One of Pop Wattenburg's first logging trucks is pictured here. It was an old federal truck. In the old days, there were many small logging outfits around the valley that would either log private timber or buy some small timber sales from the government. In later years, the timber sales that went up for bid were so large and bid so high that the smaller operations had a hard time competing. (Courtesy of Nansi Bohne.)

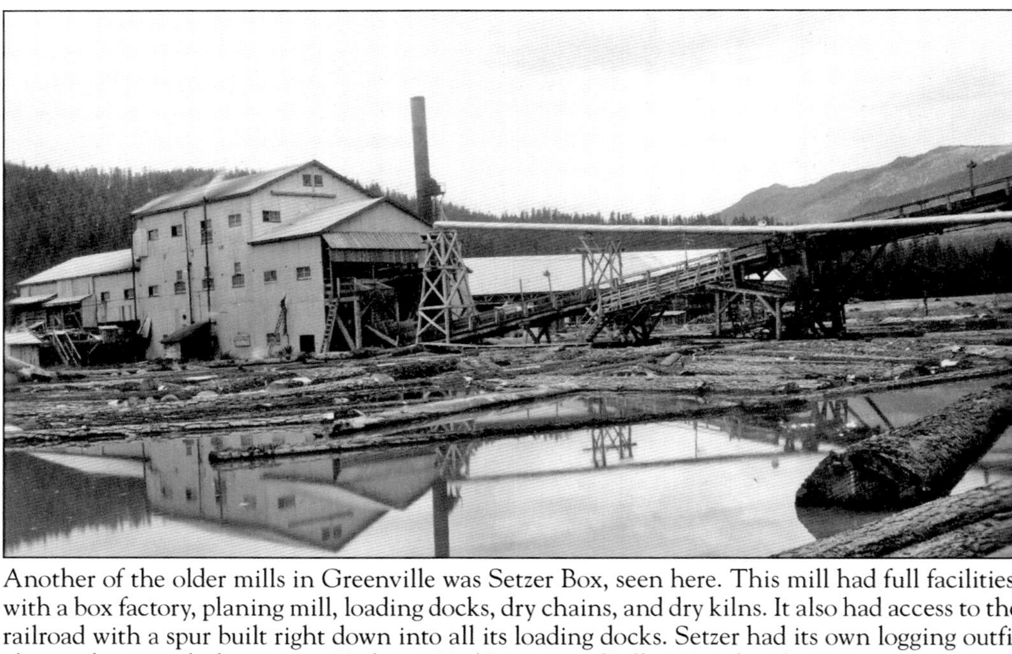

Another of the older mills in Greenville was Setzer Box, seen here. This mill had full facilities, with a box factory, planing mill, loading docks, dry chains, and dry kilns. It also had access to the railroad with a spur built right down into all its loading docks. Setzer had its own logging outfit also, with its truck shop up on Highway 89. (Courtesy of Lillian Lambert.)

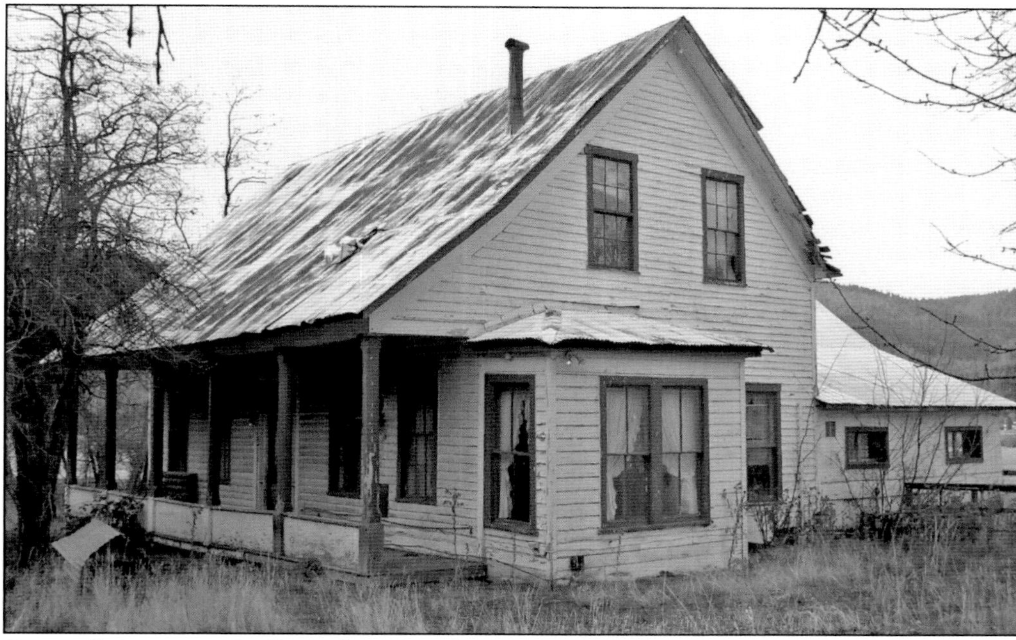

Originally known as the Deutsche or Dutchman's Ranch, the Knoll Ranch was the site of one of Plumas County's first murders when Jacob Dertsch was shot by Henry Van Orman with a shotgun in 1856. Van Orman fled and was never apprehended. Matthias Knoll, who was born in Germany in 1821, came to Indian Valley in 1867 and took up the Knoll Ranch. He married Petrolenia Geiss the same year and along with her child from a previous marriage, they had two children of their own. The house was built about this time and until recently was occupied. Unfortunately, it is now being left to decay. Across the present-day highway, Knoll also operated a brewery that supplied beer to local residents and businesses. The brewery burned in 1932. Pictured below is the brewery.

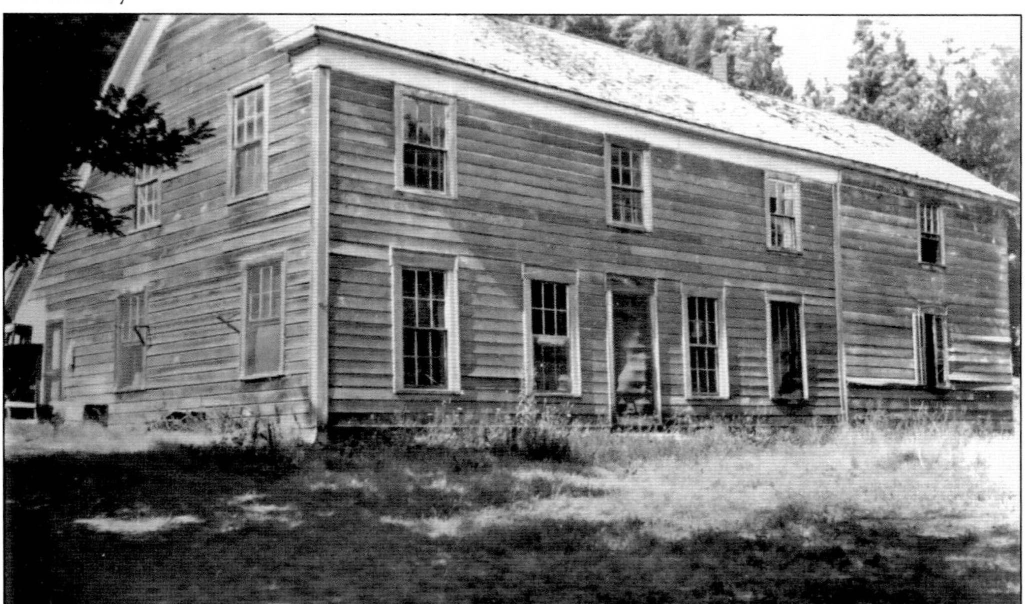

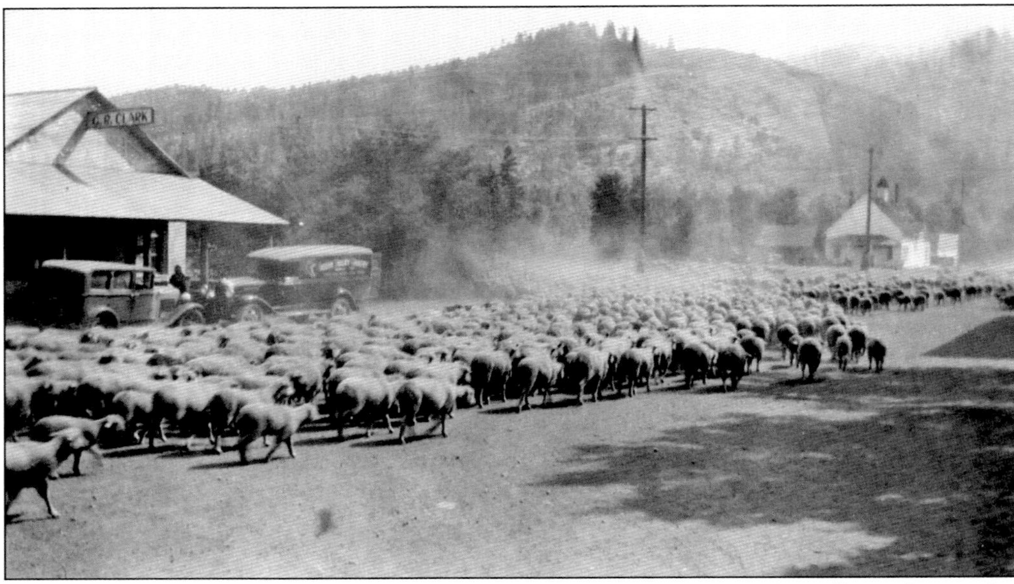

A common sight in the area was sheep grazing. This is downtown Taylorsville, and a rancher heads east with his sheep. They used to herd their sheep all through the high country. Most would hire Basque shepherds, who were great with sheep. There are still a few places up high with names posted where they camped with their sheep, including Wheeler Sheep Camp. (Courtesy of Mary Lynn Neer.)

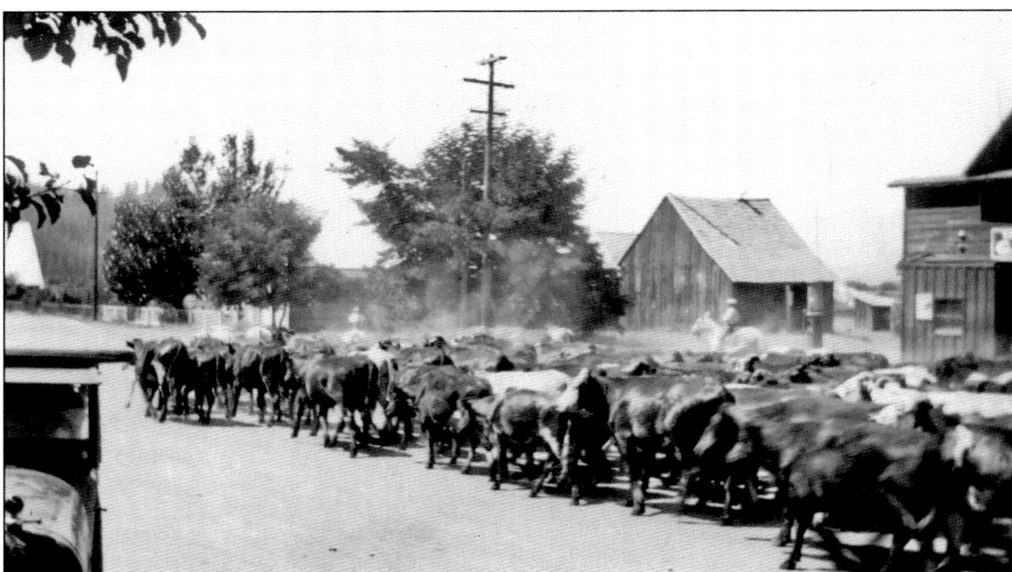

Of course the cattlemen were not going to be outdone. They also herded their cattle right through town. Here Main Street in Taylorsville is filled up with cattle. Cattle also grazed in the higher elevations until fall. Cattle have an instinct to start moving to lower elevations when the weather gets bad. (Courtesy of Mary Lynn Neer.)

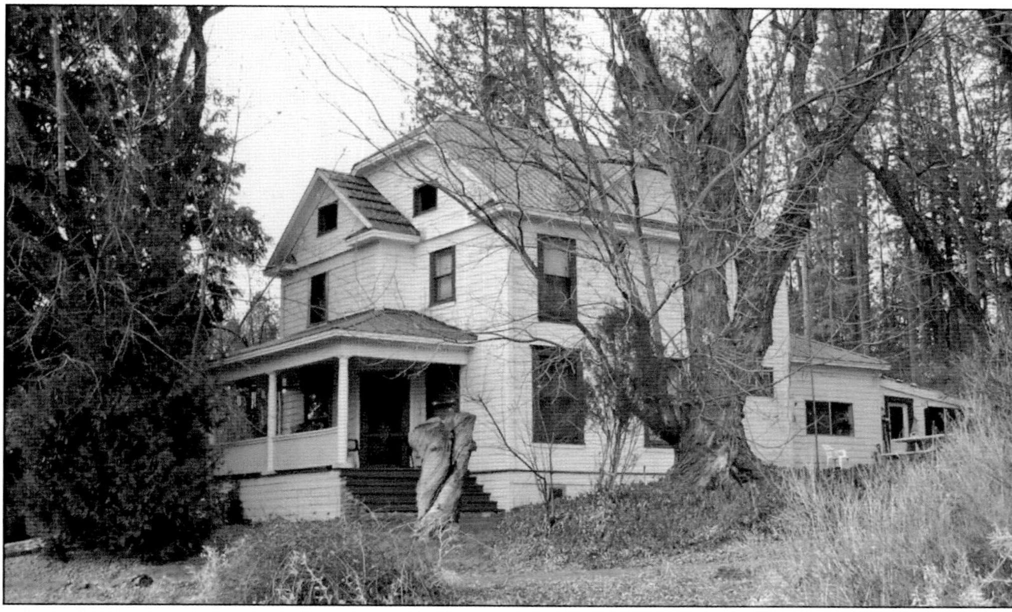

The Wheeler Ranch house was built in 1906 by the Schieser family after a previous home burned. Wesley and Ida Wheeler bought it in 1945. Wesley ran one of the dairies in the valley on what is now North Valley Road. The Wheelers had a modern dairy barn with milking machines located below the house on the other side of the road. The Wheeler Ranch house is still there today. (Courtesy of Richard McCutcheon.)

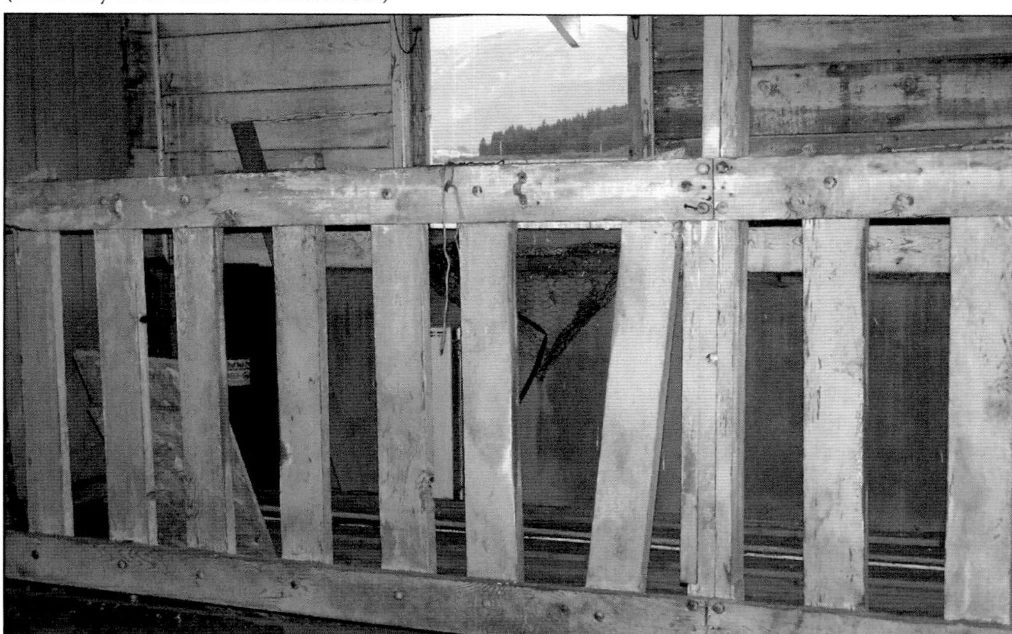

This shows the inside of the old Wheeler dairy barn that is still there but no longer in use. It has been years since this barn was used to milk cows. This brought back some memories for the author; his grandfather had milk cows and a dairy barn that looked identical to this. (Courtesy of the author.)

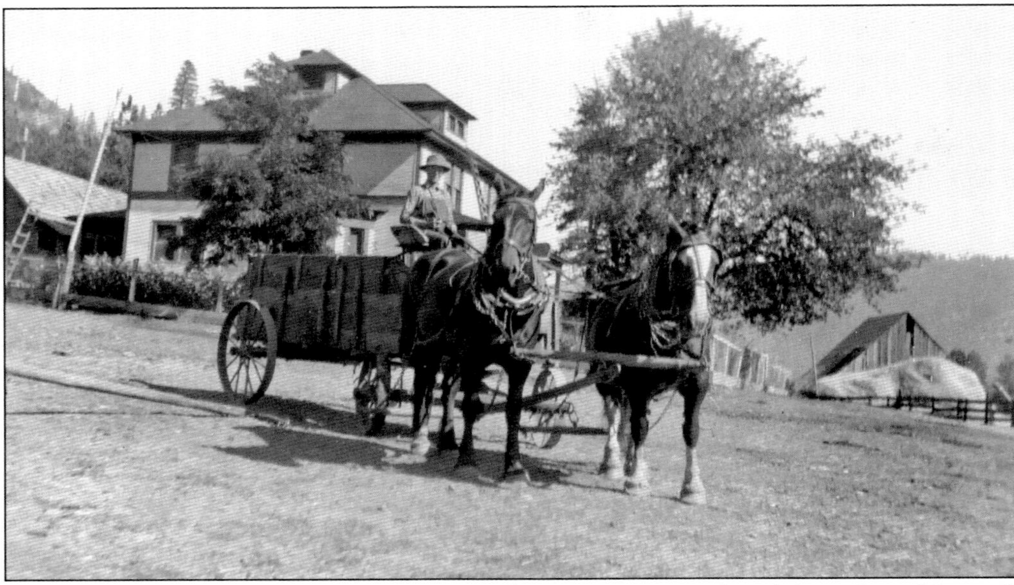

This is Bill McCutcheon at his ranch in North Arm. It was purchased from Gustaf Stampfli around 1912. This ranch was 363.4 acres and was on both sides of the road. Bill deeded it over to his wife, Icy A. McCutcheon, when they divorced. (Courtesy of the author.)

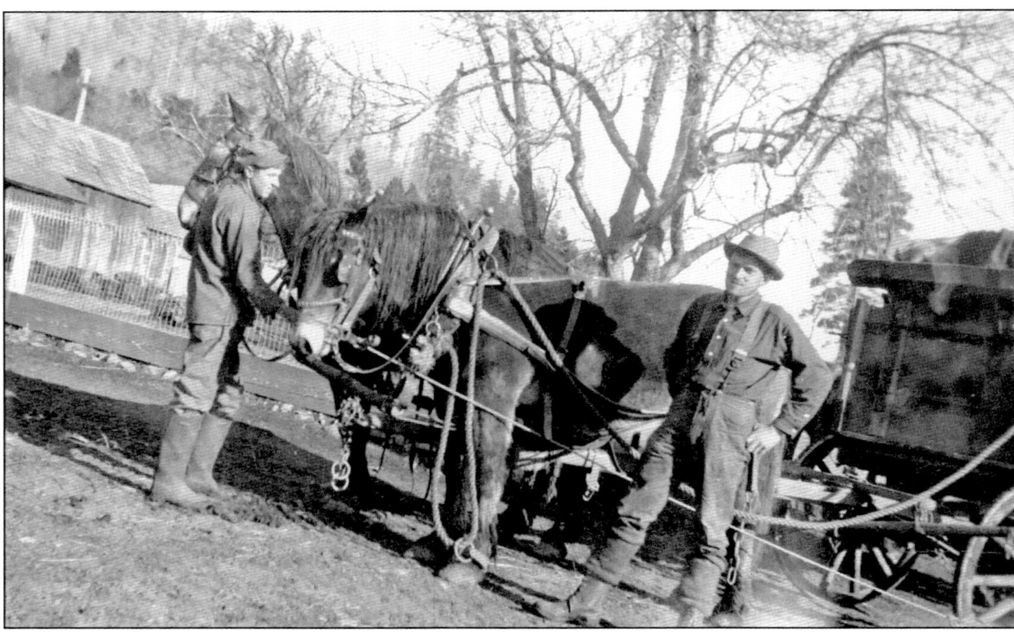

The author's uncle, Weston Scott "Wes" Quigley (right), and Wes's brother, Floyd "Skig" (left), are pictured here. Wes purchased one of the McCutcheon ranches and became the owner of this ranch when he married the author's aunt in 1917. This ranch at one time was known as the Nye Ranch.

One of the first McCutcheons to come into the North Arm of the valley was Hugh McCutcheon. Hugh was a miner for awhile then settled down to ranching around 1870. At one time, Hugh owned 700 acres with a dairy in the higher elevations. Hugh served the county as a supervisor for eight years. Because of his health, he did not seek re-election. His wife, Christeney Mack, was from Canada. (Courtesy of the author.)

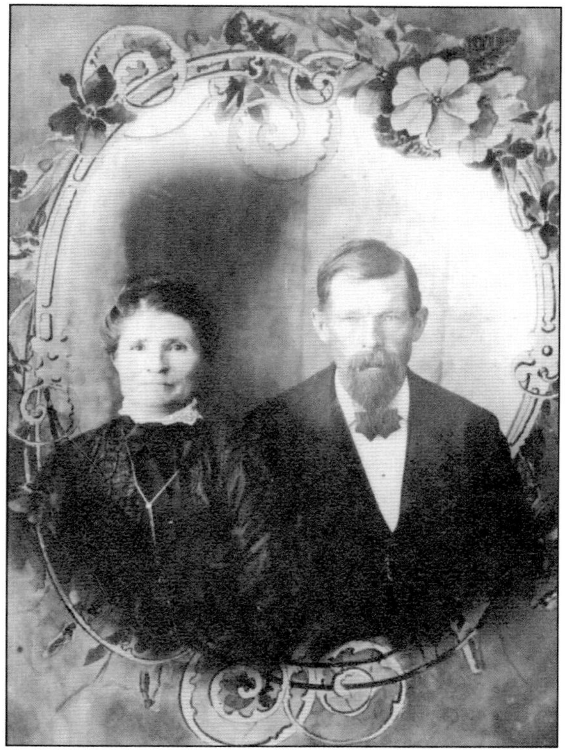

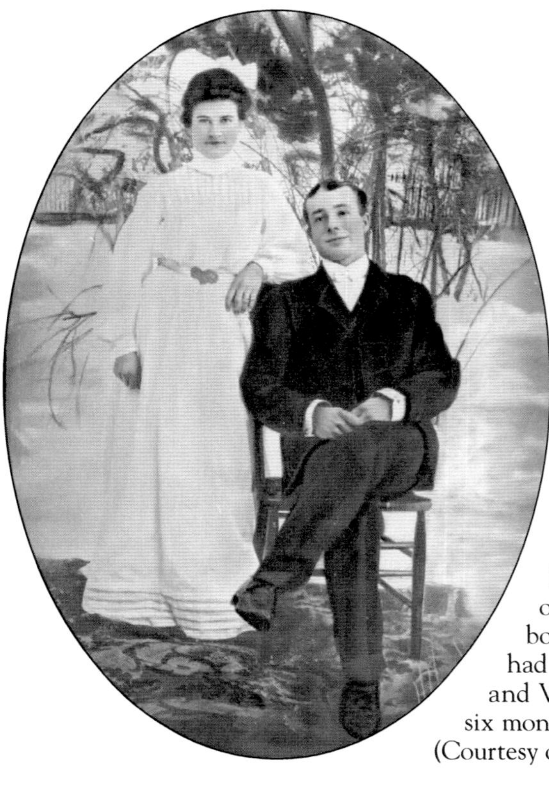

The oldest son of Hugh and Christeney McCutcheon was John Henry, the author's grandfather. John married Mercy Delilah Brown, and he ran the ranch he was born on. The author and his dad, John II, were also born in the old ranch house. John and Mercy had five children, Willard, Zelma, John II, Lois, and Vernon. When John and Mercy passed on, six months apart, John II was left to run the ranch. (Courtesy of the author.)

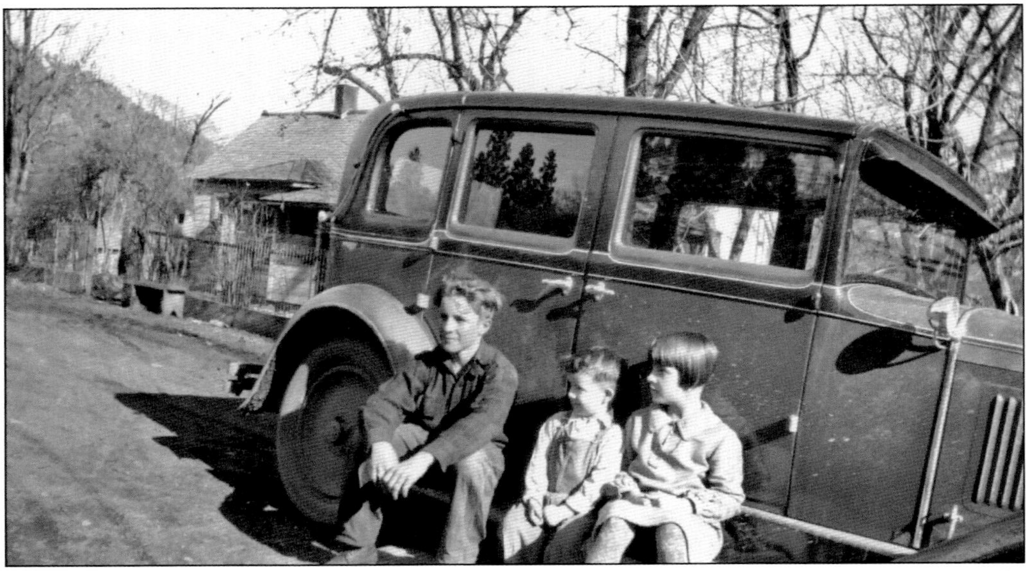

This is the front of the McCutcheon Ranch. The ranch house is to the left. From left to right are the author's dad, John II "Tuffy;" Rosie Toscani; and Helen Schieser. Both the Toscanis and the Schiesers were old ranching families in the valley. (Courtesy of the author.)

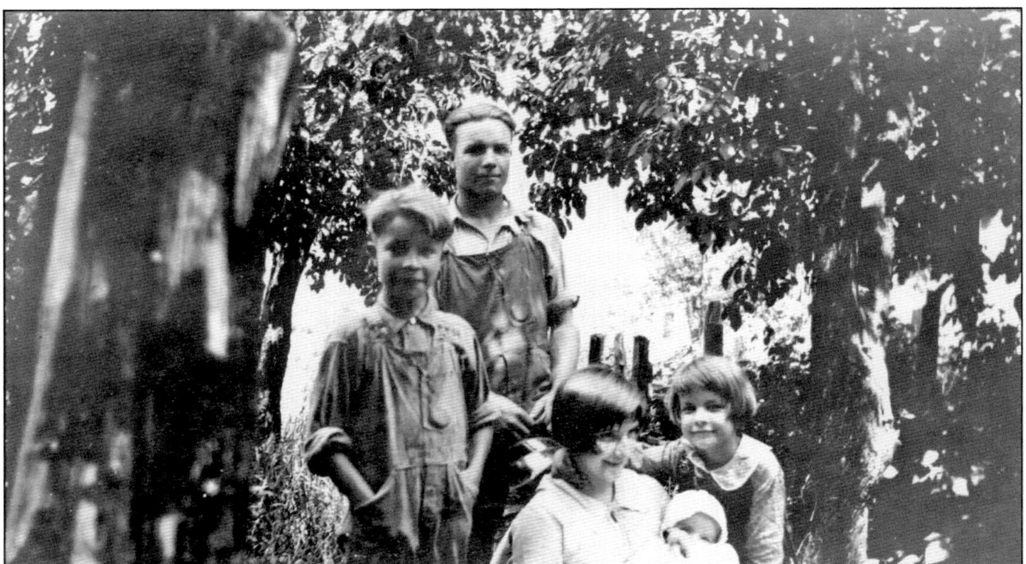

This picture of John Henry's family was taken at the McCutcheon Ranch. The children were a few years apart in age. In the back is the oldest, Willard; from left to right are John II, Zelma, and Lois; and the baby was Vernon, the last child born to John and Mercy. (Courtesy of the author.)

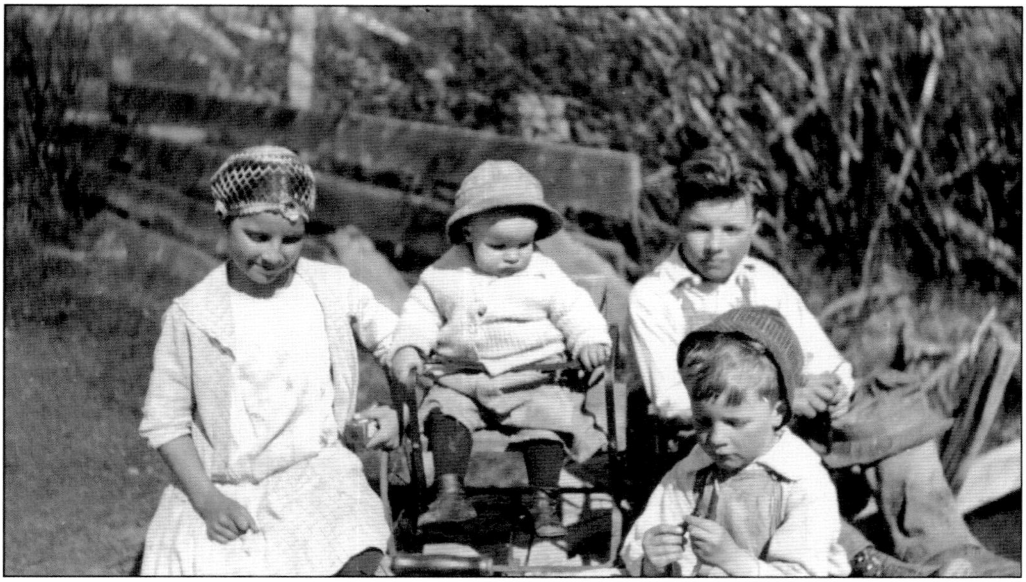

Here is another picture of the McCutcheon kids before Vernon was born. From left to right are Zelma, also known as Dutch; Lois in the chair; Willard; and John II in the front. (Courtesy of the author.)

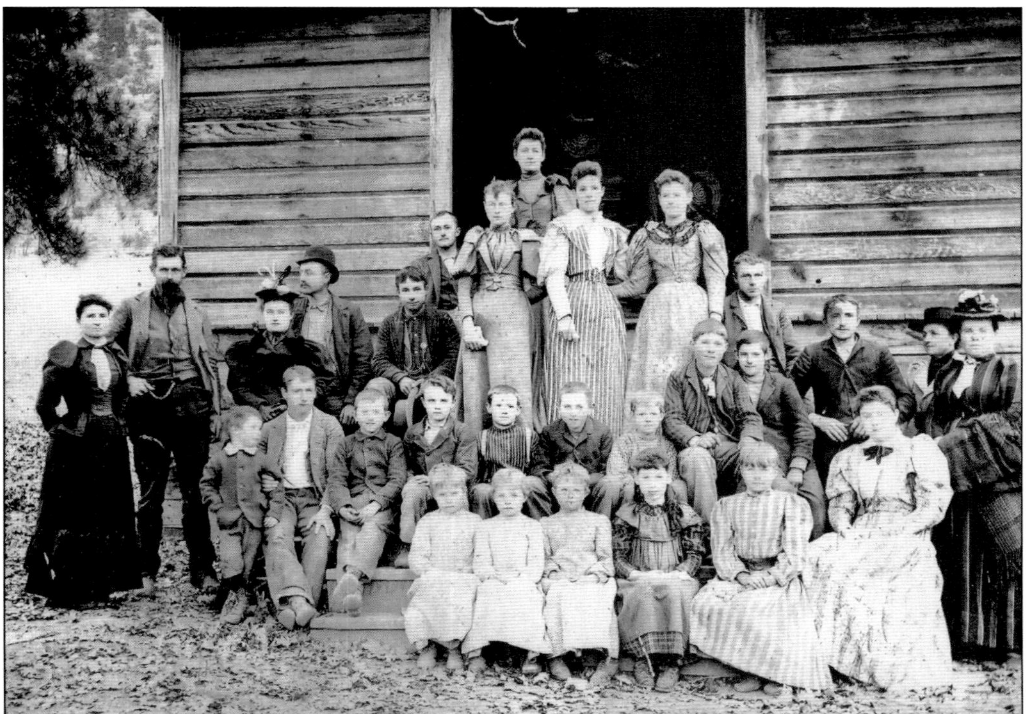

This is the oldest picture the author has seen of the old Union School that used to be in North Arm. It dates back to the 1880s. On the left are the author's great-grandparents, Hugh and Christeney McCutcheon. To the right in the dark clothes is their son John Henry. It must have been a school function to have the parents there.

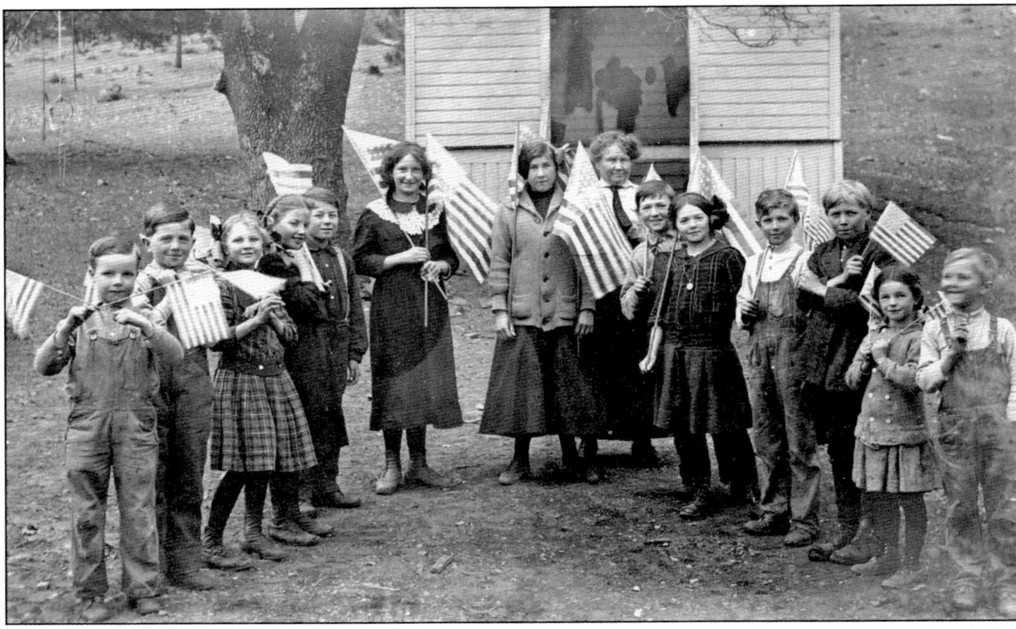

This is the Union School with possibly the entire student body in the picture. The school probably had first through eighth grades. The children were very patriotic with all the American flags. The little boy on the left is Willard McCutcheon, one of the cover picture children.

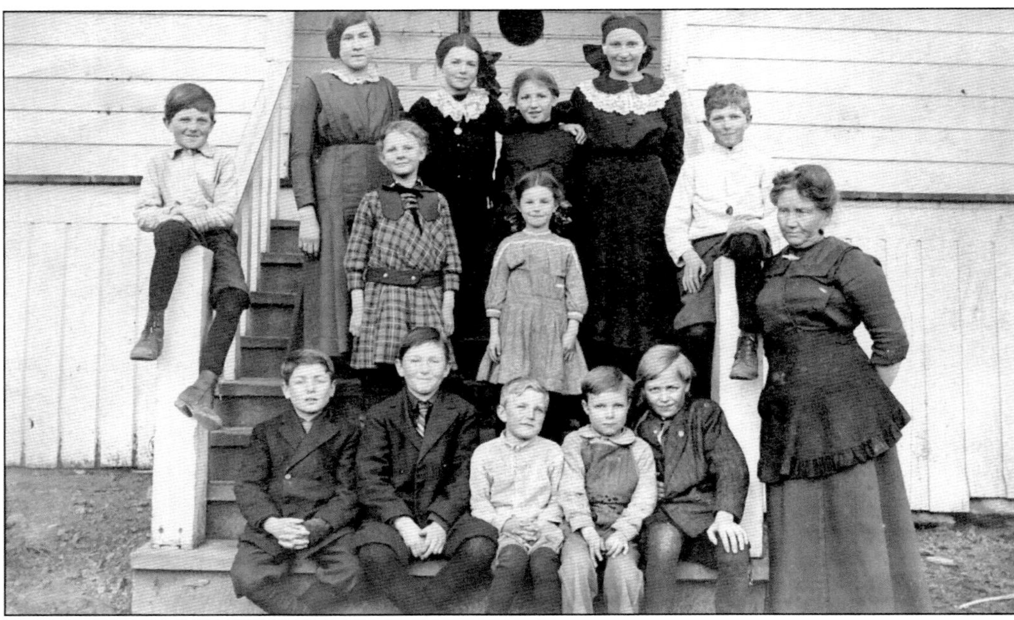

The Union School is seen here around 1913. It looks again like maybe a school function with so many adults in the picture. These pictures were from the collection of the author, passed on to him from his dad. Sitting in the front, second from the right, is Willard McCutcheon.

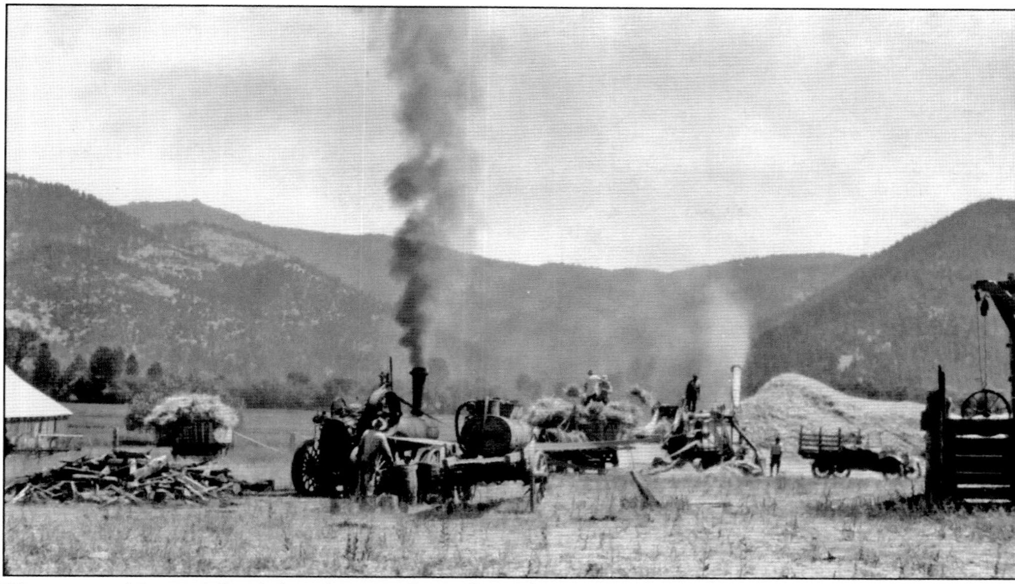

This is an old wood-fired thrasher. In those days, the grain was hauled to the stationary thrasher, usually used by more than one farmer. It was on wheels and moved from ranch to ranch. All the straw was blown into one pile. This picture was taken just west of Taylorsville.

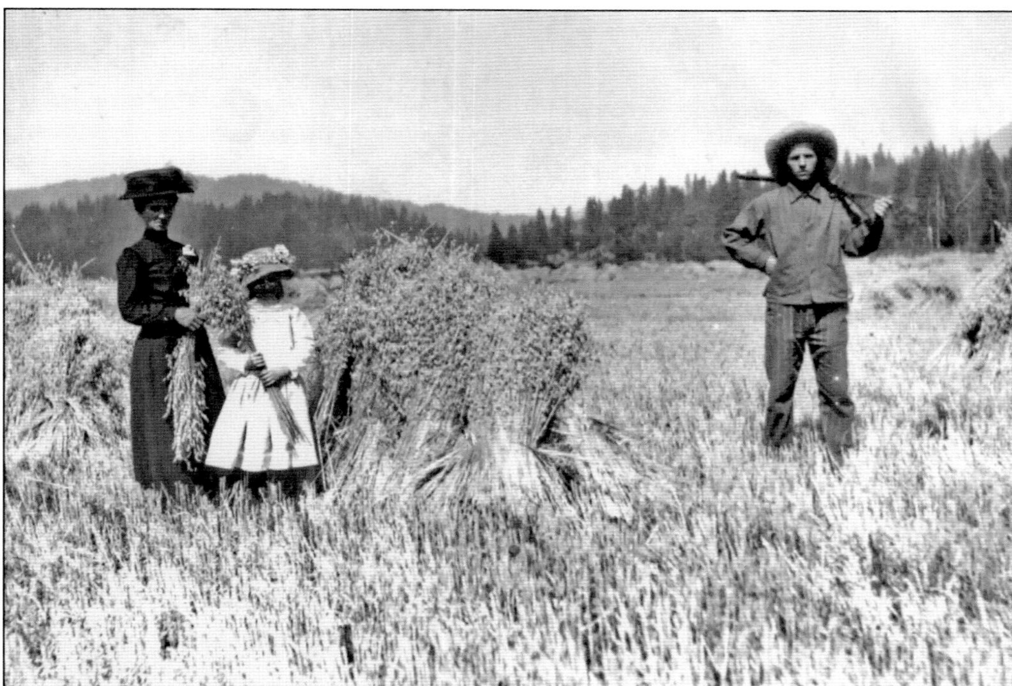

This is the way they bundled and tied the grain to take it to the thrasher. This picture of the old Schieser Ranch was taken off what is now North Valley Road, just a few miles east of Greenville. Pictured are Mary, her niece Margaret, and her cousin George Schieser.

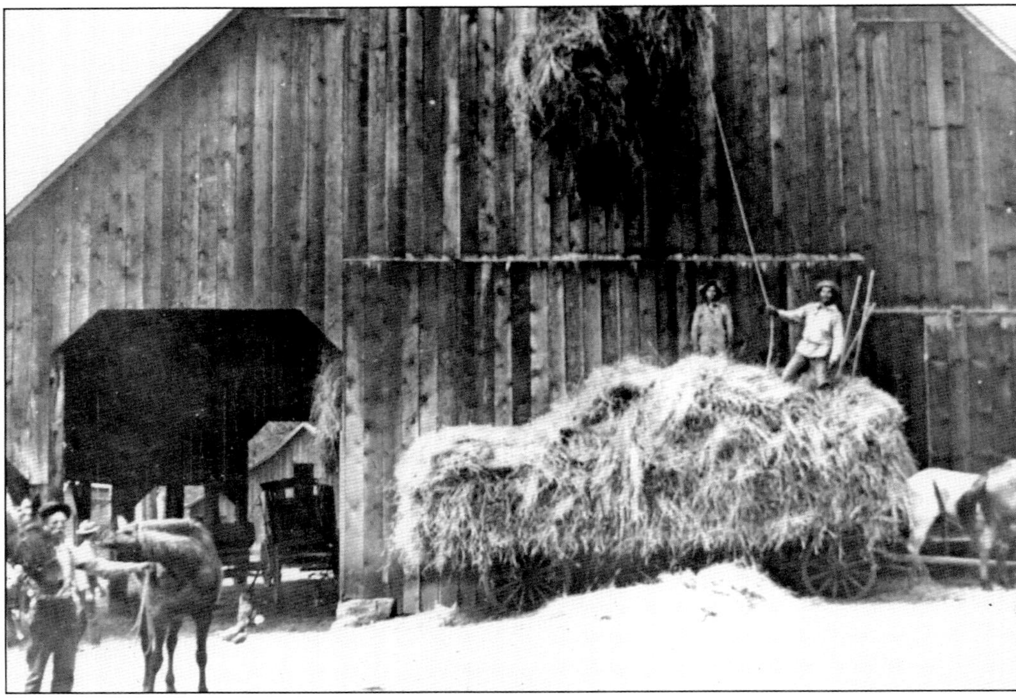

This photograph was also taken at the Schieser Ranch. It shows how they got the hay into the barns. Most was pitched by hand to load the wagons in the earlier days, but later they had a machine to pick it up and put in the wagon. The hay at the top of the picture is in what is called a Jackson fork. It was used to get a forkful of hay out of the wagon, then a derrick at the back of the barn pulled it up and through the barn.

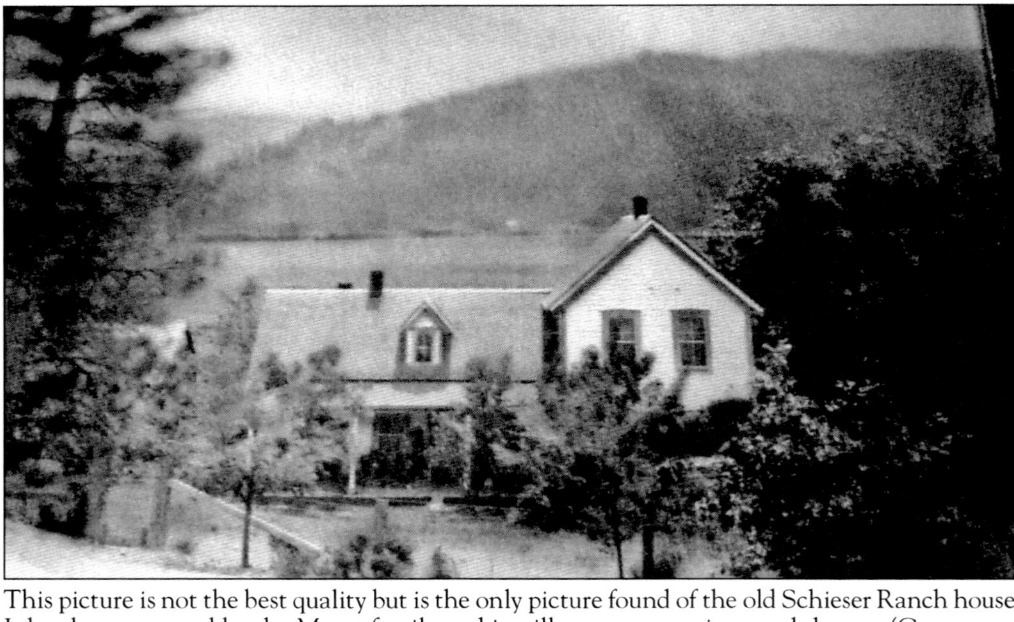

This picture is not the best quality but is the only picture found of the old Schieser Ranch house. It has been restored by the Meyer family and is still a very attractive ranch house. (Courtesy of Jim Hamblin.)

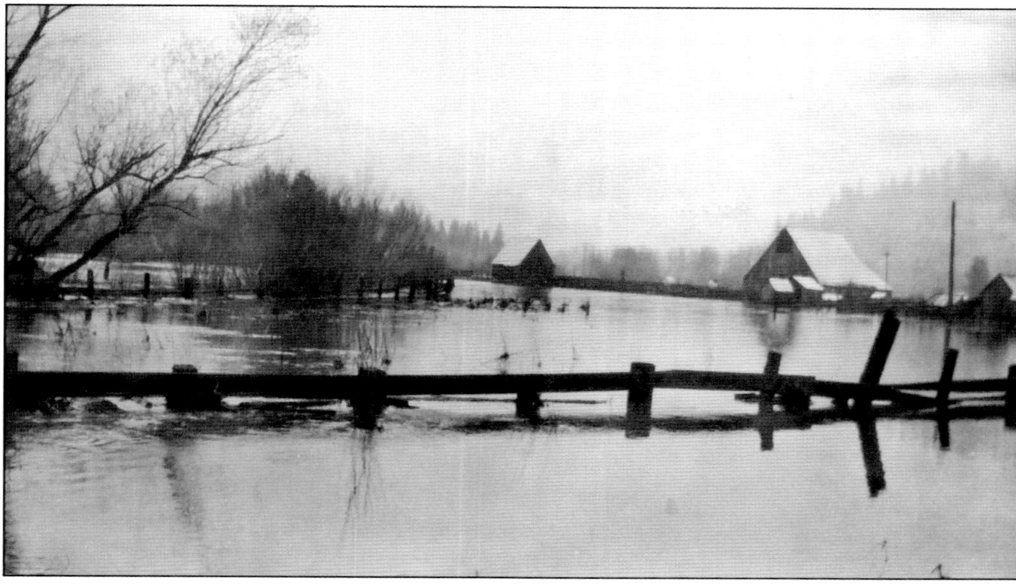

This is the Hardgrave Ranch in 1927, showing just how high the water used to get. It was not uncommon for the floodwaters to reach up into the ranches and homes. Now major work has been done on Indian Creek and it has been straightened out so the water has a straight pass through the area. This ranch is still owned by the family.

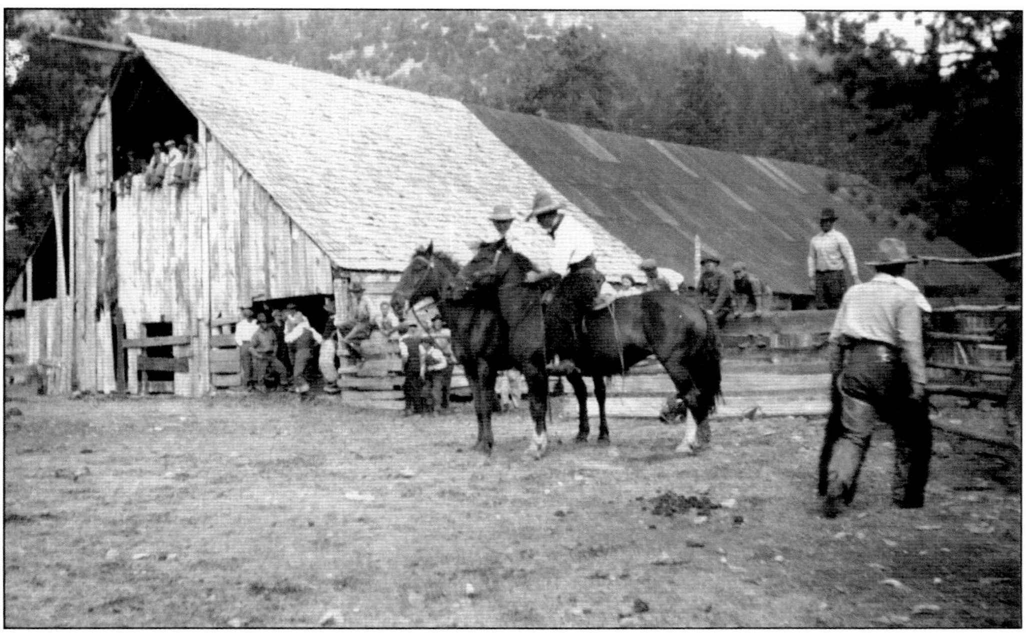

Back in the 1920s, it was not uncommon to see local rodeos held at ranches. This is the Peter Ranch holding one of those rodeos. The barn in the background is still there today, and the ranch is still owned by the family. Note the spectators up in the hayloft for a good seat. (Courtesy of Jim Peter.)

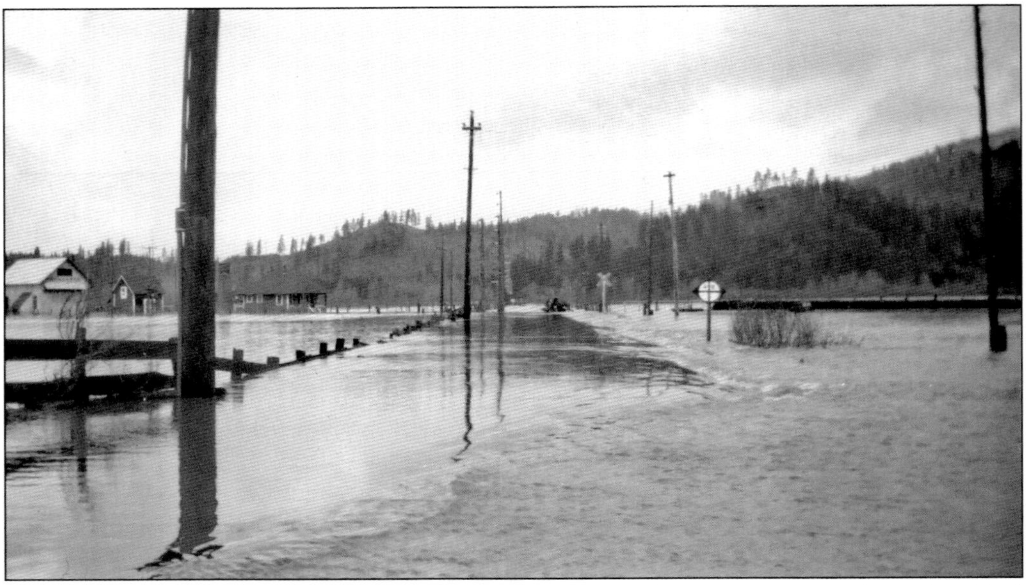

Flooding was, and is, very common in this area, but not nearly as severe today. This is Dead Fall Lane down from the Veramont Depot and Sub Station. Look closely and it is possible to see the Indian Valley Railroad sign at the edge of the flooded road.

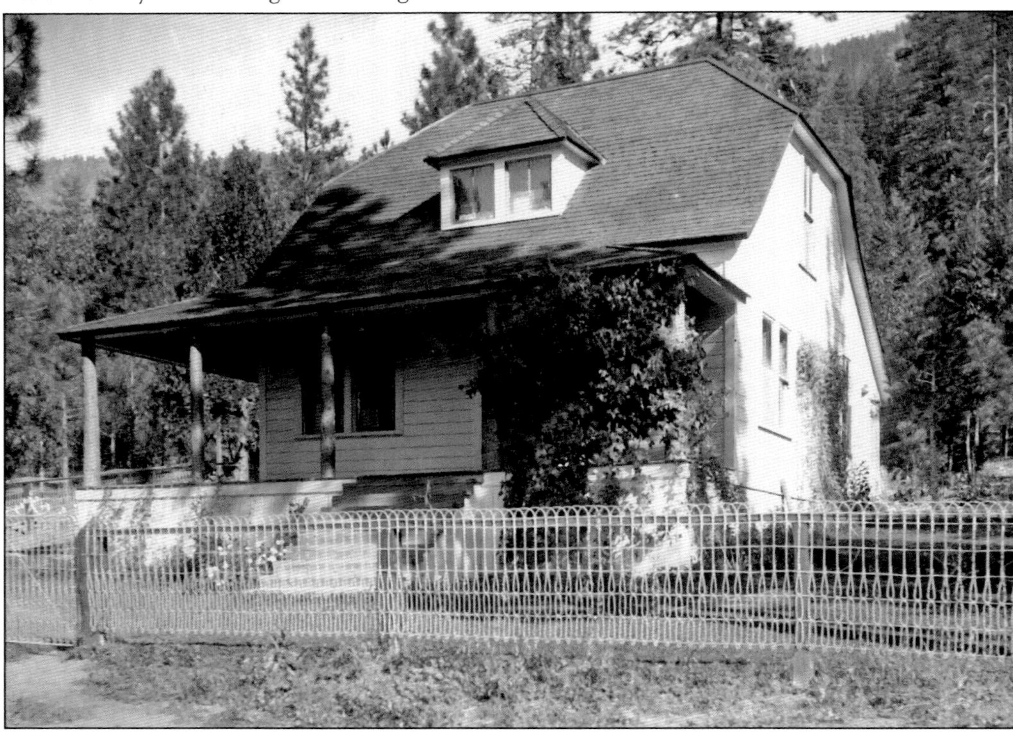

Remick and wife, Stella Herring, lived in this ranch house. The last people to run a dairy and live in this house were the Foland family. Maurice Foland is still alive today; he lives in Idaho. Maurice came through the valley around 2007 and was glad to see it had not changed much. Maurice hauled the last milk to the creamery back in late 1964 or early 1965.

William Tom Peter and his wife, Sarah Isabelle, were the first of the Peter family to settle in North Arm. William was called Tom and was the son of J. N. and Emily Peter. Tom was born in 1837 in Illinois. In 1859, Tom came to California, arriving in this county in August. Three of their boys, Russel, Arthur, and Forrest, stayed in the valley to ranch and at one time had three ranches in North Arm. (Courtesy of Jim Peter.)

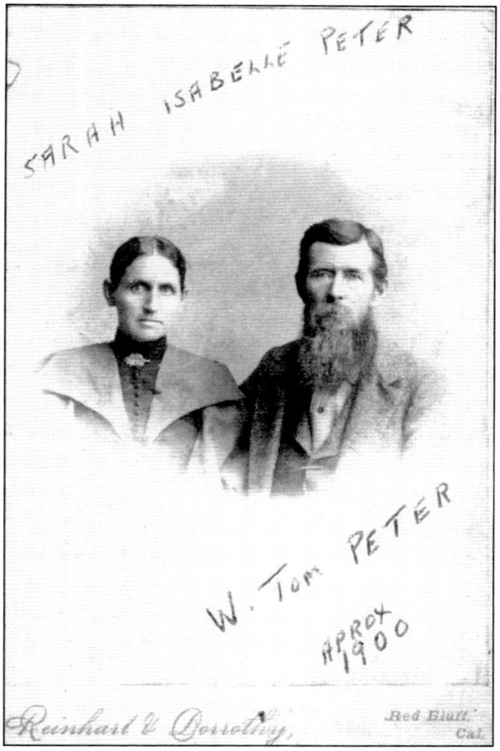

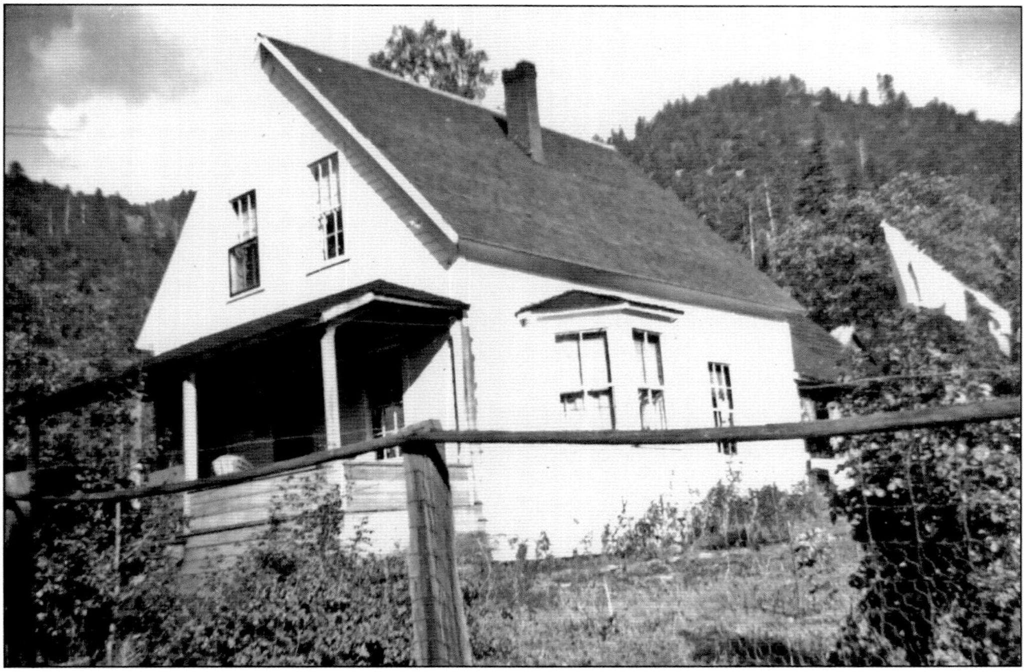

The Peter Ranch house is still there today. The house was built in 1885 after two previous homes burned down. The two previous homes were located on the flat where today there is a trailer home. The home was painted by Claude and Jim Peter around 1940. (Courtesy of Jim Peter.)

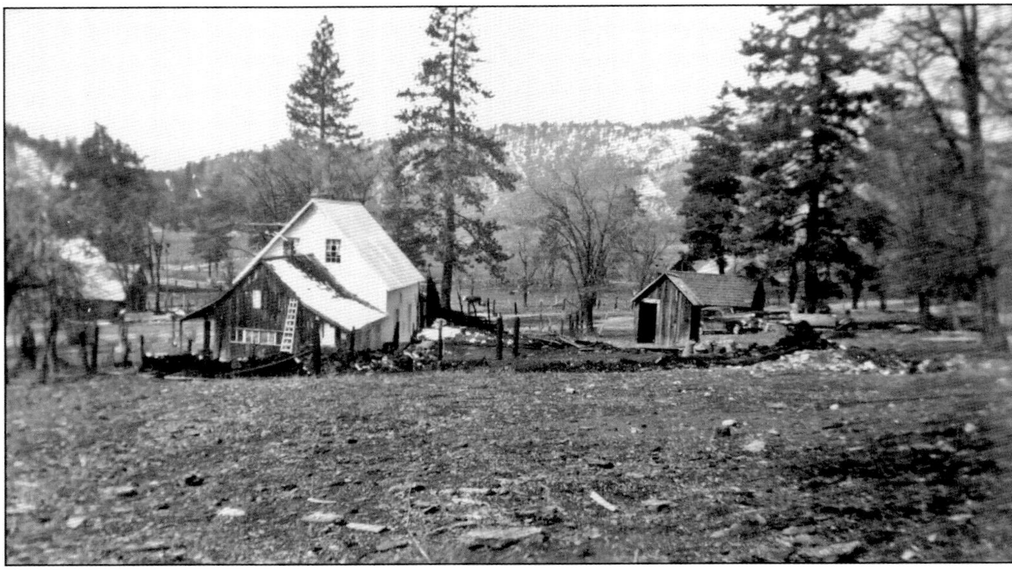

This is a picture of the ranch house from behind, showing where the outbuildings burned down. The smoke house, woodshed, and other outbuildings were lost, but the house was saved. A clinker landing on the shake roof started the fire. The responding fire truck is on display at the Indian Valley Museum. (Courtesy of Jim Peter.)

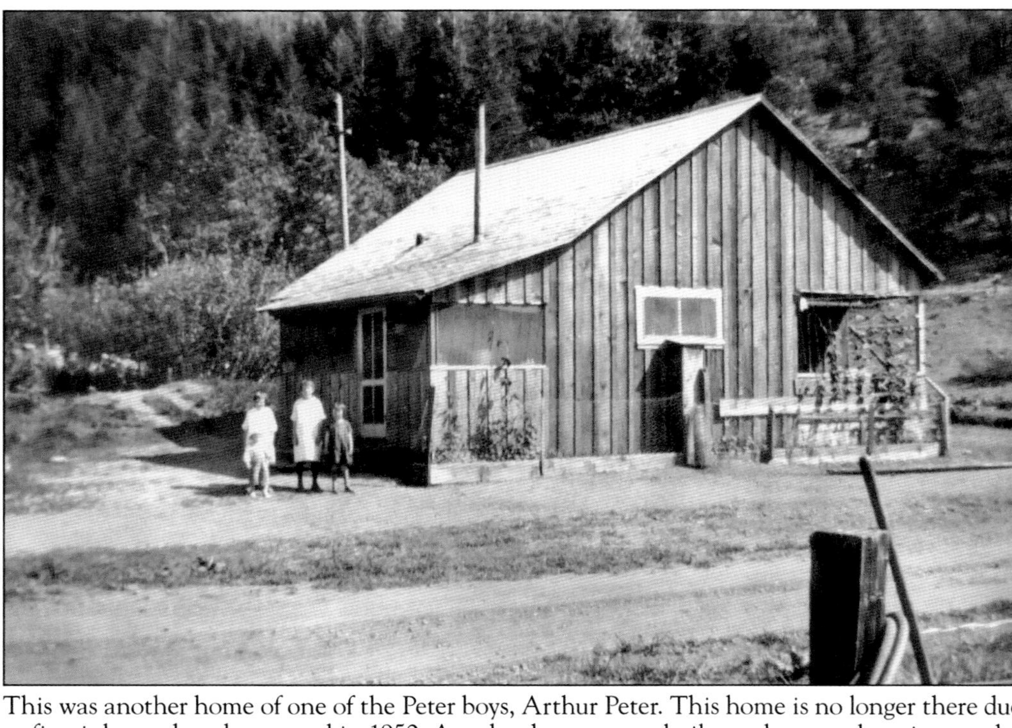

This was another home of one of the Peter boys, Arthur Peter. This home is no longer there due to fire; it burned to the ground in 1950. Another home was rebuilt on the same location on the ranch. (Courtesy of Jim Peter.)

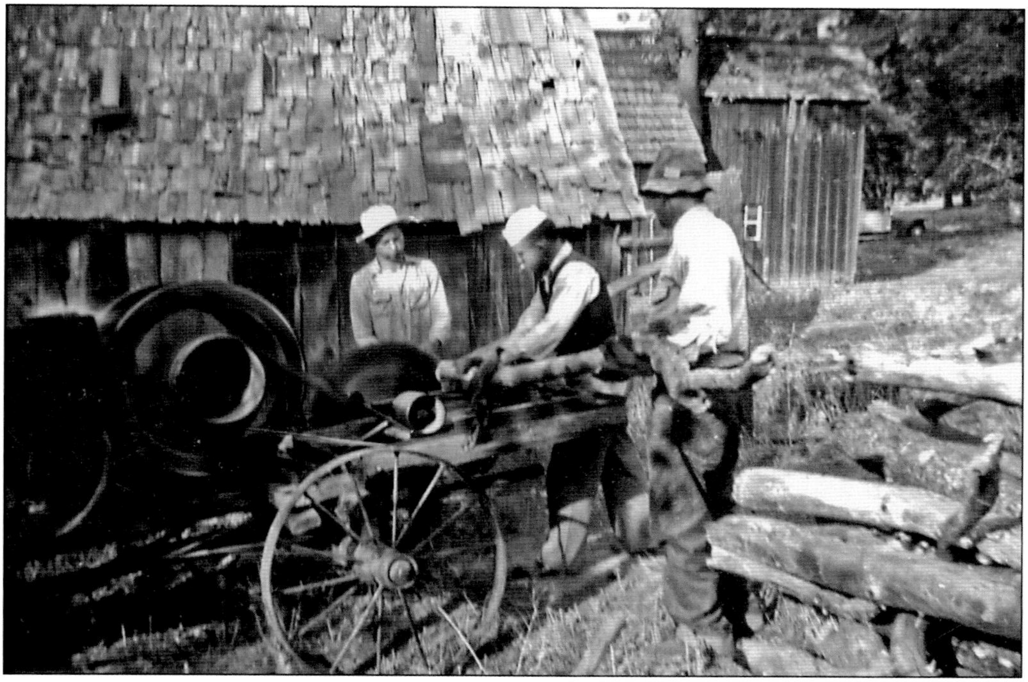

This buzz saw, a common tool in those days, had a five-horsepower, one-cylinder motor running it. It was used to cut up firewood. Pictured from left to right are Claude Peter, brother-in-law Charles Edward, and Russell Peter. In the background are the woodshed, smokehouse, and cabin. Those burned down in 1946, but the Taylorsville Fire Department saved the ranch house. (Courtesy of Jim Peter.)

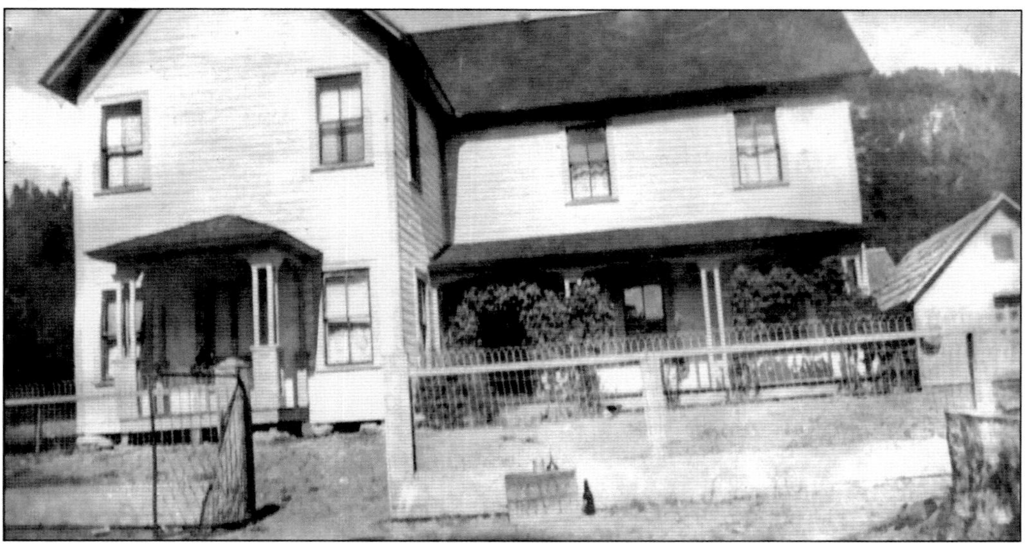

According to Feriss and Smith, early publishers of Plumas County history back in 1882, the first three farms in the North Arm of Indian Valley were those of A .C. Light, William Hussey, and James and Martha Ford. George H. Herring later purchased the 200-acre Hussey Ranch in 1871. George married Slyvia Johnson in 1873. The Herrings raised five children on the ranch and lived there until just before or after his death in 1911.

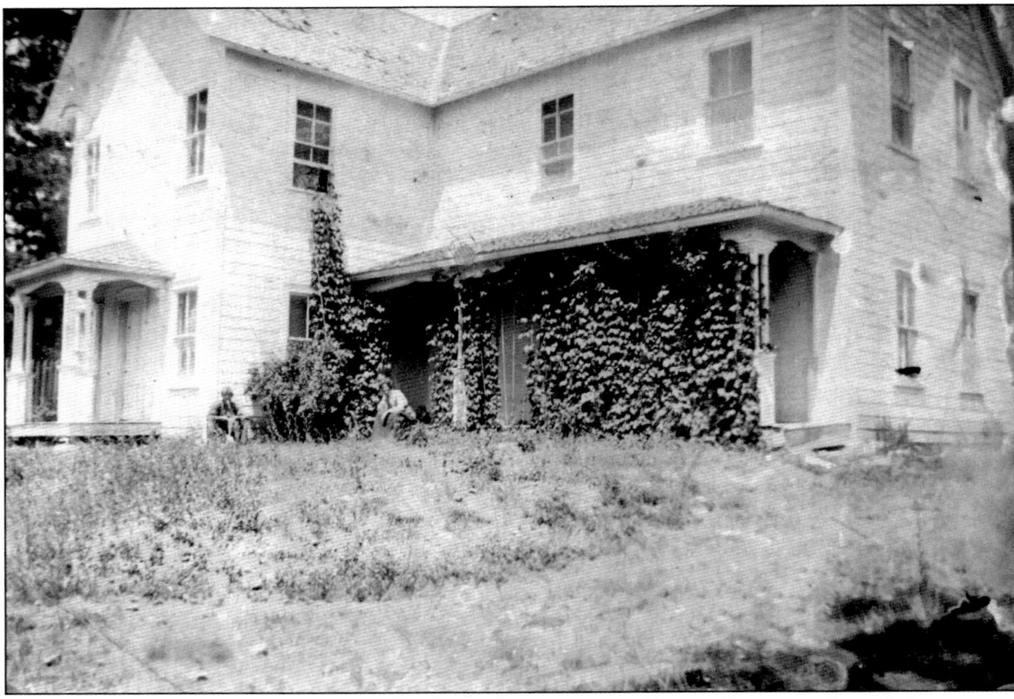

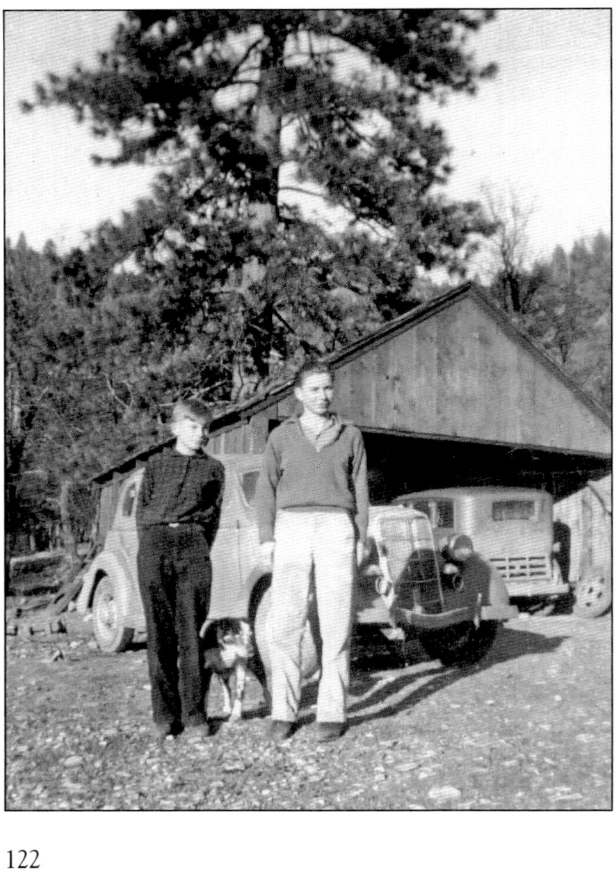

Forrest Peter purchased the Herring Ranch around 1911, thus making it the third Peter ranch on the east side of North Arm. This ranch had milk cows and outbuildings surrounding the home. One was a milk house with cold storage for fresh milk; also there was a barn and many sheds. The barn blew down around 1978. Some of the hand-hewn timbers were used in the construction of a new home.

Two of the Peter boys, Claude and Jim, are pictured here in 1940 with their dog, standing in front of a garage with some older model cars in and around it. Jim, at right, was the oldest. This garage is still standing and is located just below the road from the old ranch house.

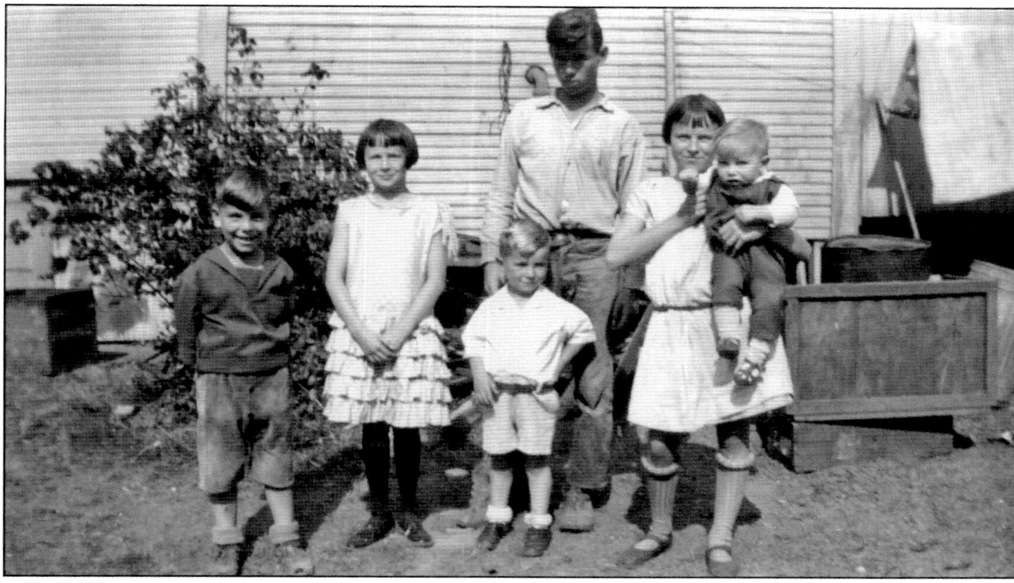

Pictured here is the Peter family. Jim Peter and his son Russell still live on the ranch today; it is the only Peter Ranch left of the original three. In the back is Russell Peter, the ranch owner, and from left to right in front are John Hall, Mary Peter, James Peter, and Wilma Peter holding Claude Peter. Today Jim is retired and leases the ranch out.

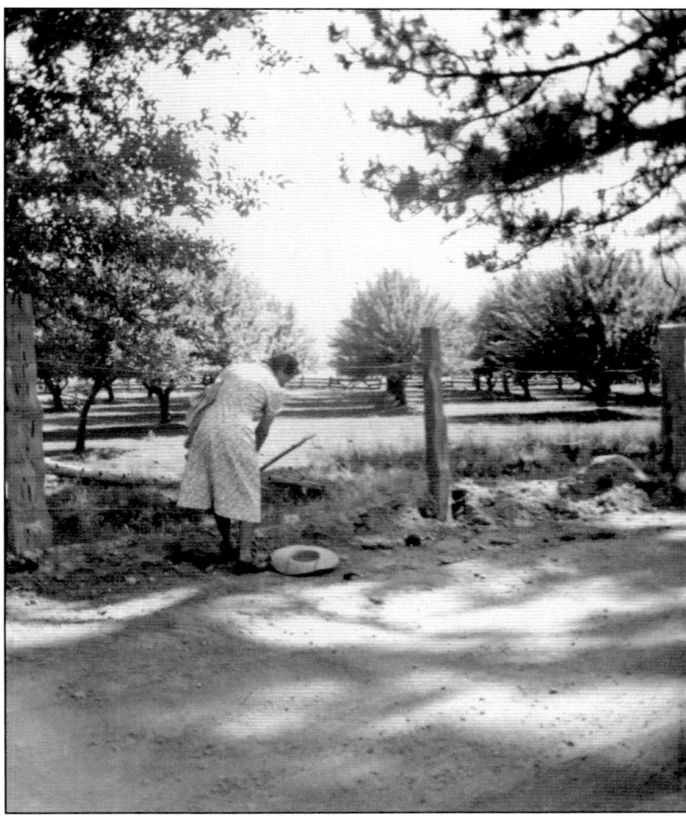

Elvetzia Defanti is shown cleaning out a post hole during fence construction. This was taken along the road by their apple orchard. The Defanti Ranch sold apples to the public. Roman Beauties, Ben Davis, Red Delicious, and Yellow Delicious were some of the apple varieties they sold. When the Defantis purchased the ranch, they brought their cattle from Nevada to North Arm via the Indian Valley Railroad. (Courtesy of Guy Defanti.)

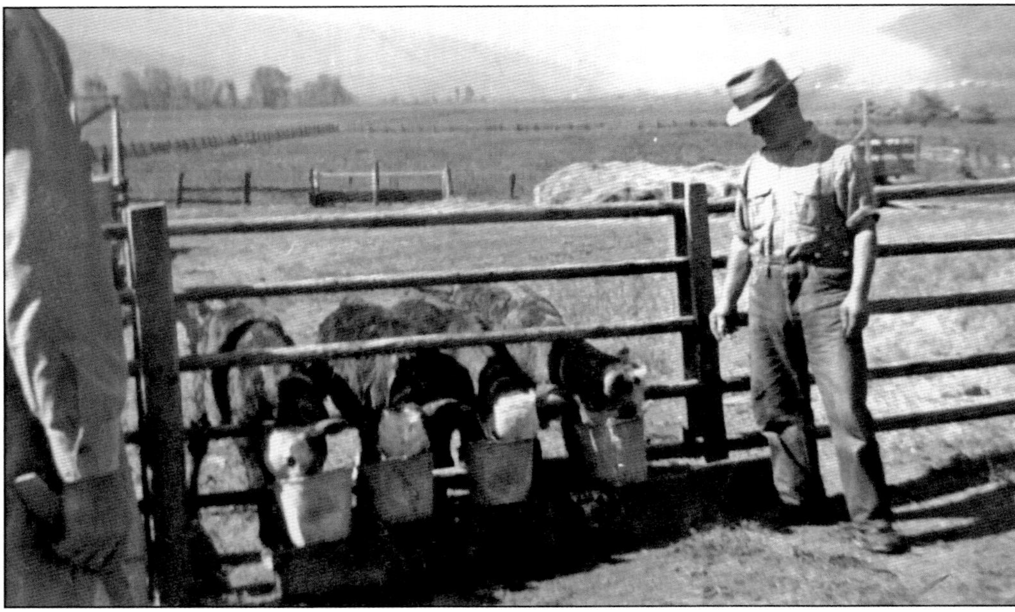

Ralph Defanti feeds the calves. He fed the calves of the dairy cows the skim milk that was left after the cream was extracted. Ralph sold the cream. In the background is an almost depleted loose haystack. The hay was piled by a portable hay derrick equipped with a Jackson fork. This photograph was taken in late winter or early spring when the haystack was almost gone. (Courtesy of Guy Defanti.)

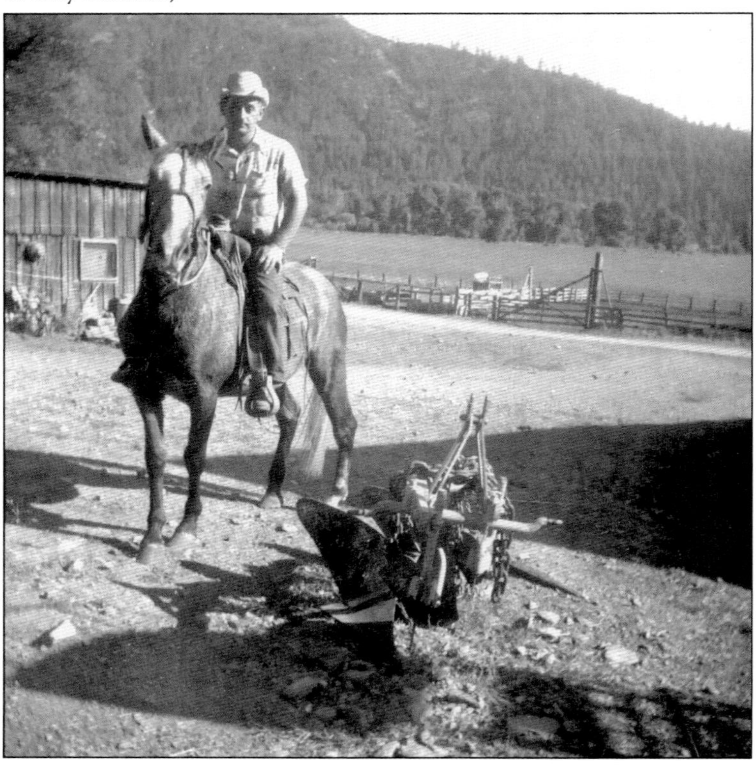

James Defanti is shown here on Jupiter, an old army horse. The structure in the background is the milk house used by Ralph Defanti to separate the cream from the milk. The cream was taken to Keddie and put on the train bound for the Crystal Creamery. Eventually, a man by the name of George Vanderhoven started a business picking up all the cream from the dairies and hauling it for the ranchers. (Courtesy of Guy Defanti.)

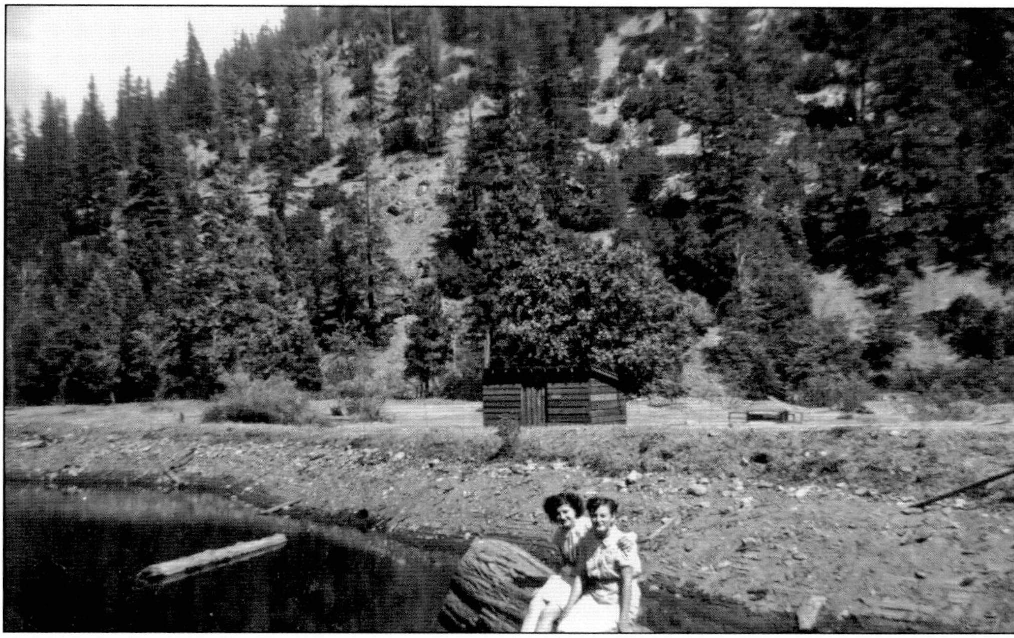

Adeline Defanti and her cousin are pictured sitting on the edge of Lights Creek just above the bridge. The land in the background has changed over the years from the high water. The Defanti Ranch was the last ranch at the head of North Arm. The Union School was on the Defanti Ranch. Up the road was Engelmine. (Courtesy of Guy Defanti.)

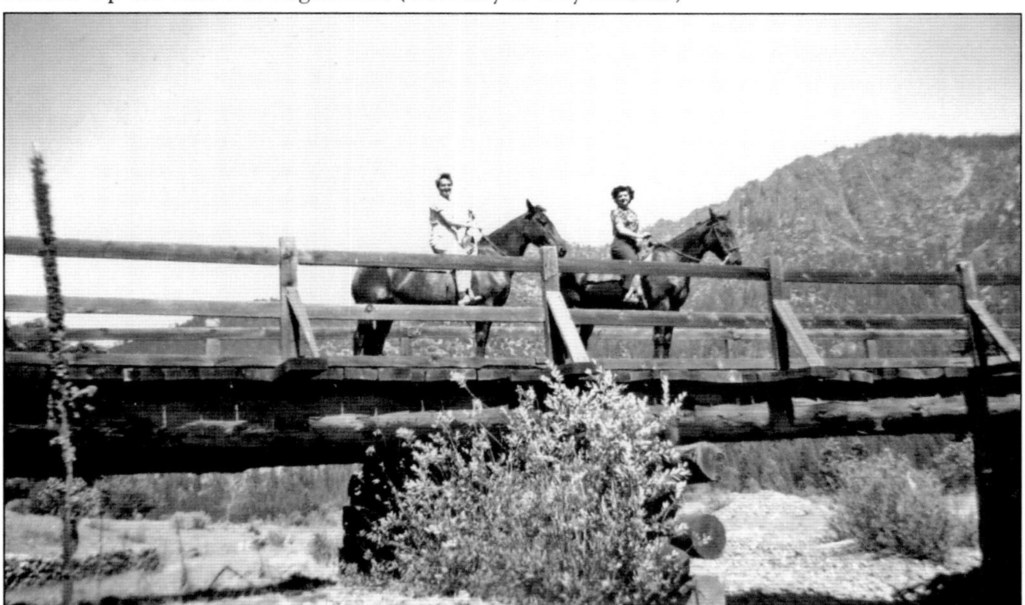

This image from the 1940s shows Adeline "Lena" Defanti and her cousin Eres Defanti riding across the original Lights Creek Bridge. The bridge was made of logs and heavy wooden planks. When the main logs became rotten, another tree would be cut to replace them. Taresh's mill was run by a man named Homer "Sandy" Hagadone, who once went across this bridge with a load of logs, and the bridge collapsed behind him. (Courtesy of Guy Defanti.)

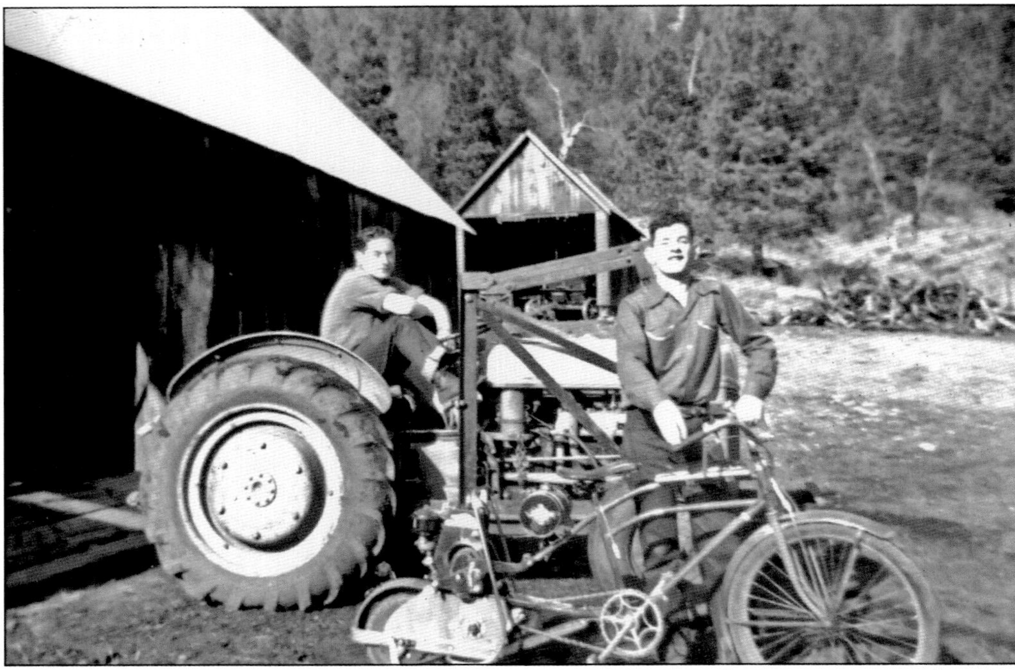

Guy Defanti is shown with his older brother Jim at the Defanti ranch. Jim is sitting on their first tractor, and Guy is smiling at his achievement of building his first motorcycle, possibly made from an old bicycle.

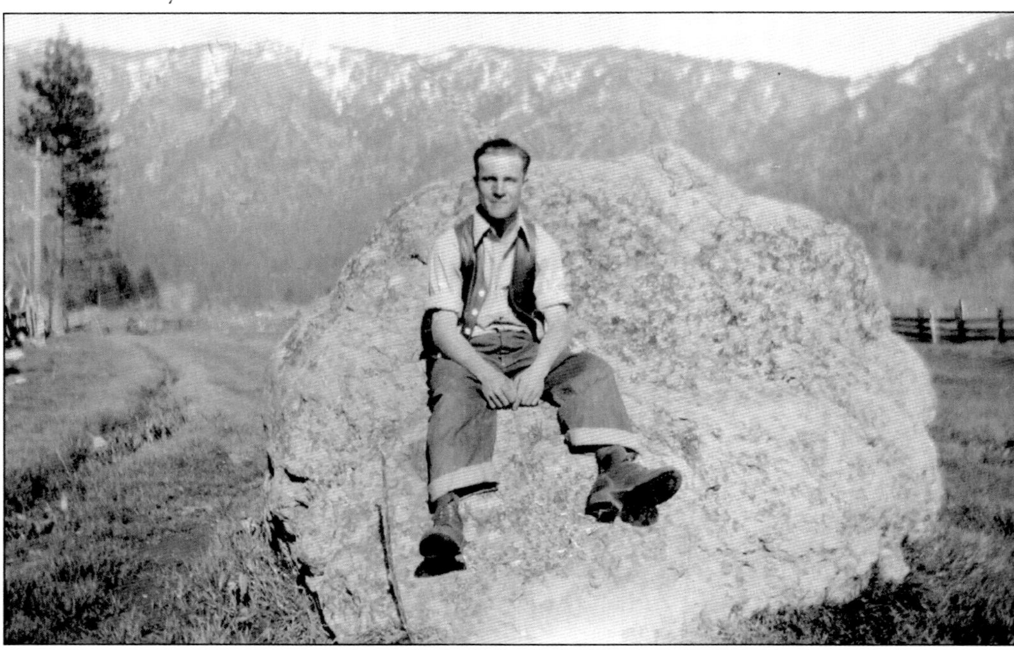

This is a picture of John Marcel McCutcheon, known in later years as Tuffy. He is sitting on a rock that is still there today. The rock is located between the old McCutcheon Ranch house and the Defanti Ranch house. This picture was taken in the 1930s when John was helping run the ranch. (Courtesy of the author.)

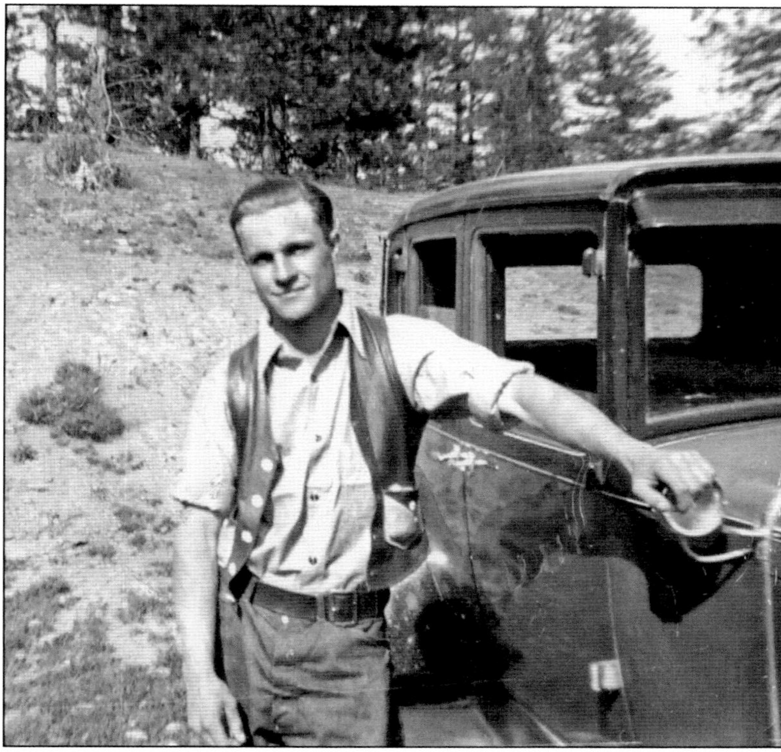

This picture was taken in the 1930s when John Marcel had a 1934 Chevrolet. The author is finishing this book with some pictures of his dad, John, because he was a third-generation resident in this valley and is buried in the quaint cemetery in Taylorsville, just below his grandparents and his parents. (Courtesy of the author.)

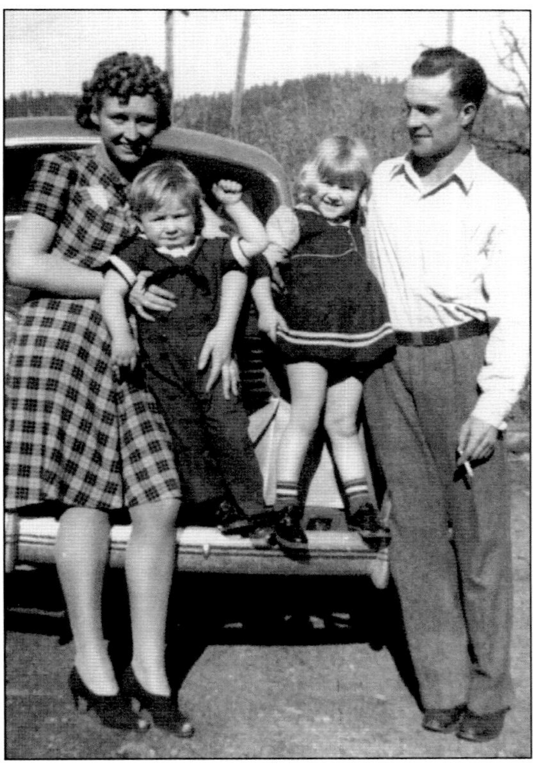

This is a picture of the author's entire family: from left to right are Lois Marie (McColm) McCutcheon, the author, his sister Barbara Gayel McCutcheon, and father John Marcel McCutcheon. In a drought year in Honey Lake Valley, Lois's parents drove their dairy cattle over Diamond Mountain into Indian Valley to lease a ranch that had water. The ranch was across the road from the McCutcheon Ranch. John and Lois went to school together and later married. (Courtesy of the author.)

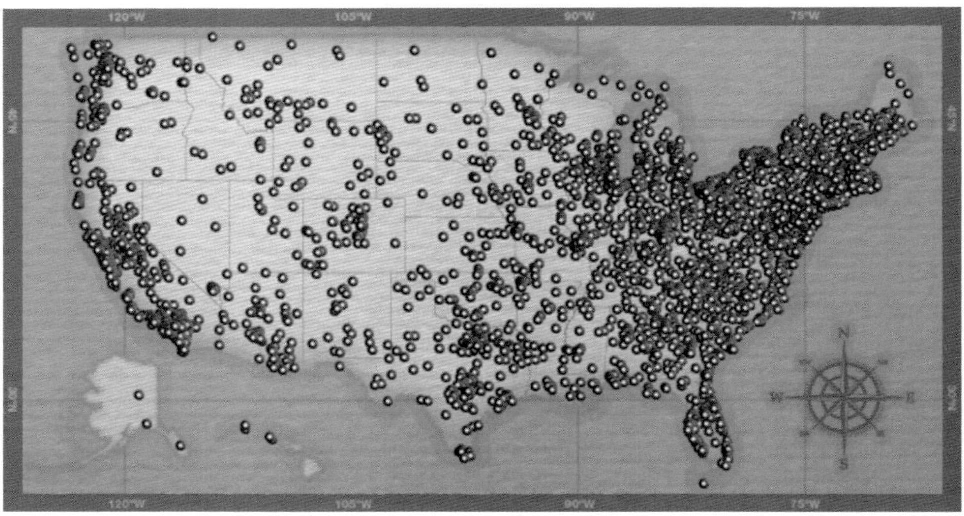

Consistent with our mission to preserve history on a local level, this book was printed in South Carolina on American-made paper and manufactured entirely in the United States. Products carrying the accredited Forest Stewardship Council (FSC) label are printed on 100 percent FSC-certified paper.